I0800141

IMAGES
of America

ALBERTVILLE

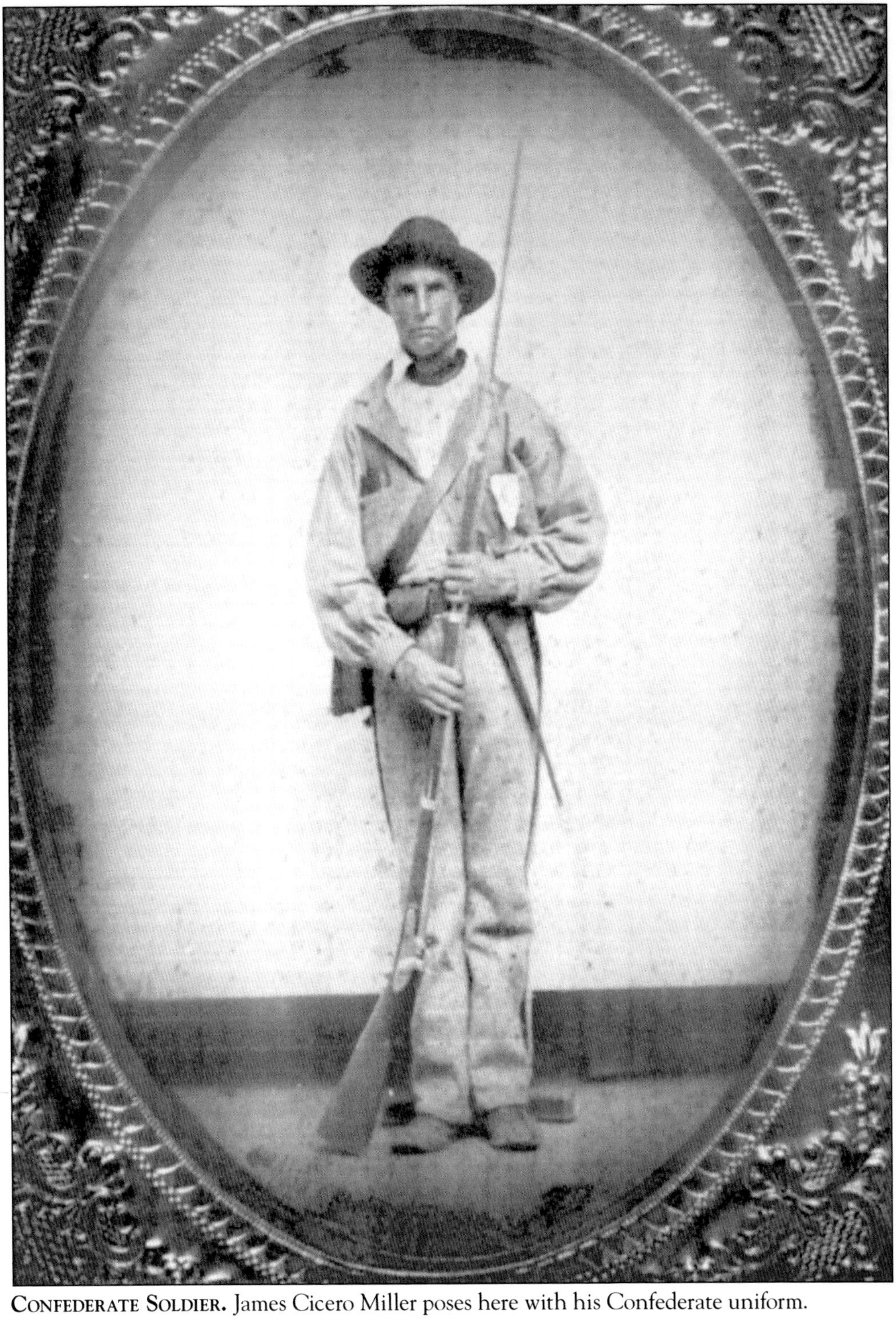

Confederate Soldier. James Cicero Miller poses here with his Confederate uniform.

IMAGES
of America

ALBERTVILLE

Dennis Burgess

ARCADIA
PUBLISHING

ISBN 978-0-7385-1664-6

Published by Arcadia Publishing
Charleston, South Carolina

Printed in the United States of America

Library of Congress Control Number: 2004104278

For all general information, please contact Arcadia Publishing:
Telephone 843-853-2070
Fax 843-853-0044
E-mail sales@arcadiapublishing.com
For customer service and orders:
Toll-Free 1-888-313-2665

Visit us on the Internet at www.arcadiapublishing.com

Contents

ACKNOWLEDGMENTS

This book would not have been possible without the assistance of numerous people. First is the photographic legacy of the Johnson Studio in Albertville, begun by J. Willie Johnson in 1908 and continued today by his son, Robert O. Johnson. Numerous photographs in this book were captured through the eyes of their cameras. I also wish to acknowledge the late J.J. Benford and his successor, Jack Thompson, a dear friend of mine whose newspaper, *The Albertville Herald*, has served as a template for this book.

In addition, I would like to thank the townspeople of Albertville, who, from the city's centennial celebration in 1991 through production of this book, have generously answered my requests for their time and the gracious loan of their prized possessions. I would like to thank my history teachers through the years, whose classes awakened my interest in history. They made it enjoyable—never dull, never boring. I wish to thank my mother and remember my late father for always reading and encouraging my writings. No writer ever had a more receptive ear than that of my dear mother. I would also like to thank my editors at Arcadia Publishing for their support and guidance.

As for my wife, Pam, the inspirational force in my life, what can I say? She is everything to me. I am one fortunate man.

INTRODUCTION

Somewhere in the hills of Virginia lies the unknown grave of James Cicero Miller. Though he died at the young age of 29, his life's legacy lies in the northeast Alabama city of Albertville. In 1852 the young Miller returned to his native Georgia and met 18-year-old Martha Anne Albert. In December of the following year the couple was married. In 1857 the couple, along with their children and Martha's parents, Thomas and Sarah Albert, relocated to the Sand Mountain plateau.

On January 13, 1860, J.C. Miller established his name for all time in the history of Albertville when he established the community's first post office out of his home at the present-day address of 406 East Main Street. Though he initially considered naming the post office after prominent Guntersville citizen S.K. Rayburn, he ultimately decided to name it in honor of his father-in-law. In May 1861 Cicero, as Martha called him, volunteered for service in the Confederate Army, although Martha pleaded with him to wait until he was called to duty. On June 27, 1862, Miller died in combat at Gaines Mill, near Richmond, Virginia. Though the location of his grave remains a mystery, a cenotaph was erected at the Old Albertville Cemetery in his honor on August 3, 1991. It was positioned near the graves of Martha's parents.

As for Martha Anne Miller, she continued to reside at the family home for another 52 years. By that time, the city had been incorporated, the downtown business district had grown, and the residential areas had begun to flourish. The houses, except for Cicero and Martha Miller's home, were becoming more ornate and more expansive. "Grandma" Miller, as everyone knew her, was conscious of the difference between her home and the rest of the town's homes. She often told people that Cicero had told her not to worry about their little cabin, that they would "fix it up" when he returned from the war. The sad thing was that she continued to utter these words, even though everyone around her knew that her husband had been dead for over half a century. Unfortunately, this episode marked the downward spiral of Grandma Miller's mental state. In 1914 her son, Thomas, received a letter from her Albertville neighbors informing him that, in their opinion, his mother could no longer live alone because of her declining mental health. Martha lived an additional four years after moving to Texas; she passed away on June 6, 1918.

As for the town the Millers spawned, subsequent generations of the "Gem City," as Albertville was at times called, have ushered it into its third century. The story of Albertville has been told through its families, its businesses, and all the things that make up human lives.

One

FAMILIES

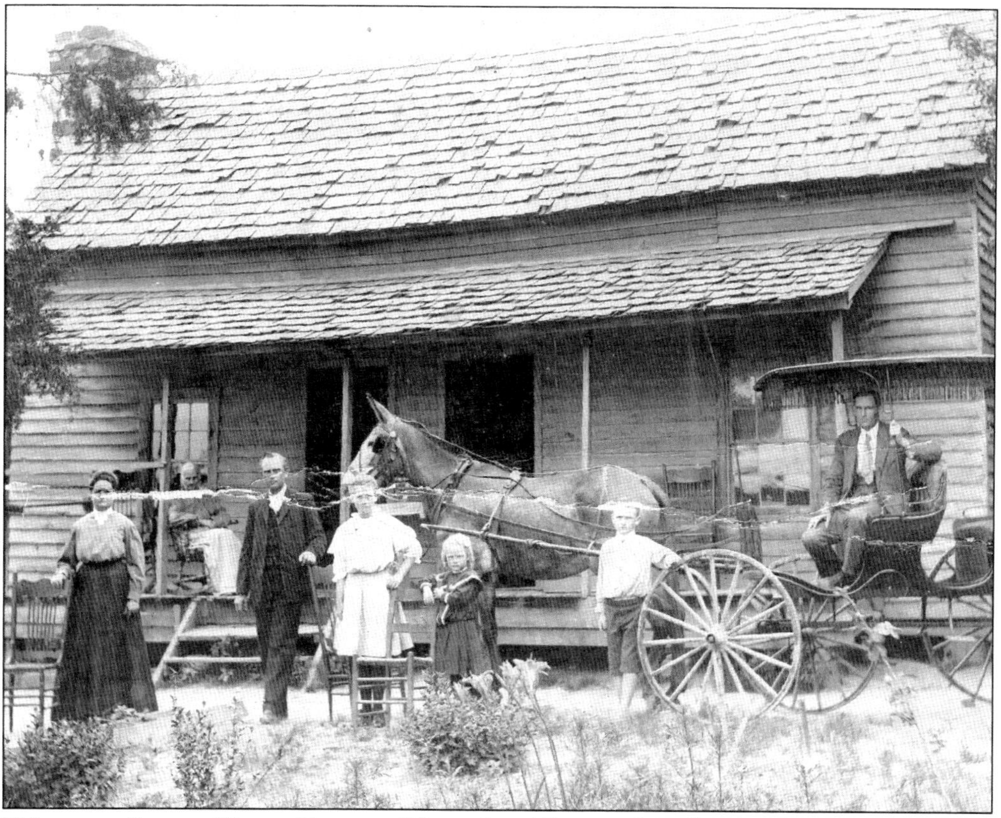

H.L. AND SARAH WELLS FAMILY. When the Albert and Miller families moved to Sand Mountain in 1857, the area was scarcely settled, sometimes averaging five to six miles between homes. During her later years, Martha Miller remembered that there were five families living in Albertville, which was then known as Jones Chapel; they were the Garrard, Bishop, Scott, King, and Bentley families. The closing days of the 18th century saw the arrival of many families whose names have become synonymous with Albertville. One such family was the H.L. and Sarah Anderson Wells family, which settled first in the Kilpatrick community after moving from Dallas, Georgia. Pictured from left to right are Sarah Elizabeth Wells, unidentified, Heflin L. Wells, Ethel Wells, Oneida Wells, Dewey Wells, and Coleman Wells.

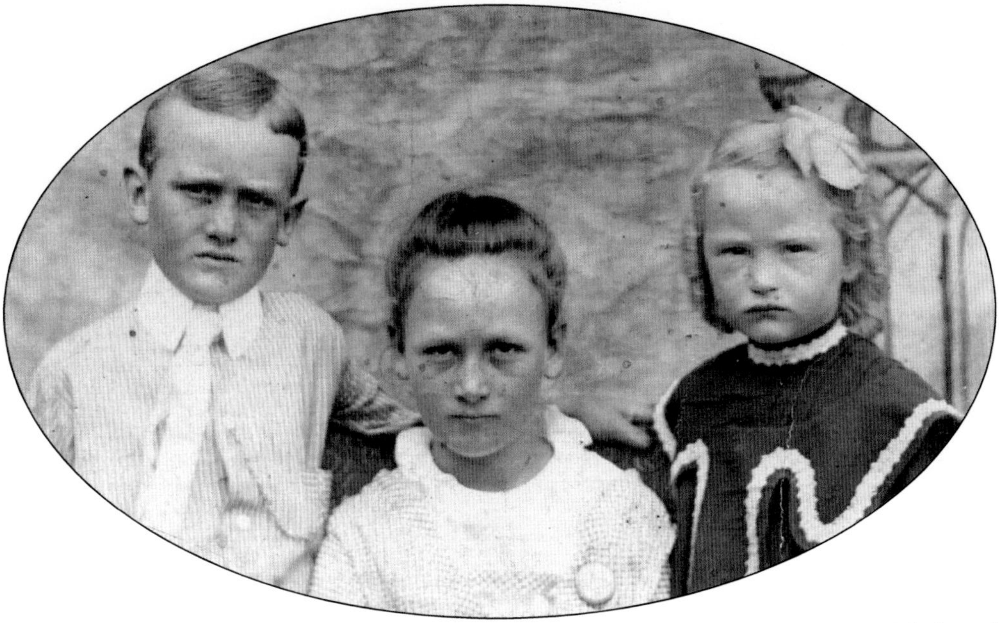

THE CHILDREN OF H.L. WELLS. Pictured from left to right are George Dewey, Ethel, and Oneida. All three of the children, as well as their spouses, distinguished themselves in the business life of Albertville.

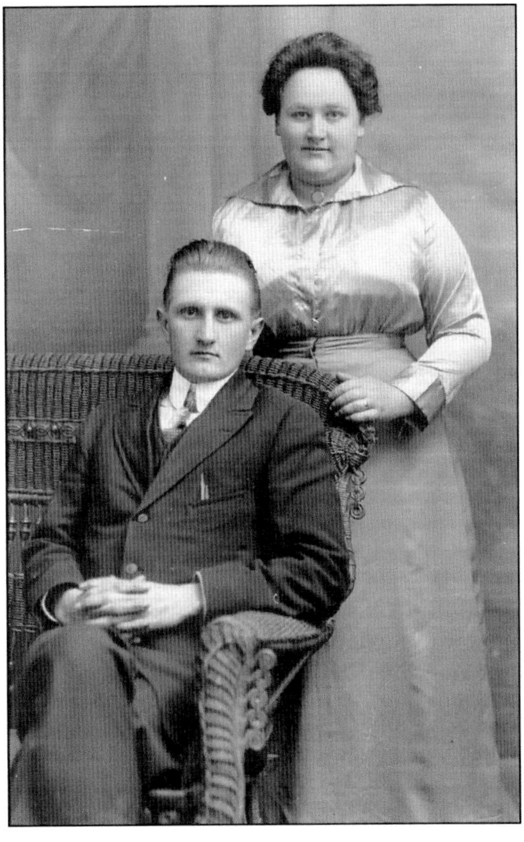

J.P. AND ETHEL WELLS COLVIN. Ethel, the oldest of H.L. Wells's children, married J. Pat Colvin, whose family had moved from Henry County, Georgia, in an old-fashioned ox wagon in 1857. Pat Colvin was one of 15 children born to a pioneer family. When the Colvins first arrived from Georgia, they settled in the McVille community, just north of Albertville. In heavily wooded areas, 15 workers, or children, was a fine thing.

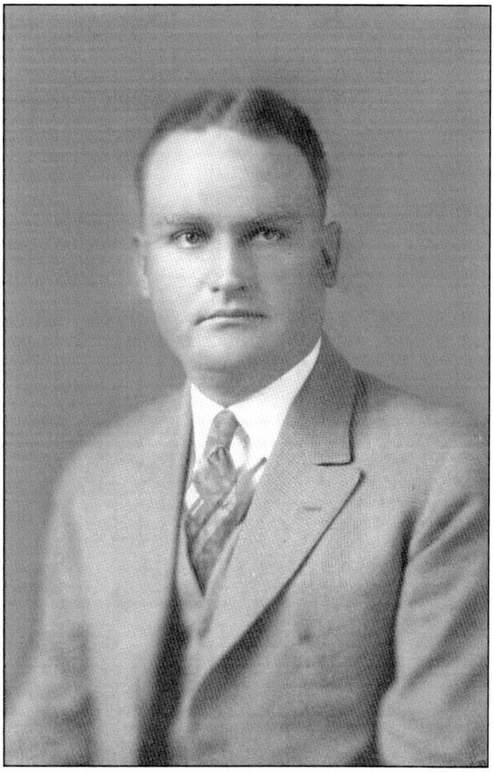

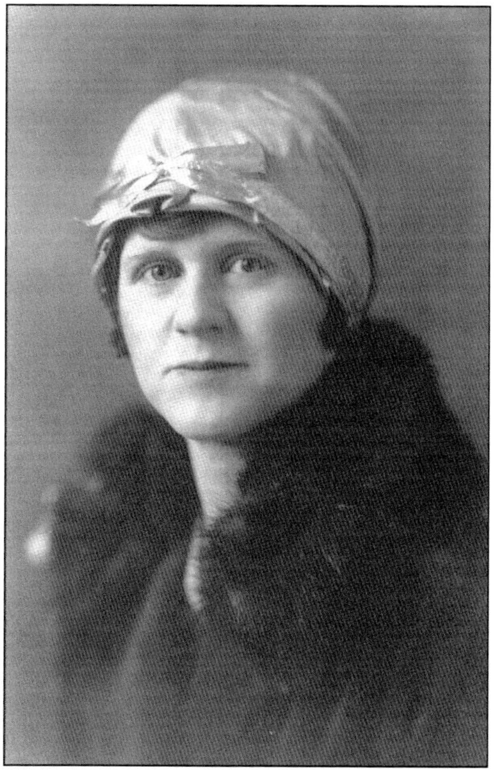

GEORGE DEWEY WELLS AND LUCILLE STARNES WELLS. The Wells son, Dewey, married Mary Lucille Starnes of nearby Guntersville. She was the sister of future U.S. Congressman Joe Starnes. The couple remained an integral part of Albertville life until their deaths. Albertville's long-standing newspaper lady, Bess Williams, once wrote in glowing terms, "Mr. Wells, one soon learns, is as much a part of Albertville and Marshall County as are the green fields, the meadows, the brooks and trees."

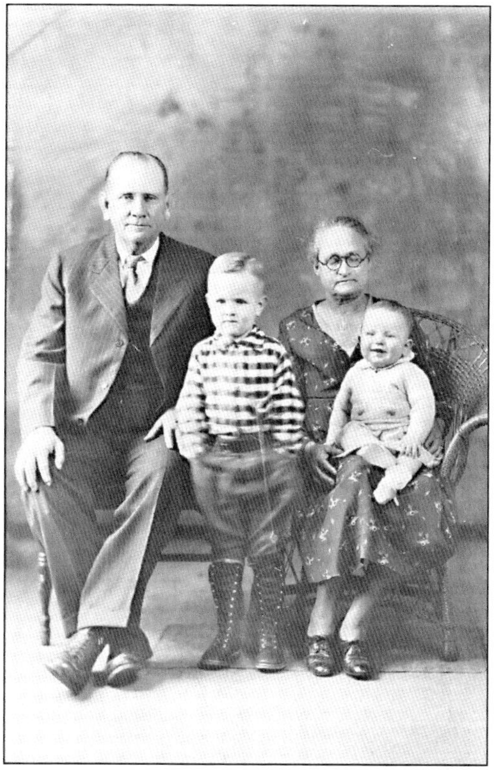

SPENDING TIME WITH GRANDPARENTS. Spending time with grandparents has always been a special time, one of indulgence and unbridled love. Pictured with H.L. Wells and his wife, Sarah, are Dewey's children, George Jr. (standing) and Jack (in his grandmother's lap). George is glad to show off his new boots in this photograph.

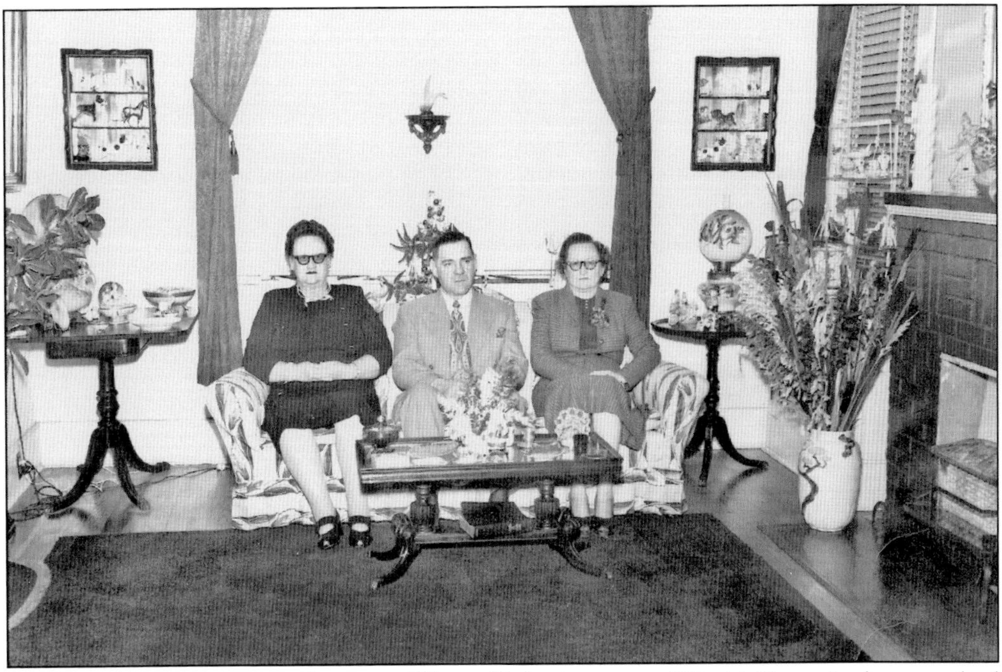

Just Have a Seat in the Parlor. Albertville businessman Olin C. Hearn is photographed surrounded by his wife, Oneida Wells Hearn (right), and his sister-in-law, Ethel Wells Colvin (left).

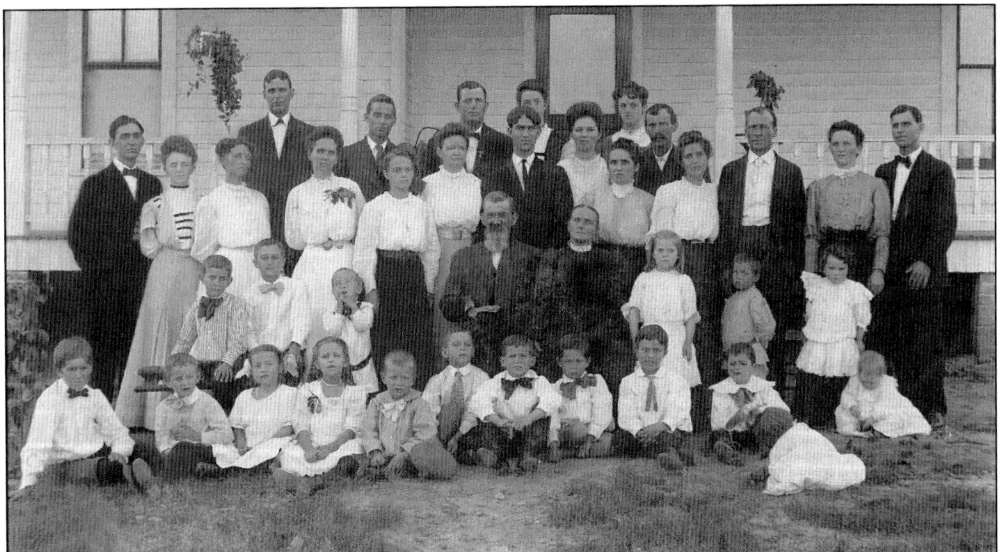

McNaron Family. During the latter part of the 19th century, members of the family of Warner Richmond McNaron began moving to the young town of Albertville. One of the first to arrive was his son, Thomas, who moved to Albertville in 1891 and became the bookkeeper for founding merchant L.S. Emmett. Another child of W.R. McNaron was Ollie. Ollie and his wife, Emma, whom he had met while attending the Agricultural School, had their lives turned upside down during the cyclone of 1908. On Ollie McNaron's birthday in September 1908, the couple moved into their new home on South Broad Street.

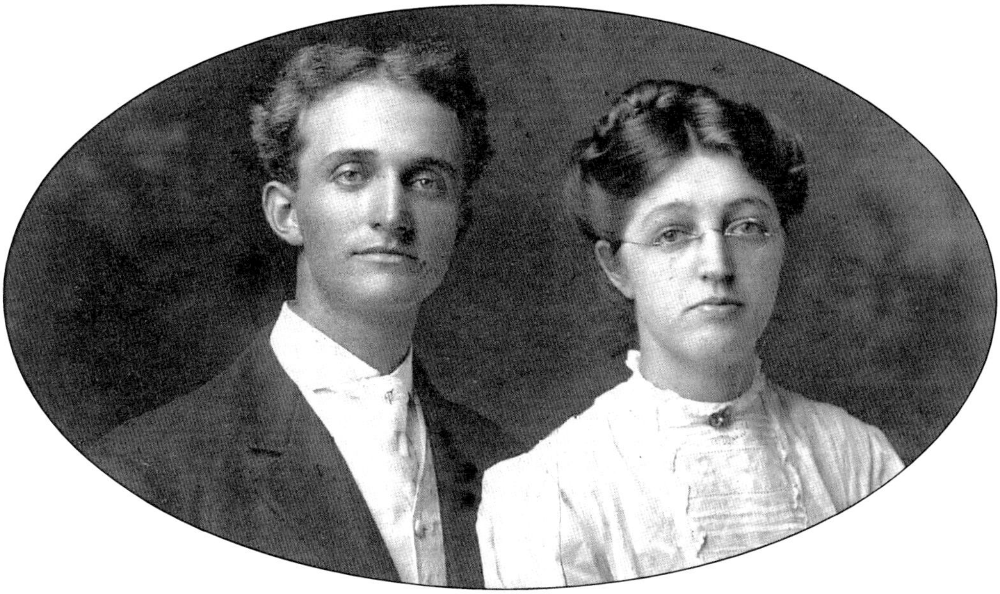

CHARLES AND DELLA HEARN. In the early days of Albertville, the Seventh District Agricultural School was responsible for bringing many people to town. One such person was Brooksville, Alabama native Charles Lycurgus Hall, who came to Albertville in 1901. In 1903 Charlie met Della Jane Hubbard, whose father had moved his family there from Heflin, Alabama. On May 9, 1906, the couple was married at the Hubbard home.

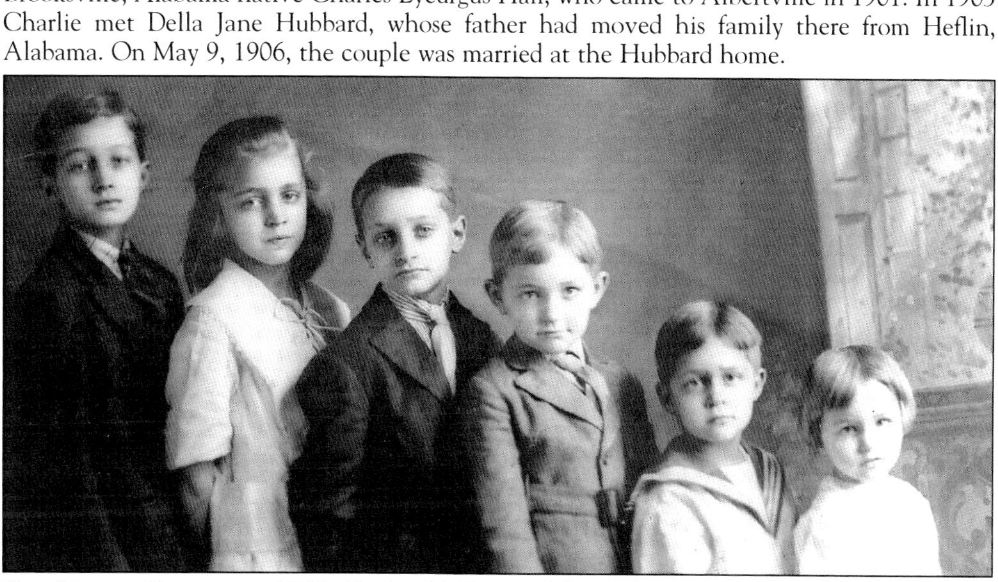

THE HEARN CHILDREN, 1918. By the 1910s six of the eight Hearn children had been born. Pictured from left to right are Aubrey, Mildred, Kermit, Fred, Glenn, and Mary Nell. Late in his life, Charlie Hearn recorded for his grandchildren the principals he had always tried to follow and wished to instill in them. He wrote to them: "Be obedient, tell the truth, keep good company, do not cheat, play the game fair, attend Sunday School and Church regularly, help with your hands and money in all good causes. Children in the home should love one another, be nice to older people, abstain from using ugly words, should read good books, make good grades in school, love Mama and Papa and help them. Care for the sick or distressed, live a Christian life, be a good citizen, upstanding, head high, in your community where you live and elsewhere and abstain from hard drinks. Cultivate good habits."

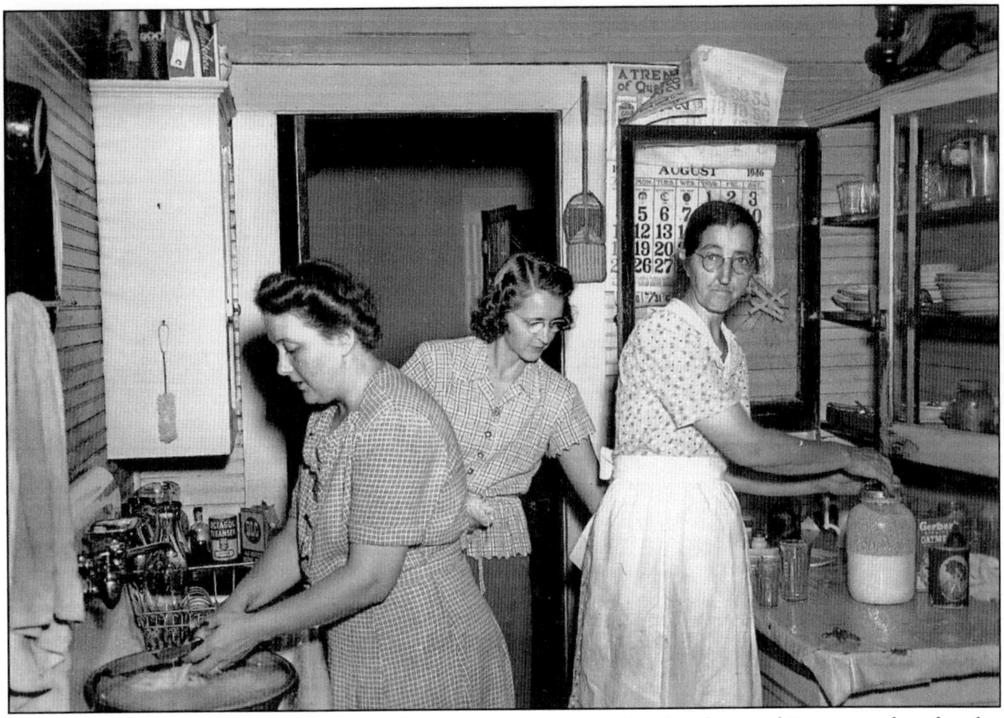

THE SOUTHERN KITCHEN. From meal preparation to canning food to making tea cakes for the kids, the Southern kitchen has always been at the center of the family home. Pictured from left to right are Florence Hearn, wife of Aubrey; Mildred Hearn Walker; and Della Hearn, family matriarch.

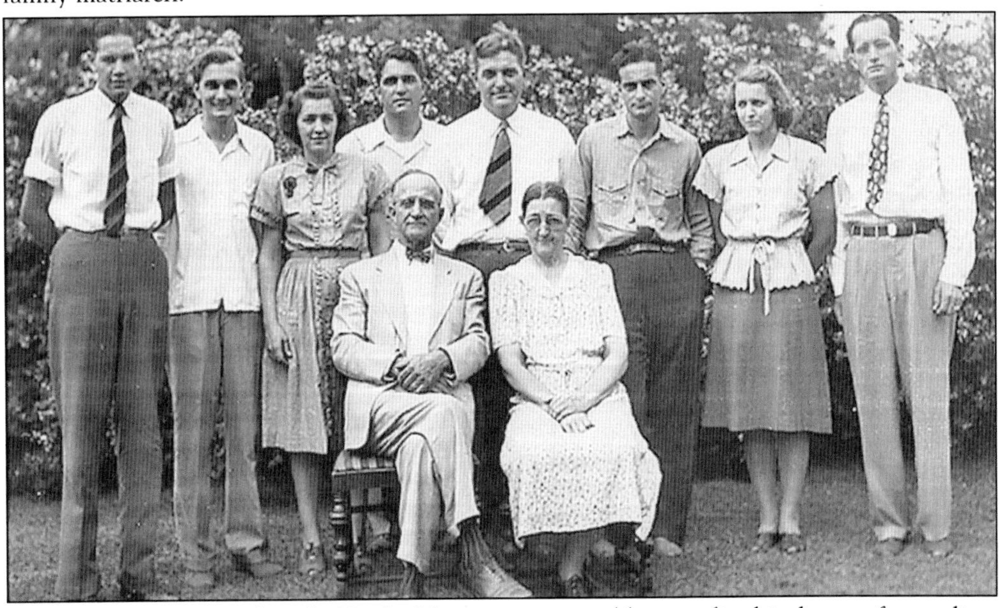

THE HEARN FAMILY. Though Charlie Hearn was never able to realize his dream of attending medical school, he and his wife were able to produce a family that yielded educators, religious leaders, and public servants. Their grandson, T.K. Hearn Jr., became president of Wake Forest University, and their son, Glenn, served as mayor of Huntsville.

DR. A.L. ISBELL FAMILY, THE EARLY YEARS. In February 1905 Arthur Levi Isbell married Cora Harris. In 1912 he began his medical practice in Whiton, in south DeKalb County. He and his family moved into a house constructed for him by the people of the community. Standing between Dr. and Mrs. Isbell are their children: (in descending order) Euclid, Dee, Hazel, Neil, Ethlyn, Quentin, Melba, Nalda, and Cora Helen.

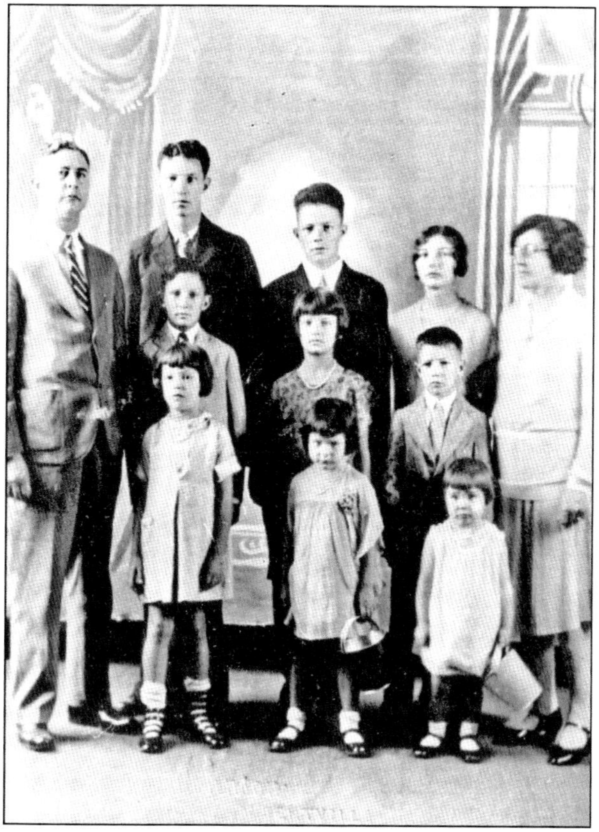

DR. A.L. ISBELL FAMILY, THE 1940S. In 1946 members of the Isbell family gathered together for a reunion at Dr. Isbell's home. With five of the nine Isbells serving in the army during the war years, reunions of the entire family were scarce. Pictured standing around Dr. and Mrs. Isbell are, from left to right, Hazel (Roberts), Nalda (Davis), Quentin, Euclid, Neil, Dee, Ethlyn (Rainey), Melba (Duke), and Cora Helen (Walker).

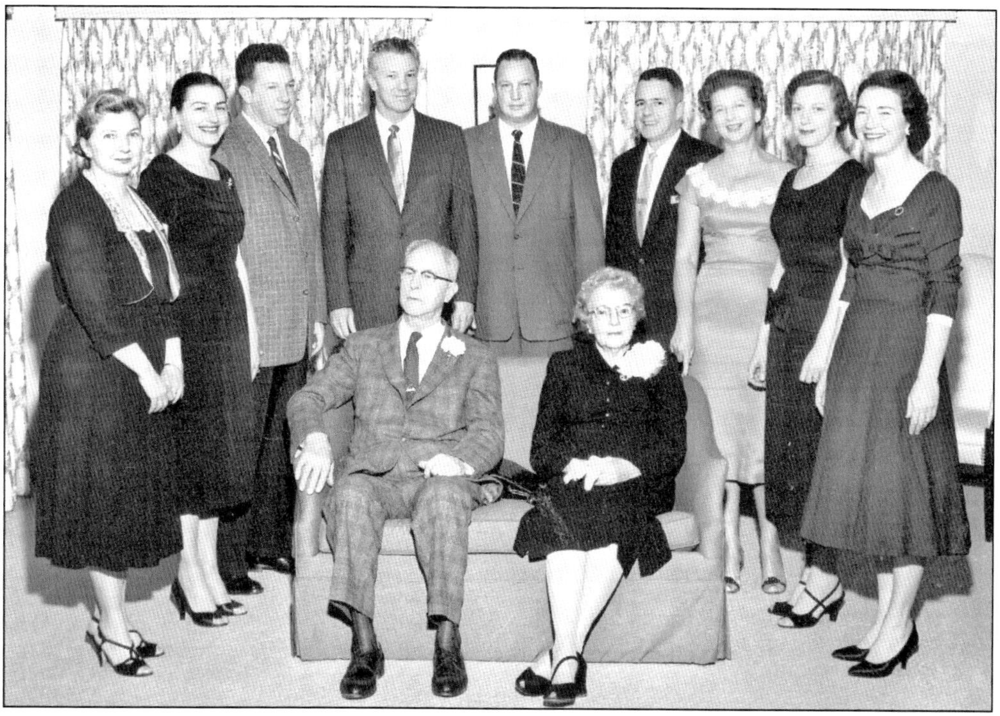

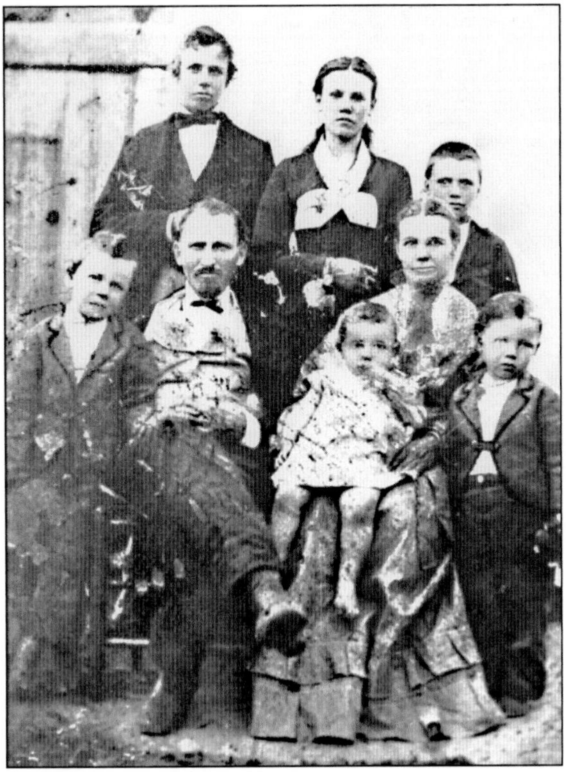

W.H.H. McCORD AND FAMILY. The spirit of public service that William Henry Harrison McCord and his wife, the former Ellen Davis (shown *c.* 1875), instilled in their children was born of their parents' character. When W.H.H. McCord died in 1909, he occupied a seat on Marshall County's Board of Commissioners.

McCORD FAMILY REUNION. During the Christmas season of 1925, members of the W.H.H. McCord family gathered at the home of E.O. McCord in Gadsden. E.O. and his brother, Tom, both served as mayors of Albertville. Leon served as a judge in the U.S. Circuit Court of Appeals, and their brother-in-law, Emory Mann, served as mayor of Boaz. In fact, it was the McCord children's mother, Ellen, who suggested the name of Boaz when Emory submitted the paperwork for a post office.

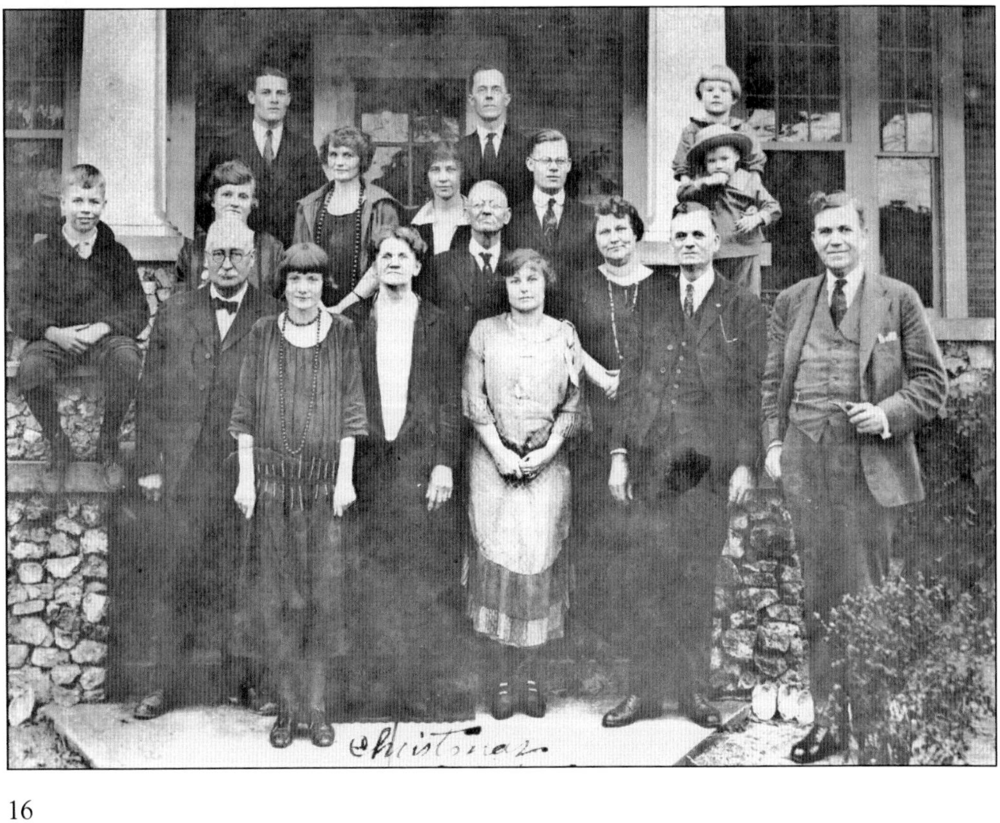

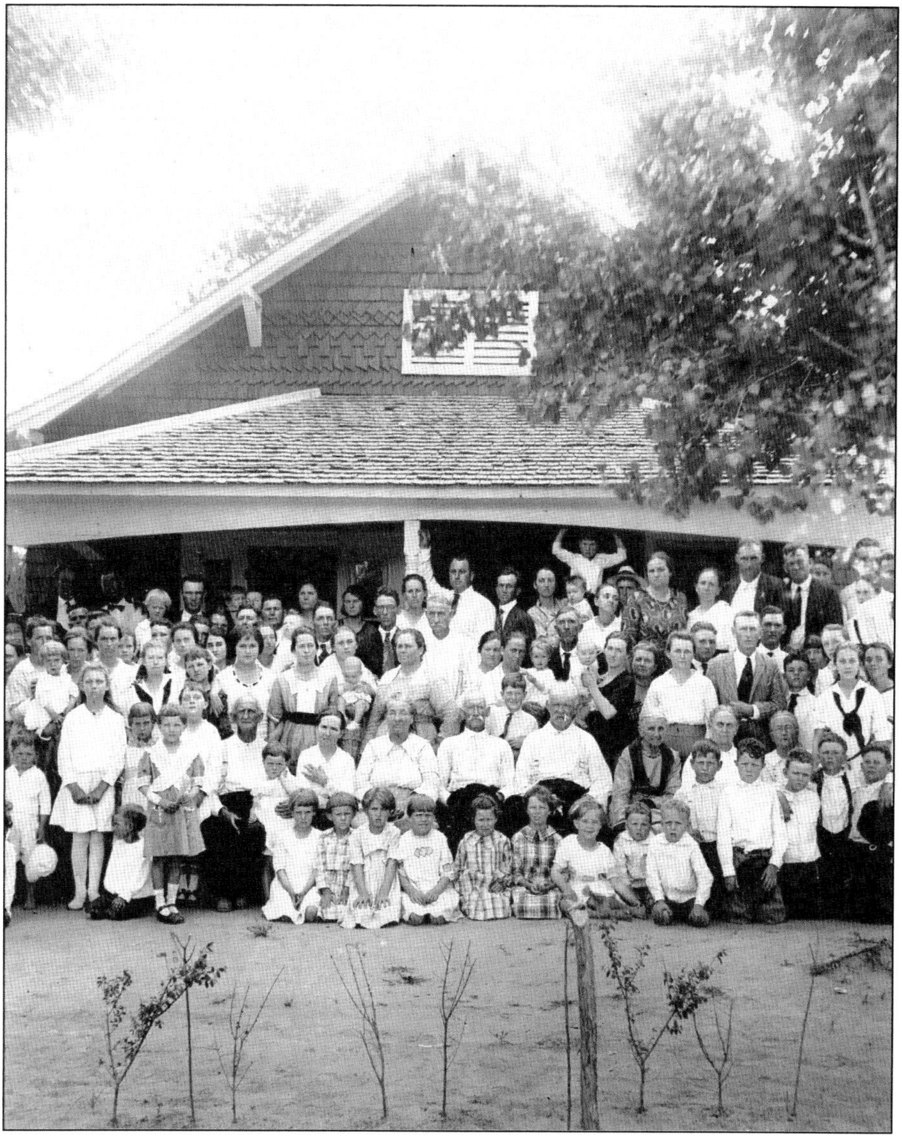

THE DOWDY FAMILY REUNION. One of the earliest families to migrate to the Sand Mountain area was the Dowdy family. In 1852 the combined families of Minerva Dowdy; her sister, Lucy; Lucy's husband, Jacob Dowdy; and the women's parents, William and Hannah Findley, moved to the New Canaan community along the Marshall-DeKalb County line. Minerva's husband, Isaac Dowdy, had passed away in their native Dahlonega, Georgia. Though three of their children died at birth, the couple had nine children before Isaac's death in 1848. Amazingly, Minerva delivered three sets of twins; however, it was one of those sets that died at birth. The second set of twins was Jane and Joe Dowdy. With the death of Joe during the closing days of the Civil War, only the third set of twins, Scott and Taylor, along with the single-birth children, Jeff and Isaac Jr. (known as "Boney"), would live to see their twilight years. During the years that followed, the birthday of Scott and Taylor, June 9, became the day for the annual Dowdy reunion. Among those pictured from left to right are (second row seated) Scott; his wife, Martha; Nancy Jane, Taylor's wife; Taylor; Jeff; and Jane, who was the widow of E.M. Isbell. The Dowdy family continues to live on in many bloodlines across the Sand Mountain area.

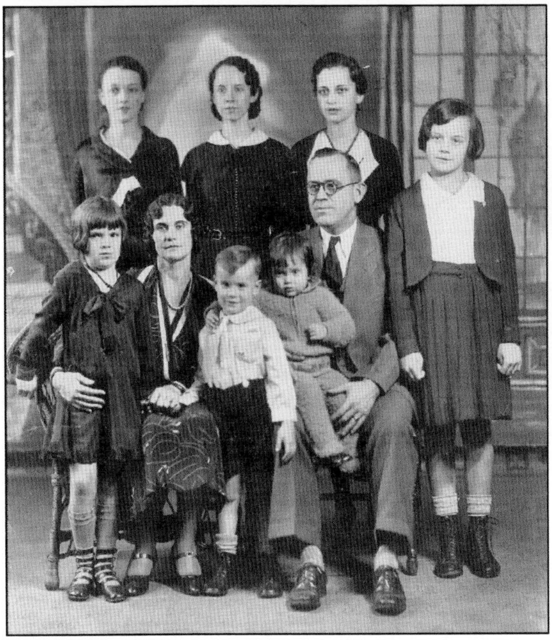

THE JAMES EARL SINGLETON FAMILY. For over five generations, the Singleton family has been active in the community life of Albertville. The following members of the Earl Singleton family are pictured from left to right: (front row) Martha Jean, Ethel Hatley Singleton, Robert Earl, Jeanine Gainer, Earl Singleton, and Dorothy; (back row) Lila Mae, Kathleen, and Earline. Earl Singleton was the son of businessman Matt Singleton.

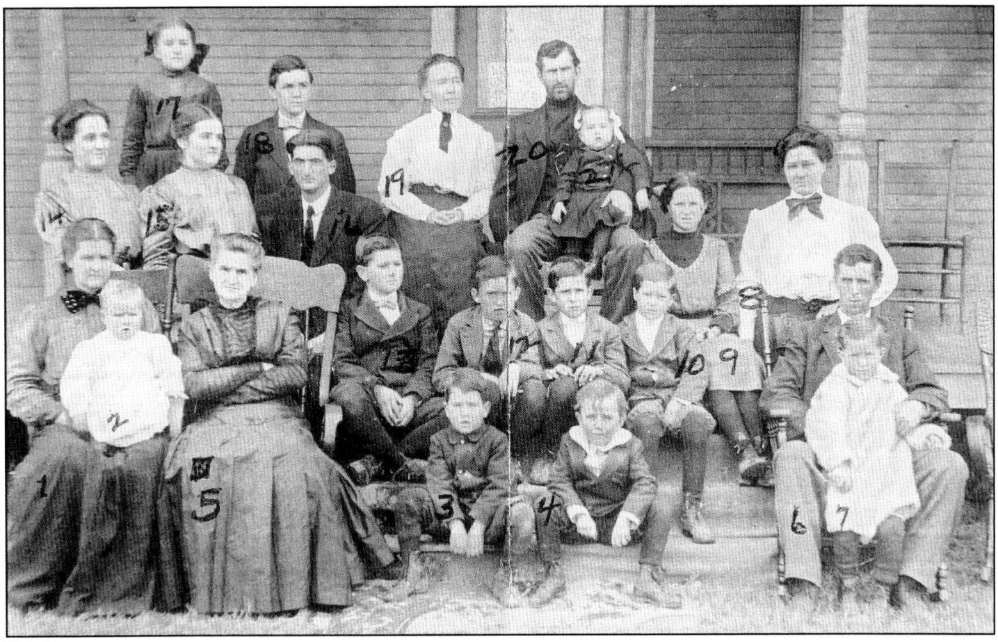

THE DAVIS FAMILY. About 1910, members of the Davis family began to arrive in Albertville. Among them were the families of J. Mercer Davis, who married Myrtle Dorsett, and Lucy Eugenia Davis, who married John H. Dendy. These families produced numerous leaders from the modern era of Albertville's business community. The following people are pictured by number: 1) Eugenia Davis Dendy; 2) Dan Dendy; 3) Cecil Dendy; 4) Eric Davis; 5) "Grandmother" Elizabeth Davis; 6) Jack Davis; 7) Ray Davis; 8) Lea Davis; 9) Faye Davis; 10) Robert Davis; 11) Foy Davis; 12) Worth Davis; 13) Jeptha Dendy; 14) Dora Davis; 15) Vesper Dendy; 16) Mercer Davis; 17) Vertis Dendy; 18) Fred Dendy; 19) Eula Davis; 20) Warner Davis; and 21) Magna Davis.

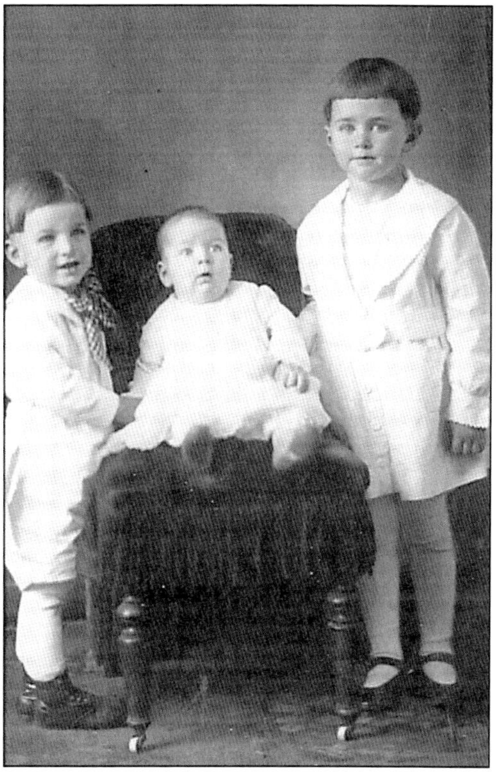

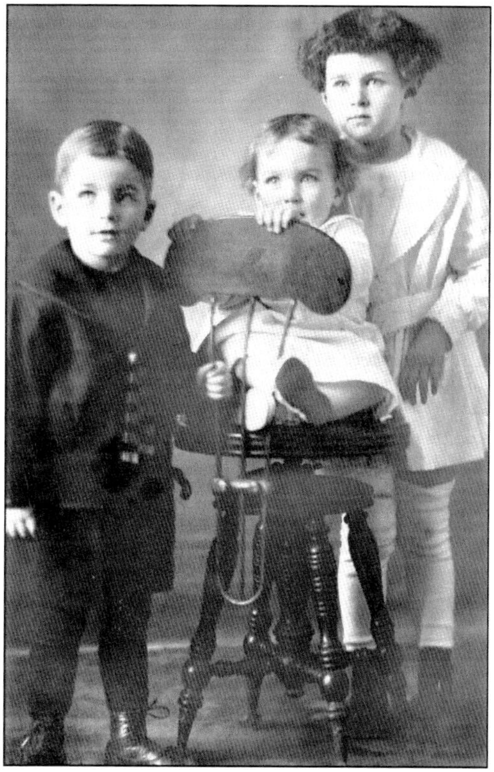

THE J. MERCER AND MYRTLE DAVIS CHILDREN. Pictured from left to right in both photographs are Joe, Dorsett, and Elizabeth. Always intensely loyal to each other, the Davis children shared the lessons of their childhood with their families. Joe passed away in 2004.

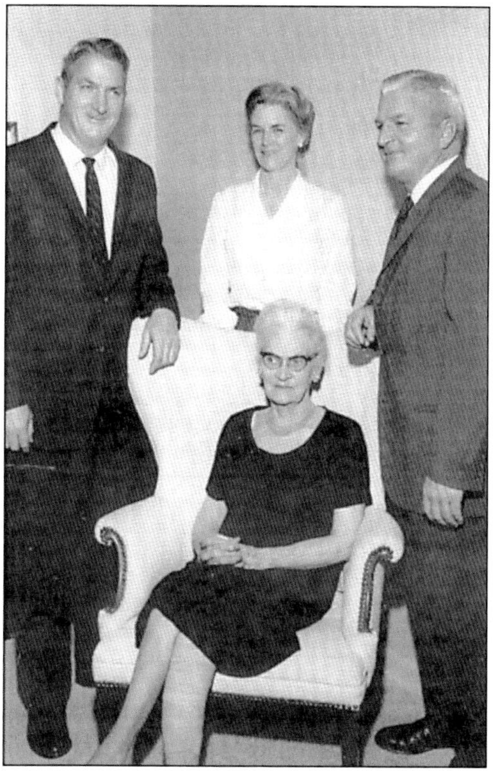

MRS. MYRTLE DORSETT DAVIS. In August 1916 J. Mercer Davis, the young secretary-treasurer in the Albertville business firm Roberts, Luther, and Company, married Myrtle Dorsett. Albertville Baptist pastor Rev. J.O. Colley married them at the church's pastorium. Myrtle survived her husband by over 35 years and died in January 1976. Her children surround her in this photograph; pictured from left to right are Dorsett Davis, Elizabeth Davis Morgan, and Dr. Joe M. Davis.

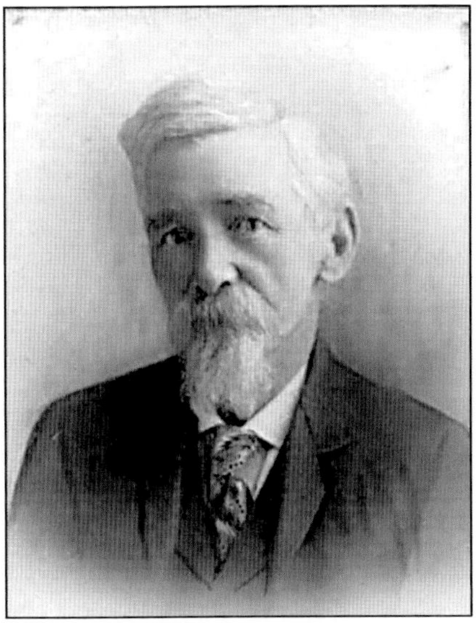

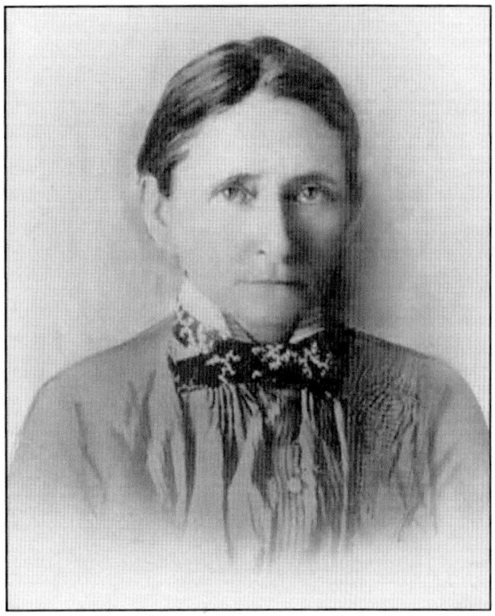

ALEXANDER CAMPBELL WALKER SR. AND JULIA VAUGHAN WALKER. Alexander Campbell Walker Sr. was born in Grangemouth, Scotland, in 1848 and became a skilled seaman aboard a training ship out of Liverpool, England. He served aboard ships with routes from London to India. At one point he was aboard a ship for 103 days without seeing land. Following this, he worked for three years in a gold mine in Australia. In 1872 he arrived in San Francisco. From there he departed for the east, settling in the Tuscumbia area of Alabama. For the next 31 years, he and his family resided at Wheeler Station, Alabama; during this time, he was in charge of tax books for Lawrence County and served as private secretary to Gen. Joseph Wheeler, famed officer of the Civil and Spanish-American Wars. In 1903 Alexander, his wife, Julia, and members of his family moved to Sand Mountain. A little more than a year after arriving in Albertville, Julia Walker died. Captain Walker, as he was known, survived his wife by 18 years.

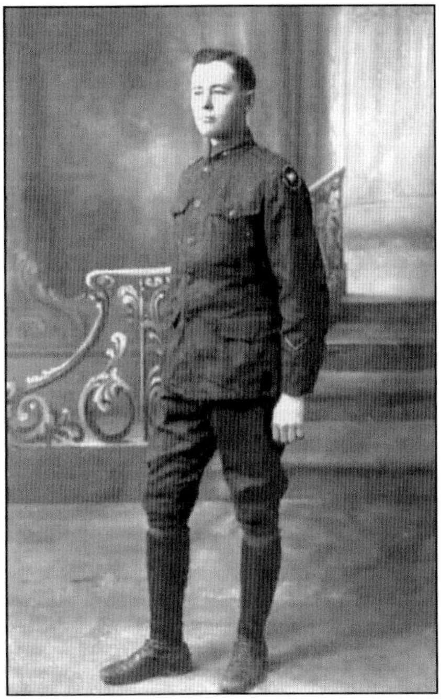

"OVER THERE, OVER THERE, SEND THE WORD, SEND THE WORD, OVER THERE, THAT THE YANKS ARE COMING, THE YANKS ARE COMING. . . ." Sitting in a Roman Catholic chapel in Europe during the closing days of World War I, young Christie Walker wrote his brother, Jim, about his experiences. He wrote about the soldiers' sleeping accommodations, describing that they slept on "what was left after the horses, cows, goats, rats, cats, dogs, chickens, and cooties had selected their home." He also remarked how disappointing it would be for "Papa" if he did not have a chance to go to Scotland to visit their ancestral home.

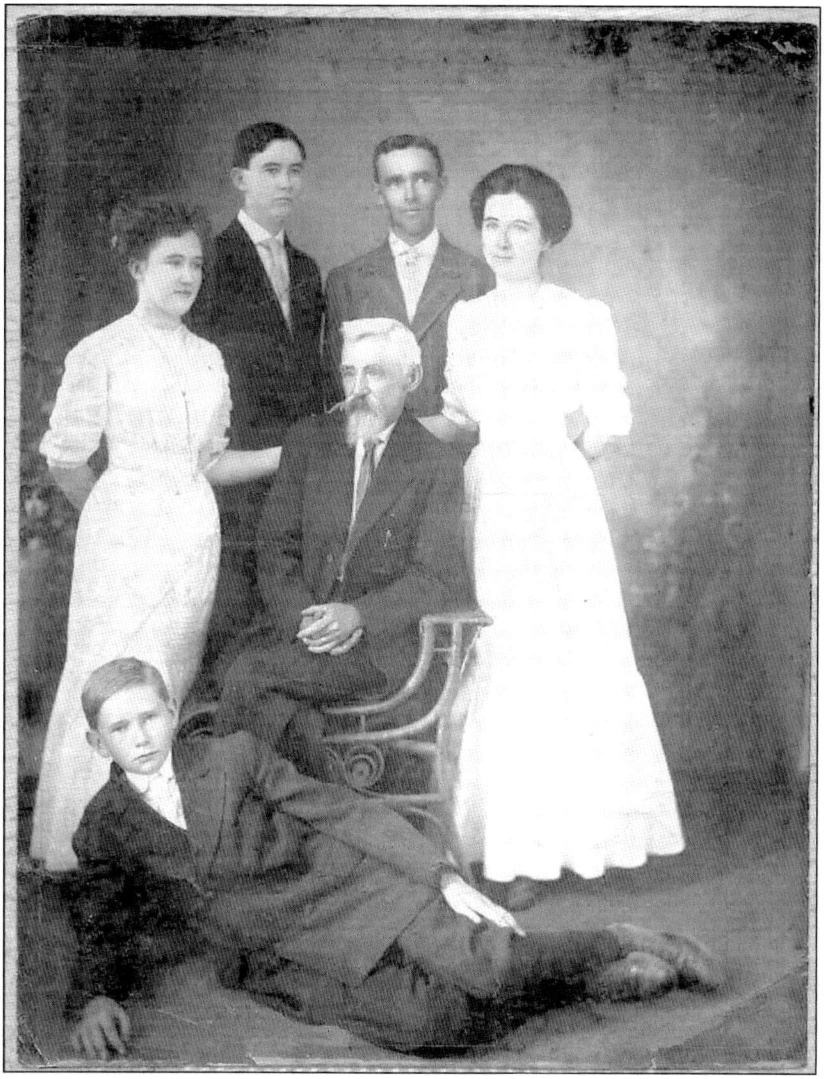

ALEXANDER C. WALKER SR. WITH FIVE OF HIS CHILDREN. One of the youngest of the Walker children, Madison, pictured lying on the floor in front of his father, died in 1934 as a result of complications of a tropical disease he contracted while serving in the army in the Panama Canal Zone.

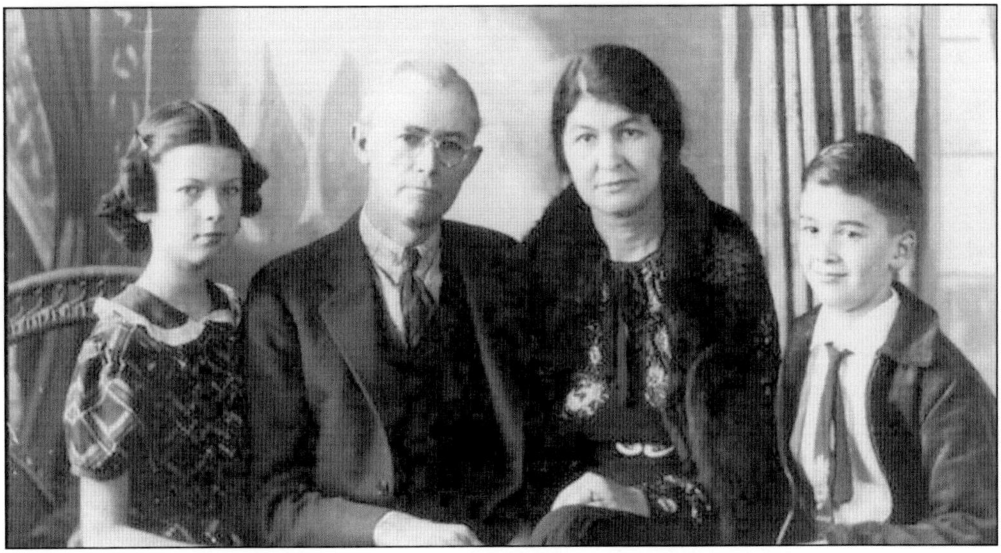

CHRISTOPHER J. "CHRISTIE" WALKER SR. AND FAMILY. Shown with C.J. Walker and his wife, the former Berty Baker, is their daughter, Martha (Davis), and son, C.J. Jr., better known as Kit. In 1955 the couple took a seven-week tour of Europe. One of the highlights for Christie was the journey to his father's hometown in Scotland. The couple also concluded that they enjoyed ship travel, namely on board the *Queen Elizabeth*, more than airline flights.

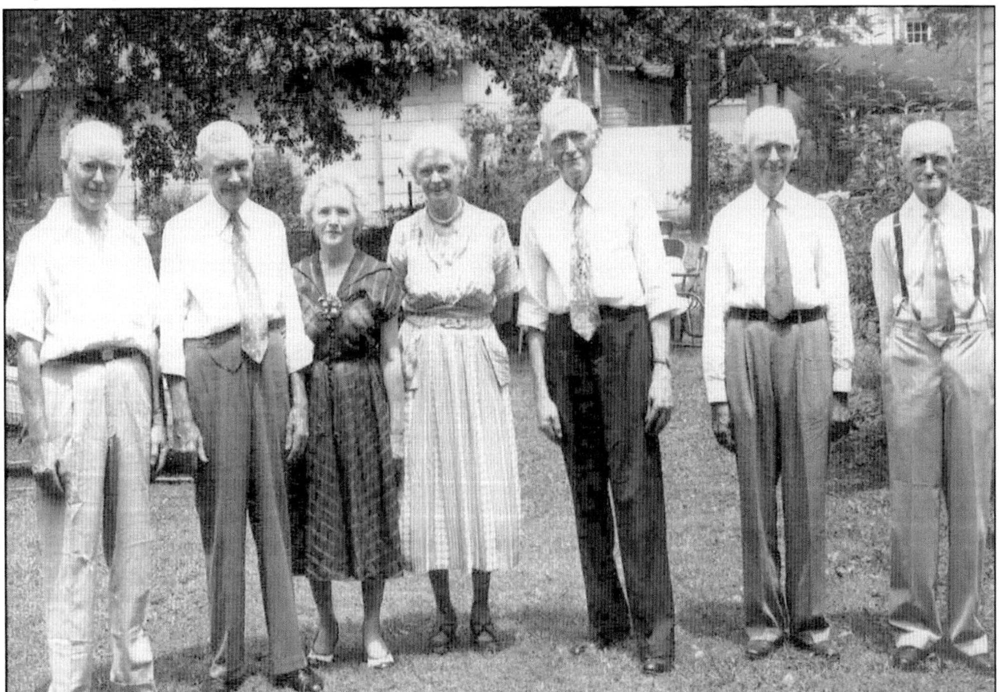

FAMILY PORTRAIT. Less than a century after Capt. A.C. Walker arrived in the United States, his family had become established members of American society. Shown here with their siblings are Christopher J. Walker Sr. (left) and James Walthall Walker (right), both of whom became prominent businessmen in the Albertville community.

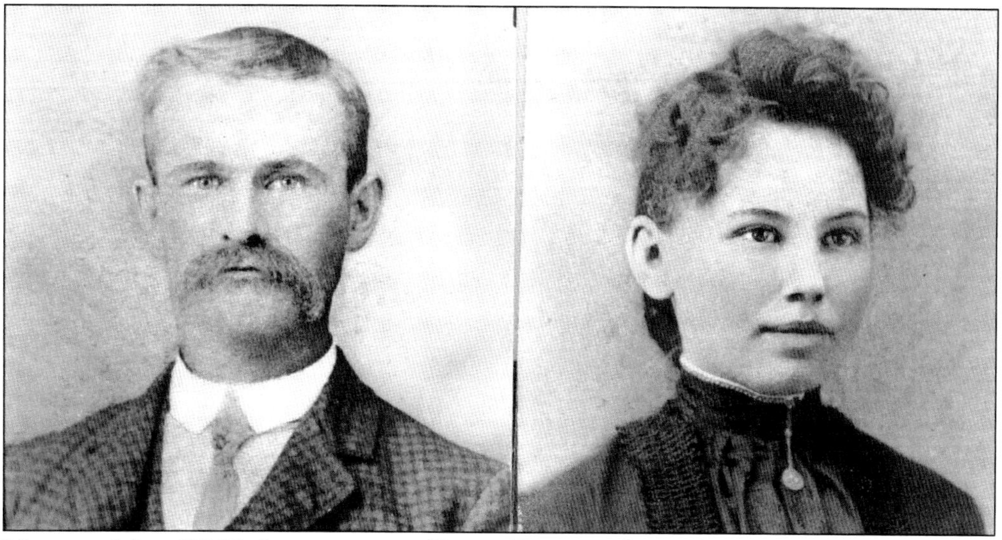

MR. AND MRS. J.B.H. LUMPKIN, THE EARLY YEARS. When John Berry Hay Lumpkin and Mattie Wakefield were married, Albertville was still a pioneer town. By 1893 the town was dotted by some 20–25 stores; however, it was still strongly geared toward its agriculture base. Over the years, J.B.H. Lumpkin distinguished his reputation through agricultural pursuits, achieving the title of Master Farmer by the farmer's association.

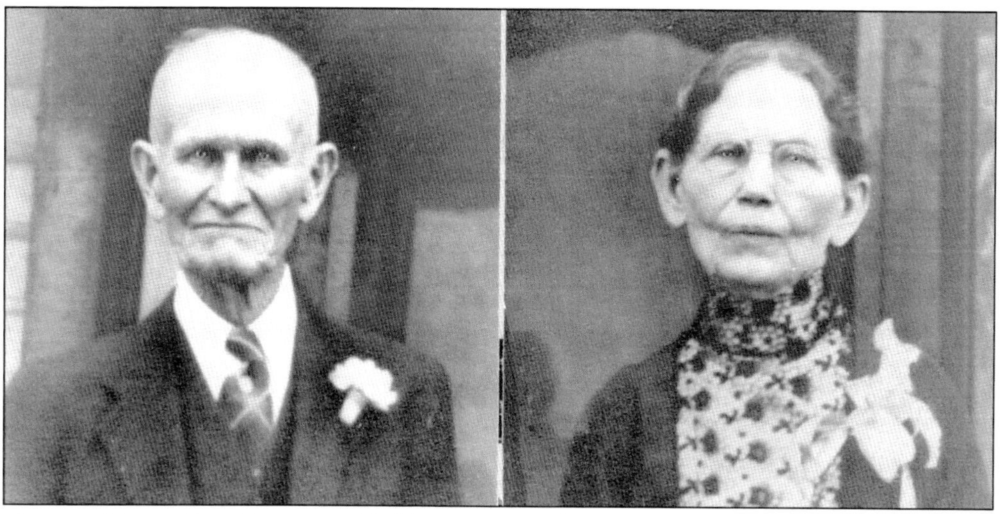

MR. AND MRS. J.B.H. LUMPKIN, 50 YEARS LATER. By the couple's 50th wedding anniversary, the city of Albertville, and the world as a whole, had changed immeasurably. In 1949 Mattie passed away. In 1954 at the age of 94, Lumpkin, with assistance from his fellow church members, broke ground for the church's new educational wing. Rev. Brady Justice, a pastor at First Baptist Church of Albertville, always remembered being interviewed by Lumpkin and the church's pastoral search committee in 1926. Reverend Justice recalled one exchange in which Lumpkin made the following comment: "Brother Justice, some of the ladies are concerned that you are not married, but we just feel that you were just waiting to get a church and you will tell her to come on." Reverend Justice answered, "Brother Lumpkin, you tell the committee that I don't even have a prospect, and if they call me, they will have to call me without being married." That must have been a satisfactory answer; Reverend Justice served the church as pastor from 1926 to 1931. He married within a year of moving to Albertville.

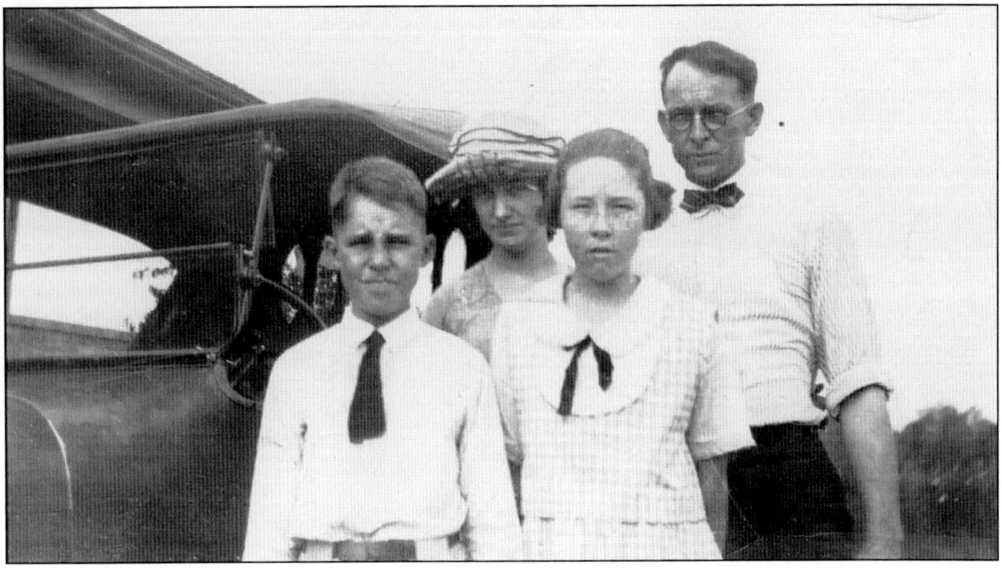

B.A. Alford Family, Part I. In 1920 B.A. Alford, a Childersburg, Alabama native, moved to Albertville and became a buyer for the Robinson Brothers firm. In 1921 Alford married Emmie Sue Lumpkin, daughter of J.B.H. Lumpkin. He had been married twice before, but both wives passed away before his move to Albertville. Though Alford had no children by his second wife, he had two by his first, Vivian (Walker) and James, pictured above with their father and his wife, Emmie. In 1929 B.A. established the Alford Cotton Company.

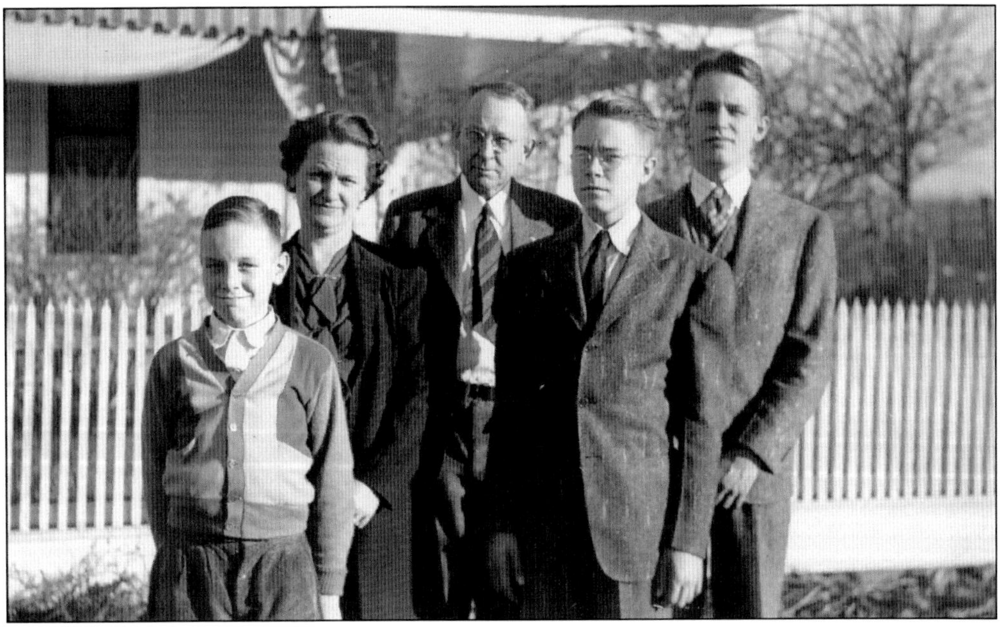

B.A. Alford Family, Part II. Pictured with B.A. and Emmie Sue Alford are their sons, from left to right, Harold Bennett, William Lumpkin, and John Frank. On January 2, 1967, B.A. died after 47 years in his adopted home of Albertville. A long time had passed since the first day he arrived in Albertville. A family friend, Bess Williams, later recalled that first day when a Roadster, driven by a widower carrying his two young children, stopped on the dusty road in front of their home to ask directions.

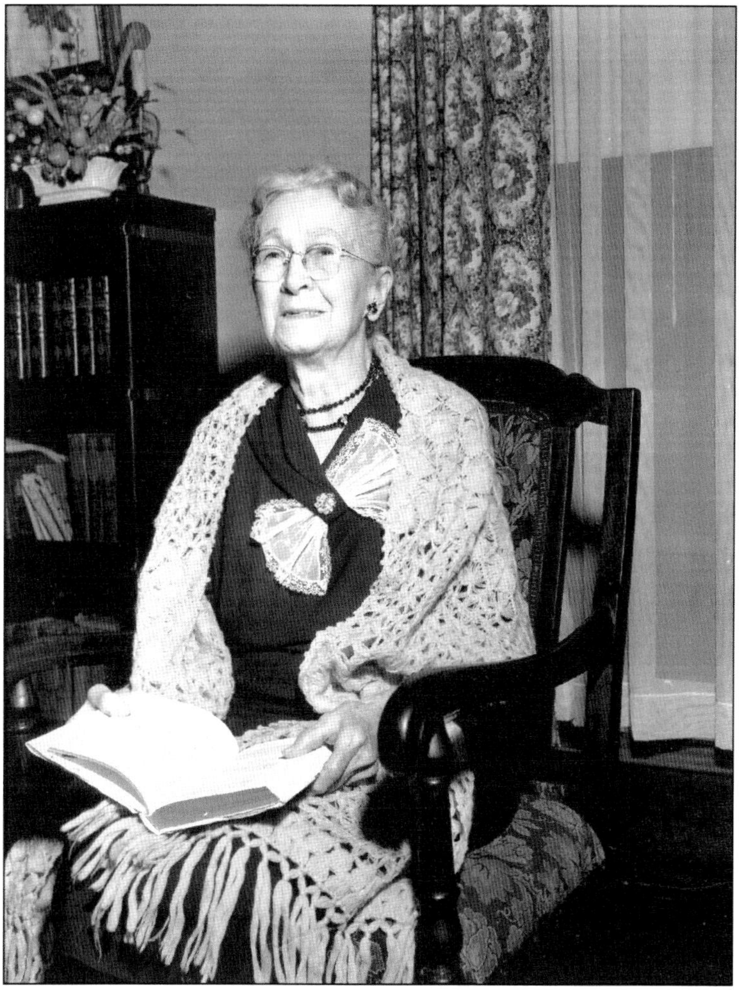

MRS. J.B. ROBERTS SR. As a result of the Civil War Centennial, the early 1960s were a time of renewed interest in the days of the Confederacy. Many newspapers printed commemorative editions for the anniversary; one in particular was *The Birmingham News*. One of the readers of that paper was Albertville citizen Mrs. J.B. Roberts Sr. While reading a section of the paper concerning Jefferson Davis, Mrs. Roberts said something that took her children completely by surprise; she described an event that had happened 67 years earlier. Looking up from the paper, in a matter-of-fact tone, she told her daughters, Eloise and Gail, "I remember meeting Jefferson Davis." After gathering their collective breath, the two of them asked, "You what? You knew him?" Almost speechless, Eloise said, "But Mother, all these years, and you never told us." The former Abigail Stanley was born in 1870 in Cusseta, Alabama, where her father owned a 500-acre plantation. She attended high school in West Point, Georgia, 10 miles away. During the spring of 1885, when "Abbie" was 15, school was dismissed for a day as the former president of the Confederacy, Jefferson Davis, would be passing through town. Students were allowed to go to the railroad depot to see him. She remembered him standing on the back platform of the train and the many cheers that went up from the students. Abbie recalled how this once-great man appeared to be so tired and, as a result, said only a few words. From there, Davis traveled on to his next destination and, ultimately, into history. Shortly after this event, Abigail's father, Alphonso Stanley, sold his plantation and moved his family to Lafayette, Alabama, where Abbie met her future husband, James Bailey Roberts. In 1900 she and her husband moved to Albertville.

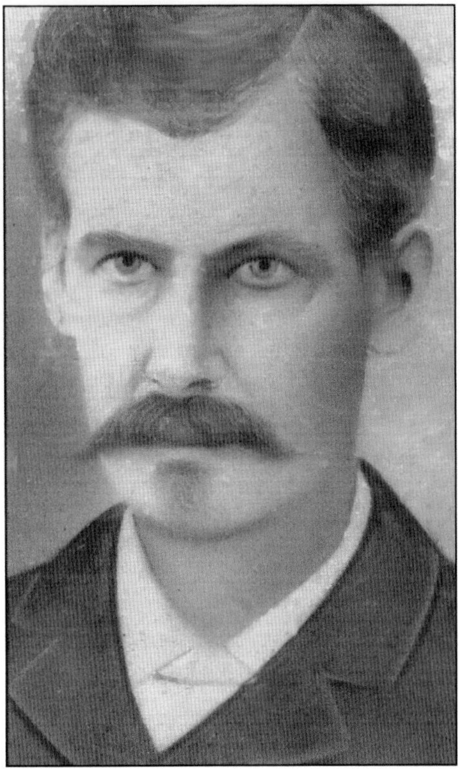

JOEL LELAND GRAHAM. About 1893 Joel Graham decided that it was time to move his family from their home in Conyers, Georgia. Years later his son, Charlie, said that his father wanted to move to an area where everyone was not related. To make an informed decision about moving, he journeyed first to Gadsden, then Boaz, and finally to the family's future home, Albertville. Returning home to Georgia, he loaded the oldest children on wagons to travel with him and the youngest on a train with their mother. Before long, he would become one of the town's businessmen, constructing a cotton gin, a grist mill, and a sawmill. In 1910 another son, Pink, established a drug store on the south side of Main Street. In 1916 Joel Graham died suddenly while visiting his son's drug store.

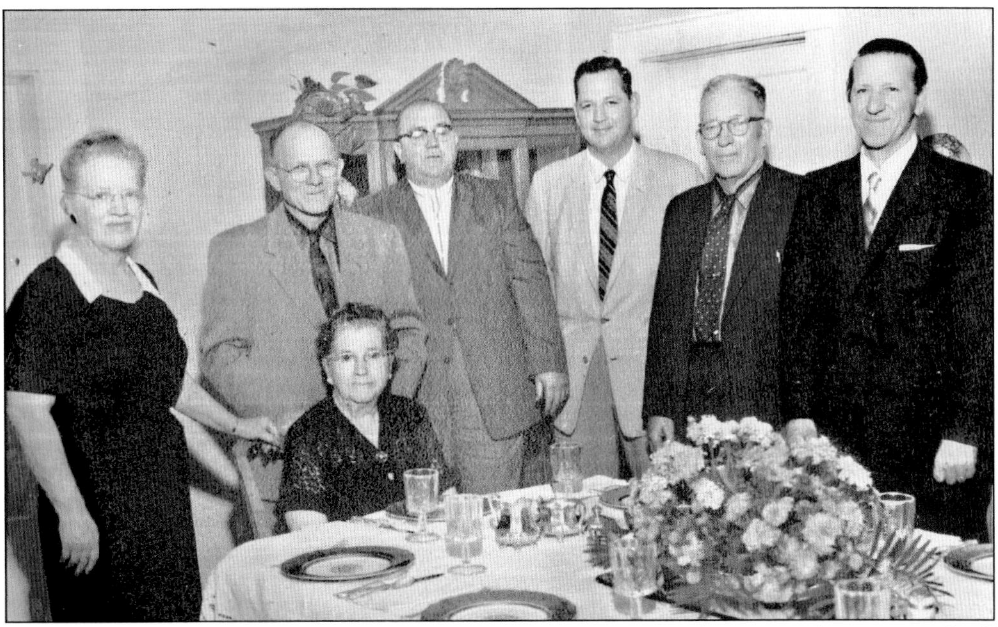

THE J.B. AND IDA THOMAS FAMILY. After J.B.'s death in 1942, the times of reunion with all five of Ida's children were few and far between. Though two of her children, John Aubrey and Josie, lived close by, distance was an issue with her other four children. Roy lived in Los Angeles, Lester lived in Akron, Carl lived in Daytona Beach, and James lived in Equality in south Alabama.

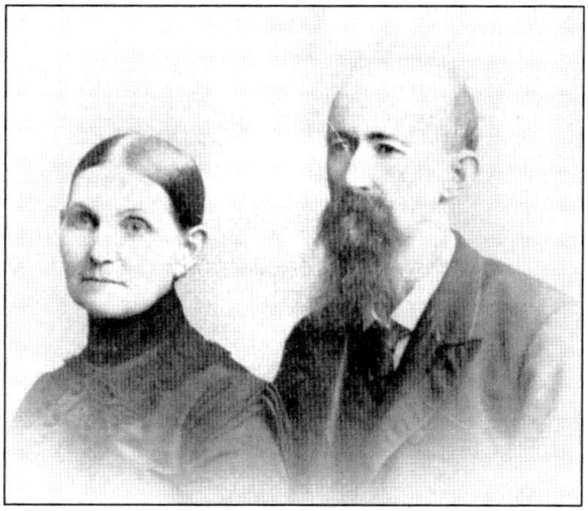

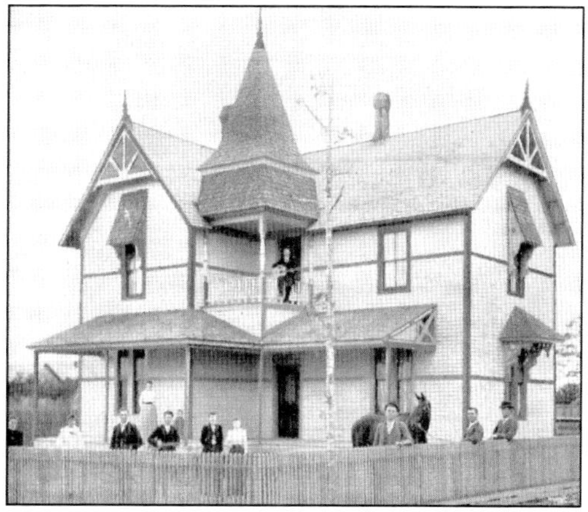

L.S. AND MARY EMMETT. On September 2, 1881, Gainesville, Georgia native L.S. Emmett and his family settled in the pioneer town of Albertville. Later recalling his first impressions of the area, he wrote, "I beheld a country with no attractions in sight except fine timber, balmy breezes, pretty land, splendid roads and pure water." Their caravan consisted of seven loaded wagons that served as the nucleus for his new mercantile store. Though others settled the town and gave it its name, L.S. Emmett sparked expansion in the business community. In 14 years his store grew into a thriving business with three departments—dry goods, grocery, and a third part, housed in a new building, consisting of furniture, cotton weighing, and undertaking. His entire family became active in the town's business affairs. From the small department of the Emmett store carrying handles and other hardware for those who built caskets grew the Emmett Funeral Home, which was run by his oldest son, Perino. His daughter, Lula, married Thomas McNaron, who first worked for her father as a bookkeeper and later became a prominent businessman. Above right is the Emmett family home.

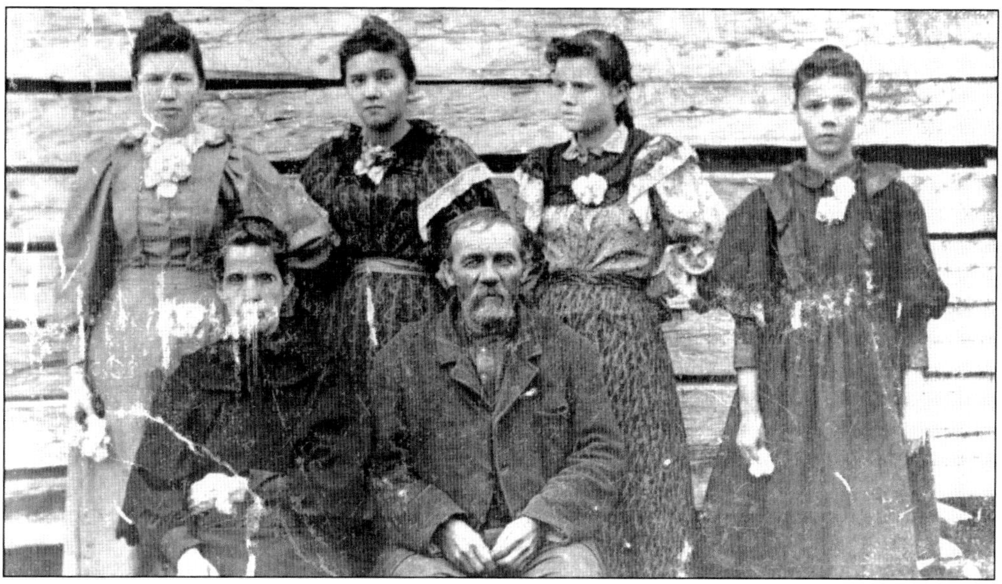

THE AMBROSE NALL FAMILY. Old Bethel Cemetery, northeast of Albertville, is the resting place for three veterans of the Civil War. Like many others from the area, these gentlemen enlisted in the Union Army, rather than the Confederacy, because of their political beliefs. Two of the three, Elijah Miller Isbell and John Houston Bearden, served in the Union Cavalry, and the third, Ambrose Nall, served in the Union Navy. Ambrose is pictured above with his family.

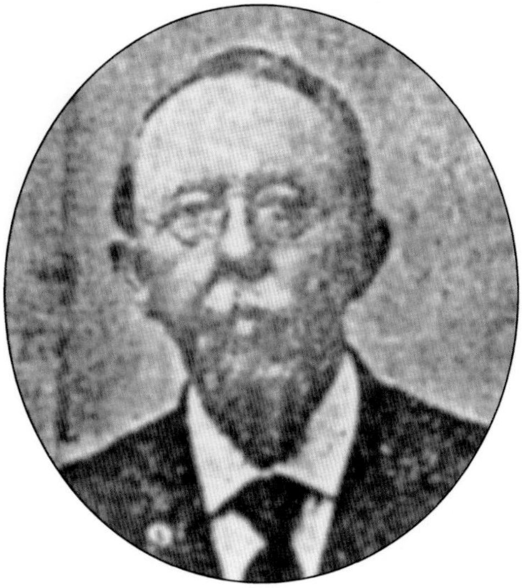

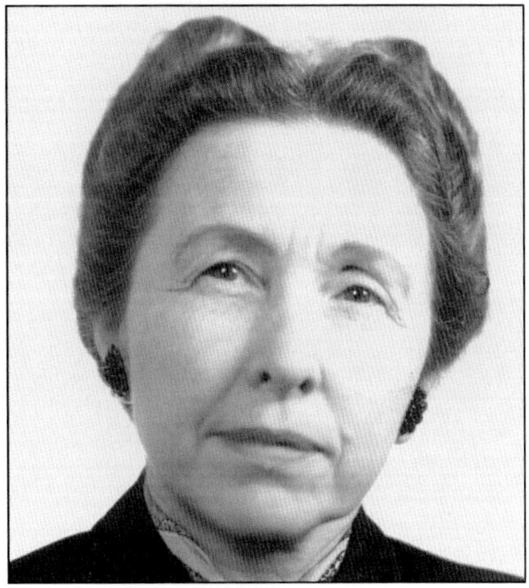

The Family Spirit, Rev. Sam Phillips and "Miss Kittye" Thomason. Many Albertville families contributed in different ways to the growth and welfare of the town for generations. One such family began with Rev. Sam Phillips, who ministered to residents and served in the Alabama legislature. He married Martha Perkins. Among their children was Katherine Phillips, wife of L.C. Adkins, who built a Coca-Cola bottling plant after the turn of the century. Their daughter, Mary Katherine Adkins, taught at Albertville High School. She married W.D. "Bill" Thomason and was a member of the First United Methodist Church of Albertville and a charter members of Albertville's chapter of the United Daughters of the Confederacy.

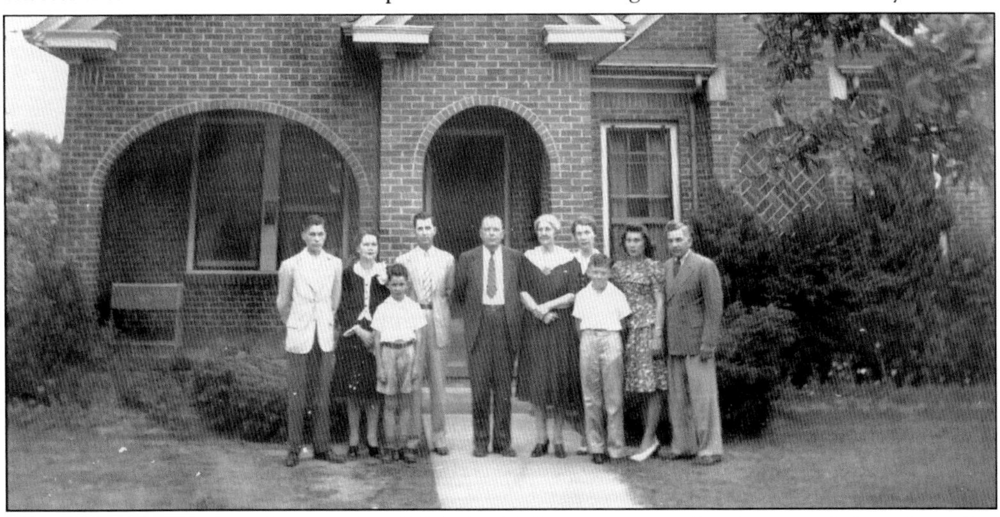

The T.D. Thompson Family. In 1906 the T.D. Thompson family moved from Brindlee Mountain to Albertville. In 1920 Thompson and his sons, Henry and Luther, purchased F.N. Archer's Albertville furniture business. He continued the business with Henry until Henry's untimely death during a college vacation in Florida. As a young man, Luther was asked by banker Hogan Jackson to work in his Arab bank. Well-received by the residents of Arab, Luther was elected mayor and is one of the youngest people in Alabama ever elected mayor. The Thompsons also had one daughter named Mayme, who married F.R. Ingram. From left to right are Jack Thompson, Mary Emma Thompson, James Thompson, Luther Thompson, T.D. Thompson, Willie Thompson, Mayme Ingram, Tommy Ingram, Jean Ingram, and F.R. Ingram.

DASHING YOUNG MEN. The sons of James Frank and Mattie Machen Rains of the Asbury community are pictured from left to right as follows: (front row) Burley, Carl, and Montgomery; (back row) Ester, Chester, Leslie, and Fred.

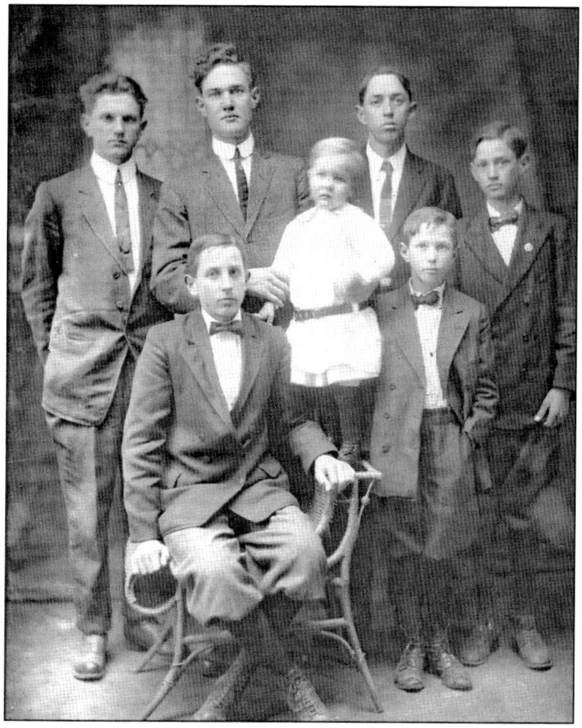

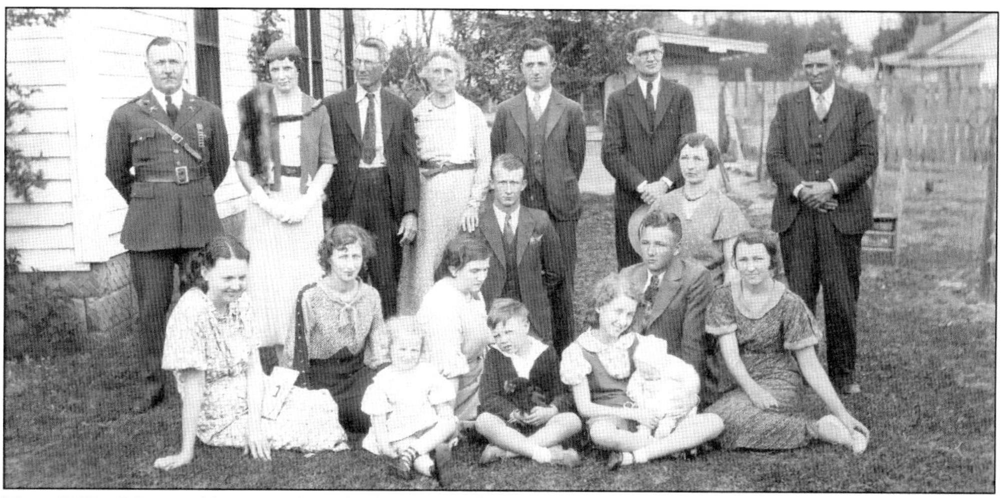

THE T.L. MANN FAMILY. In 1916 T.L. and Amanda Mann moved to Albertville from the Whiton community. Before buying an interest in one of the town's leading stores, The Starr Company, T.L. operated a grist mill near the current site of the Marshall County Courthouse on West Main Street. One of T.L. Mann's hobbies was hunting. One day, he and his son, Morgan, also known as "Kluxie," went hunting for squirrel near Rice's Mill. After deciding to go separate ways, Morgan thought he had found his mark when he saw some leaves rustling, so he fired. Suddenly, he heard his father call out, "Morgan did you fire your gun?" He answered excitedly, "Yes, Papa, I shot a squirrel." His father replied, "You shot me!" At the infirmary, Dr. B.C. Scarbrough removed 16 number-four shots from T.L. Mann's scalp and shoulder. In this photograph, Mr. and Mrs. Mann are pictured third and fourth from the left in the back; Mrs. Mann has her hand on Morgan's shoulder.

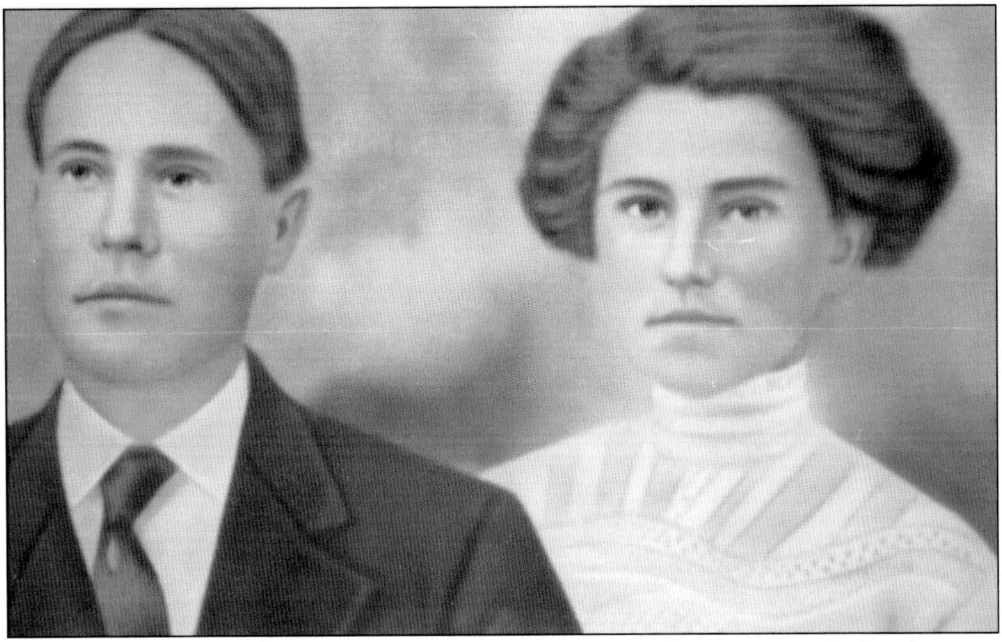

CHARLIE AND NEELY GRAHAM. In June 1911 a most unusual marriage took place between Albertville resident Charlie Graham and Neely Isbell of the Whiton community. They were married, according to a newspaper of the time, in the public road near the Marshall-DeKalb County line. Charlie Graham was the son of Joel Leland Graham, who had moved his family to Albertville c. 1893.

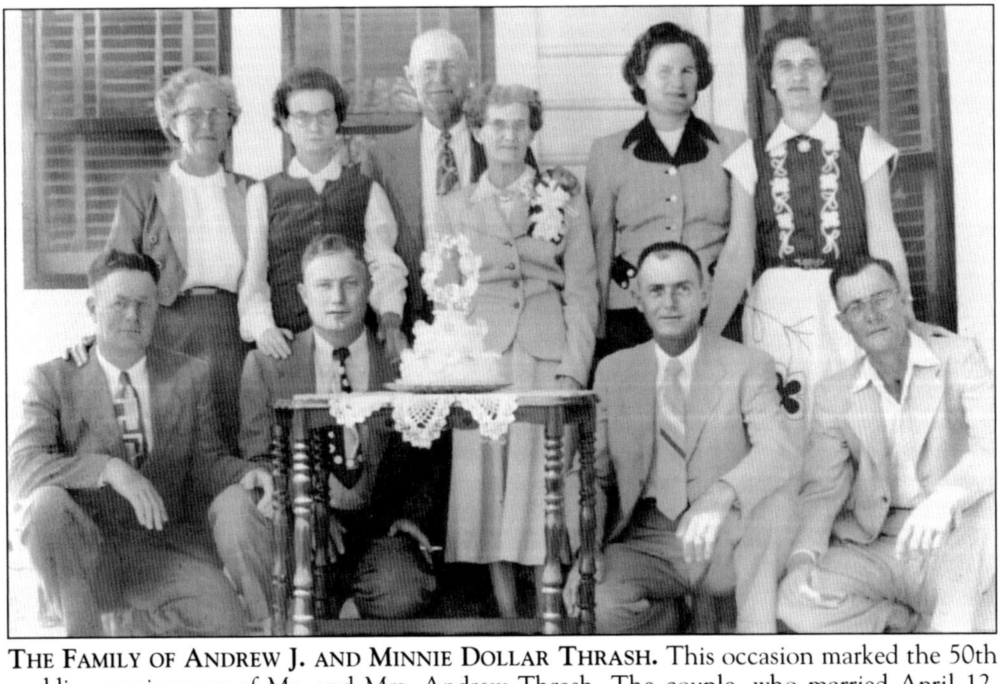

THE FAMILY OF ANDREW J. AND MINNIE DOLLAR THRASH. This occasion marked the 50th wedding anniversary of Mr. and Mrs. Andrew Thrash. The couple, who married April 12, 1903, is shown with their children, Connie, Marie, Alma, Gladys, Fillmore, Thomas, Delmus, and Houston.

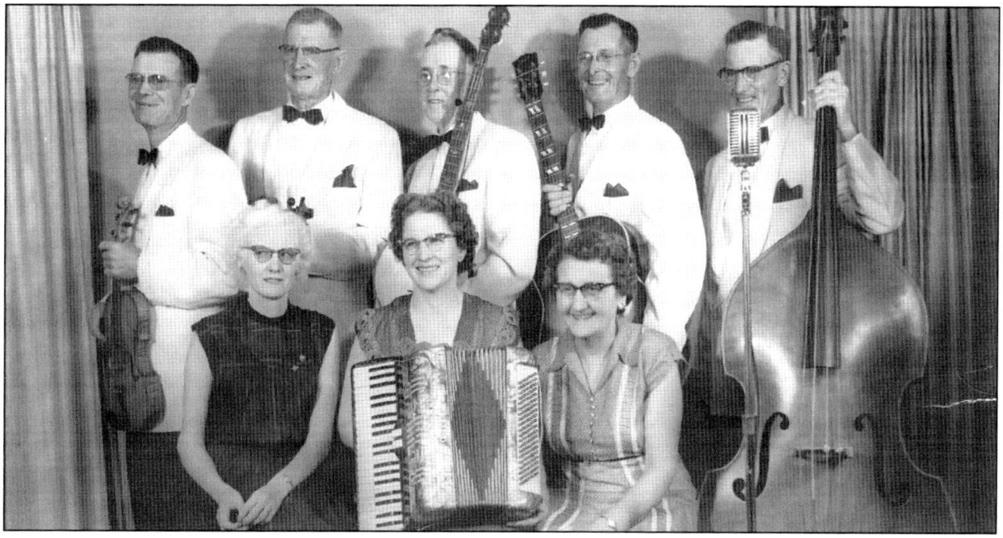

THE JOHNSON FAMILY BAND. For years, the premier musical group on Sand Mountain was the Johnson String Band from the Hustleville community, just north of Albertville. Originally, the group consisted of the six sons of George and Elizabeth Jane Johnson. The following members are pictured from left to right: (seated) Imogene Pledger; Mrs. Leo Johnson (Imogene's mother), who played the piano and accordion; and Mrs. Ras Johnson, the vocalist; (standing) Leo, who played the violin; H., the oldest, who also played the violin; Bert Stevens, the only non-related member, who played the banjo; Ras, who played the guitar; and Adous, who played the bass violin. In addition to their musical talent, members of the family also crafted beautiful violins.

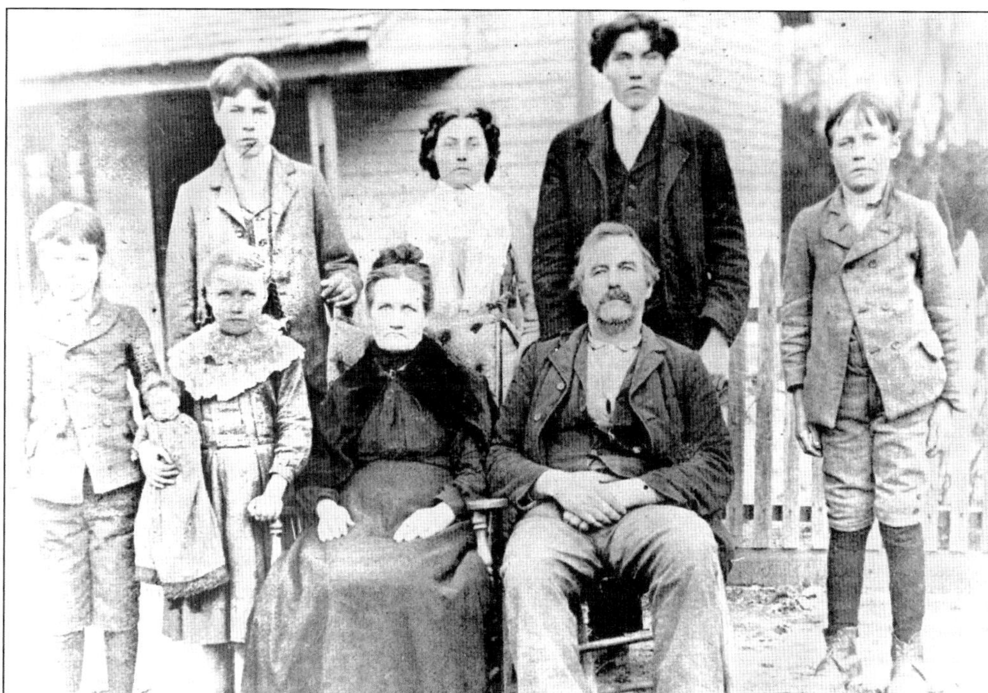

THE GEORGE SLATON FAMILY. Shown is the family of George and Sarah Horton Slaton. Numerous descendants still reside in the Poplar Springs community north of Albertville.

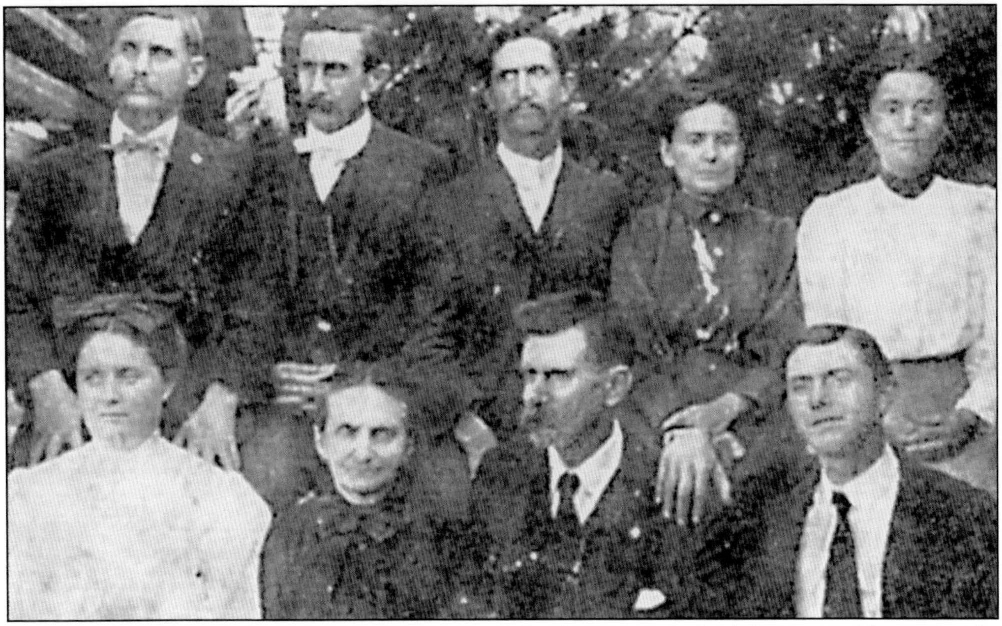

The Joel Brown Family. Around the turn of the last century, Joel Brown and his wife, the former Lourana Bice, settled in the Martling community north of Albertville. Shown here are from left to right (front row) Minnie, Lourana, Joel, and Eddie; (back row) Will, Lonnie, General, Elizabeth, and Lula. Their son John Will established the store known as Brown and Company,which operated in Martling for many years; he eventually passed it to his stepson, Howard Jackson. Another son, Jesse Elonzo, moved to Albertville and later served as mayor.

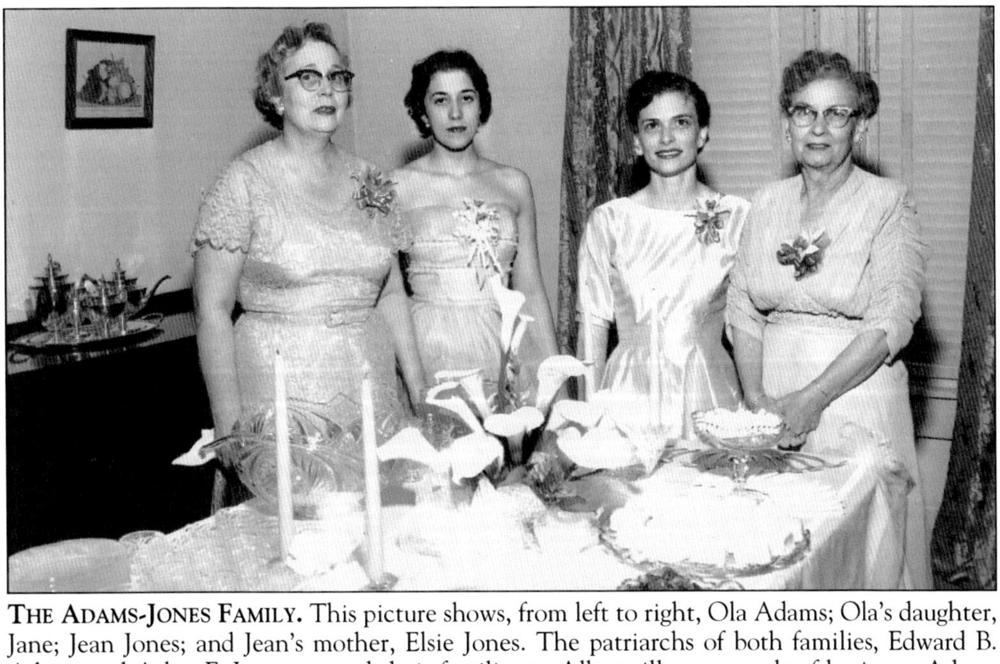

The Adams-Jones Family. This picture shows, from left to right, Ola Adams; Ola's daughter, Jane; Jean Jones; and Jean's mother, Elsie Jones. The patriarchs of both families, Edward B. Adams and Arlen F. Jones, moved their families to Albertville as a result of business. Adams was founder of the Adams Funeral Home, and Jones came to Albertville with the railroad. The two families were united in June 1950, when Jean Jones married Richard Adams.

Two
BUSINESS

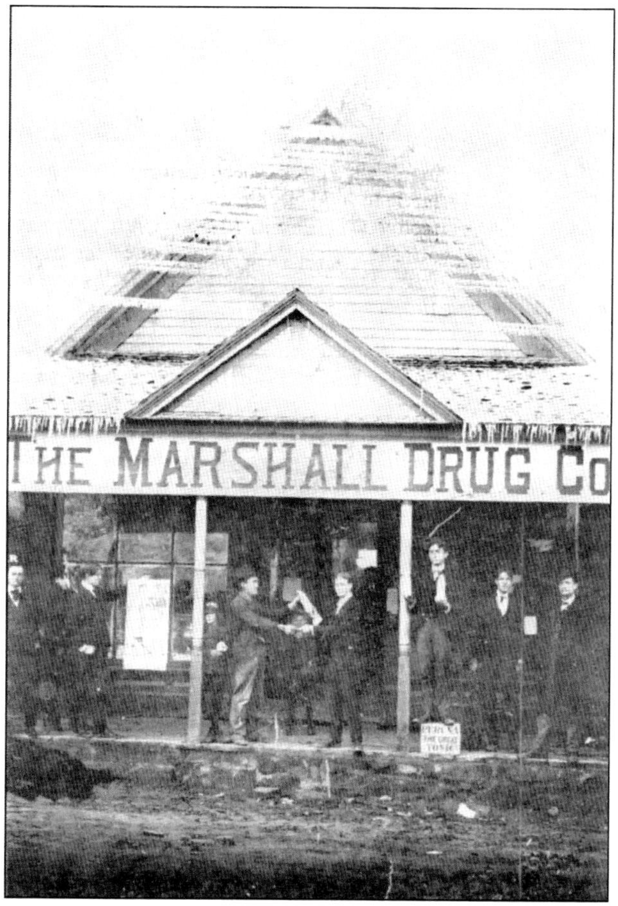

THE MARSHALL DRUG COMPANY. By 1896 Main Street had witnessed a proliferation of stores and businesses operated by men like Gran Hall, Charlie Parker, Dr. Agrippa Scott, and J.L. Graham. One business was the Averyt Drug Company, established by Dr. E.W. Averyt. For three days 23-year-old James Walker traveled the dusty roads, trails, and byways before ultimately arriving in Albertville on December 13, 1900. His move to the burgeoning town had come at the request of his business mentor, Dr. Averyt. In 1901 the business was reorganized and the more familiar name of The Marshall Drug Company was adopted. In 1919 Walker attained controlling interest in the company.

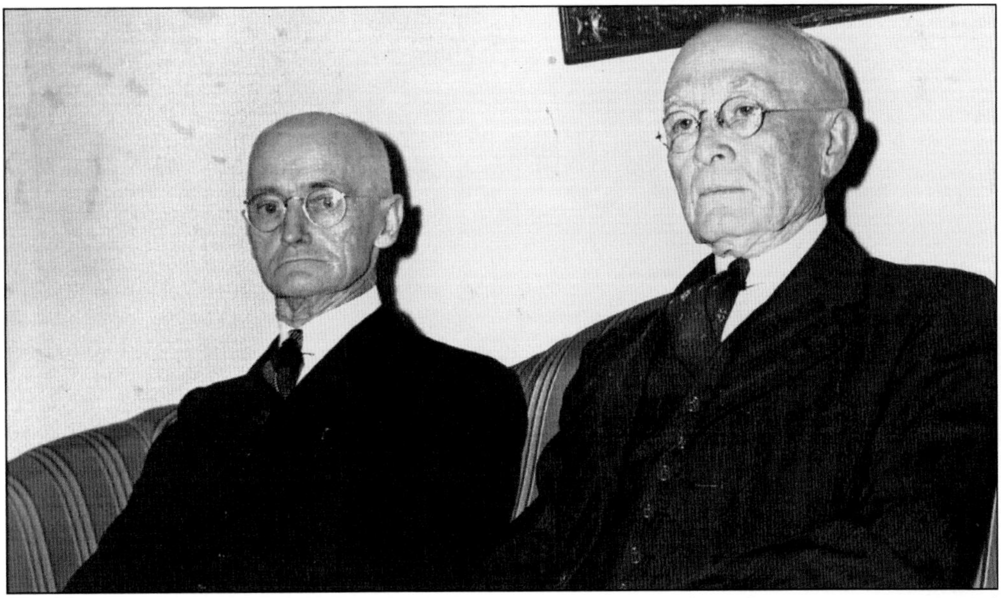

SOMBER TO SAY THE LEAST. Not undertakers, not ministers, but pharmacists are pictured here—James W. Walker (left) and his mentor, E.W. Averyt. Though Averyt eventually sold his interest in the drug store to Walker, he remained connected to Albertville, both through his farm, known as Paradise Farms, and his eventual interment at Memory Hill, the Albertville city cemetery.

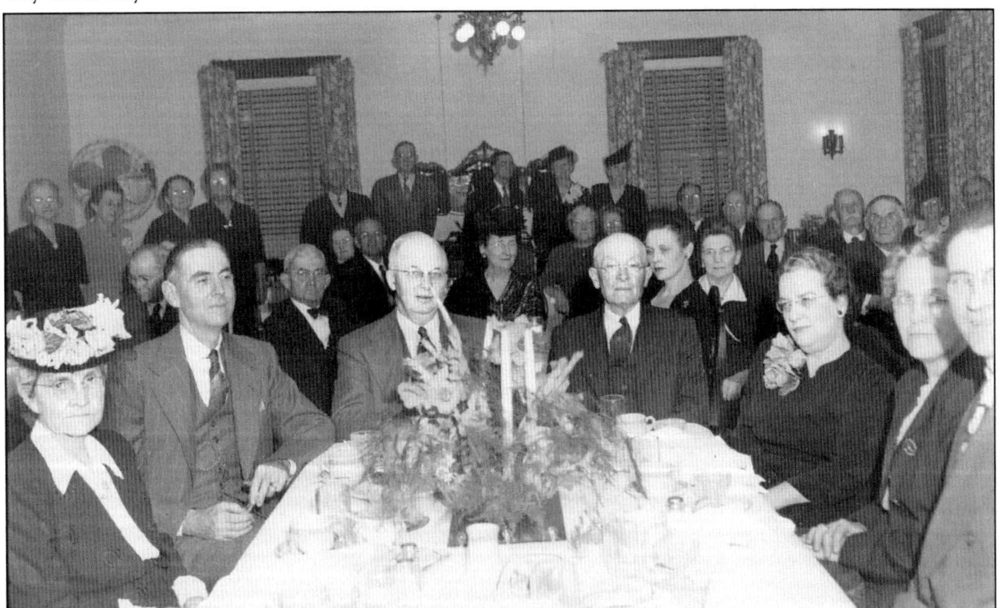

GOLDEN ANNIVERSARY CELEBRATION. On December 19, 1946, a celebration was held at Albertville's Saunders Hotel to honor the 50th anniversary of The Marshall Drug Company. The invited guests for the evening were townspeople who had known and traded with E.W. Averyt and J.W. Walker for decades. Representing the town's medical community were Dr. B.C. Scarbrough and Dr. A.L. Isbell, as well as Pink Graham, who had operated a pharmacy directly across the street for years.

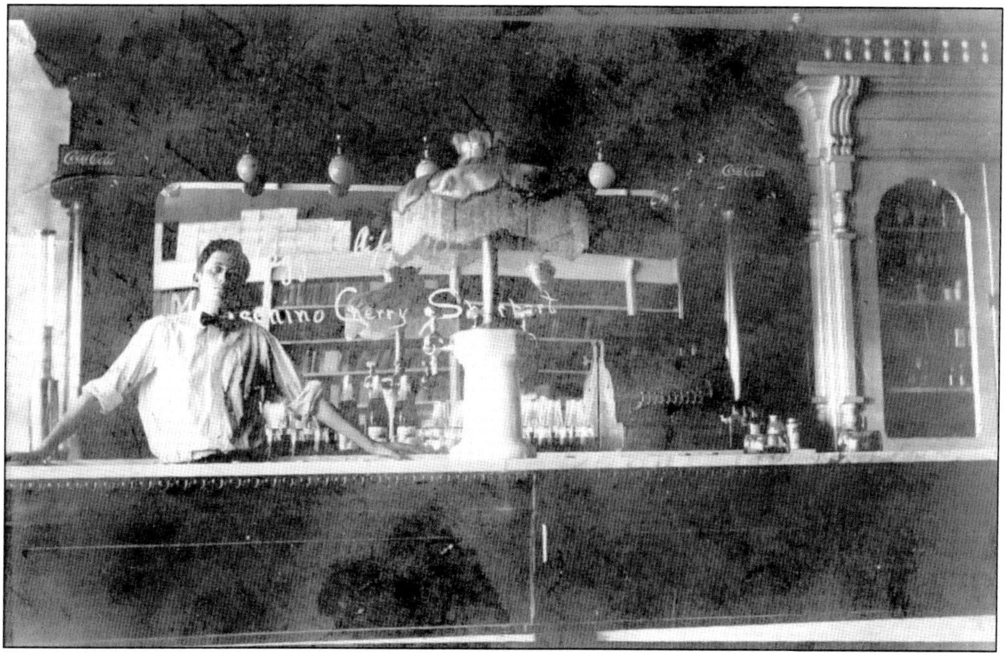

The Marshall Drug Company Soda Fountain. By 1915 Marshall Drug had established itself as a center of activity in Albertville, a reputation it retained until its closing day. One can almost taste the maraschino-cherry sundae advertised on the mirror.

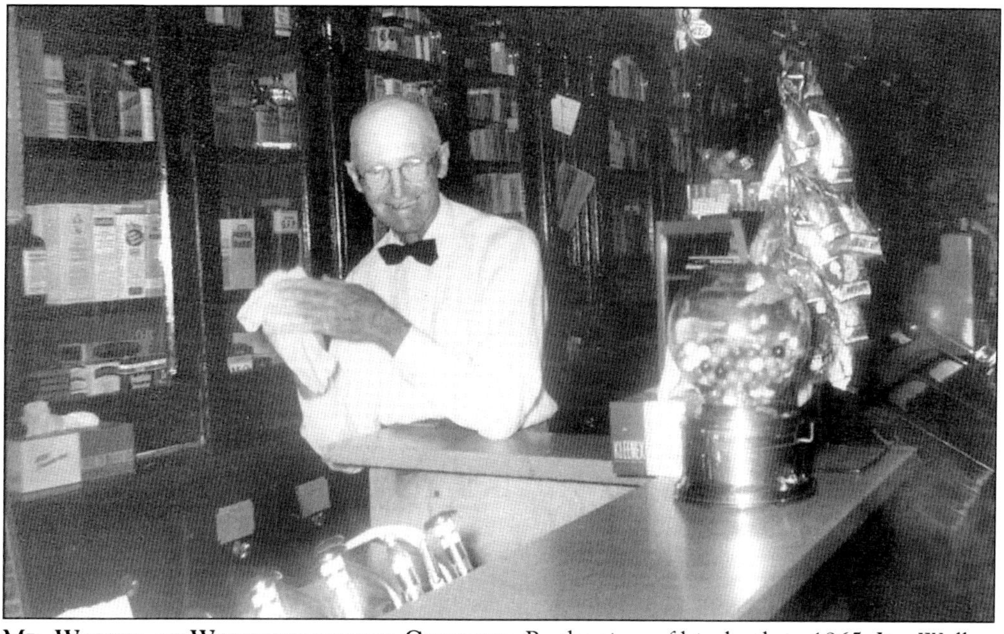

Mr. Walker at Work behind the Counter. By the time of his death in 1965, Jim Walker had "rolled," as it was called in the early days, a lot of pills. In addition to serving his customers and numerous physicians, he trained many young men for the profession of a pharmacist. He saw it as a profession, not an occupation. His son, J.W. "Pat" Walker Jr., followed in his father's footsteps and, with Albertville native John Aubrey Thomas Sr., established another Albertville institution, P&J Pharmacy.

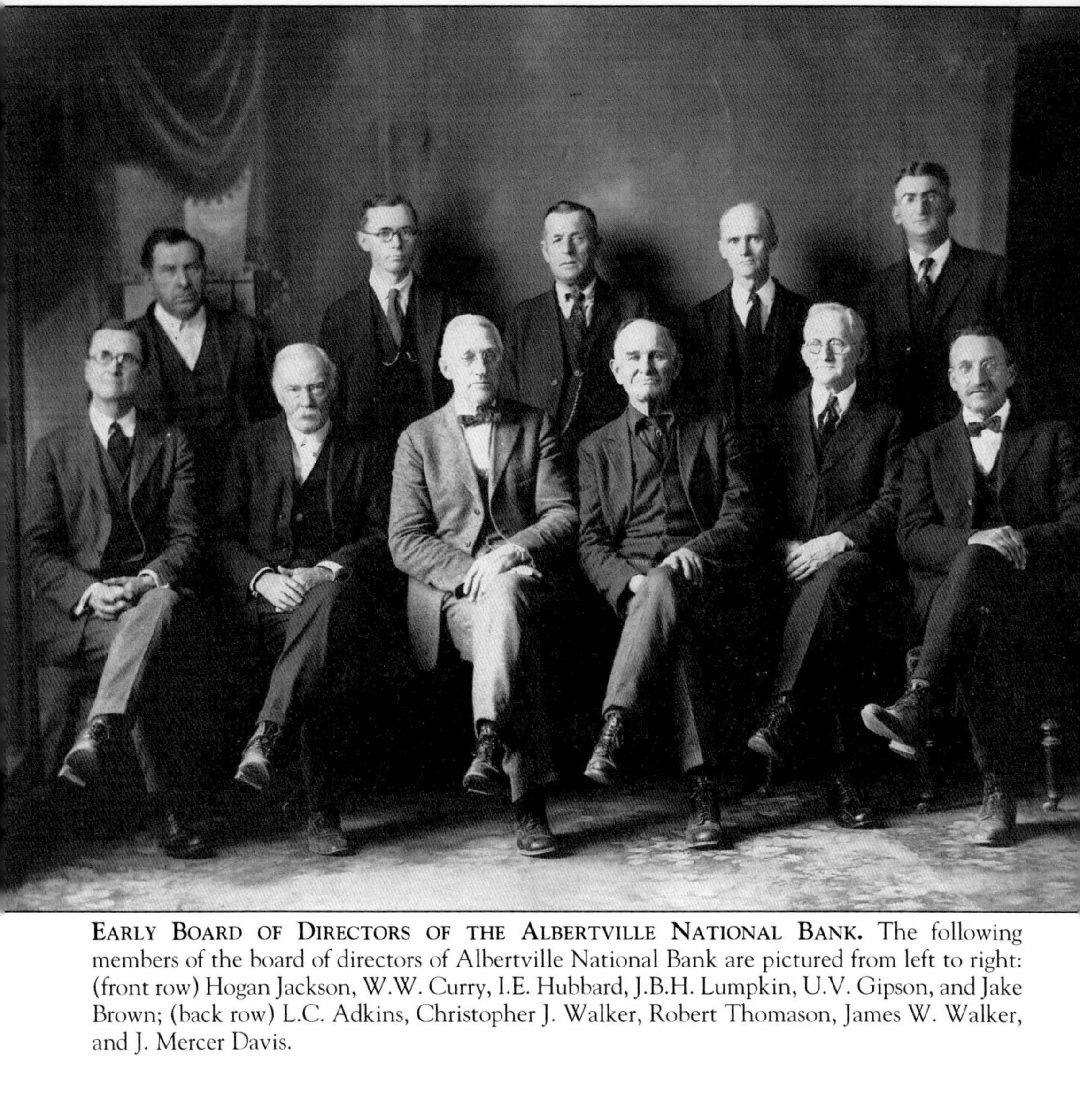

EARLY BOARD OF DIRECTORS OF THE ALBERTVILLE NATIONAL BANK. The following members of the board of directors of Albertville National Bank are pictured from left to right: (front row) Hogan Jackson, W.W. Curry, I.E. Hubbard, J.B.H. Lumpkin, U.V. Gipson, and Jake Brown; (back row) L.C. Adkins, Christopher J. Walker, Robert Thomason, James W. Walker, and J. Mercer Davis.

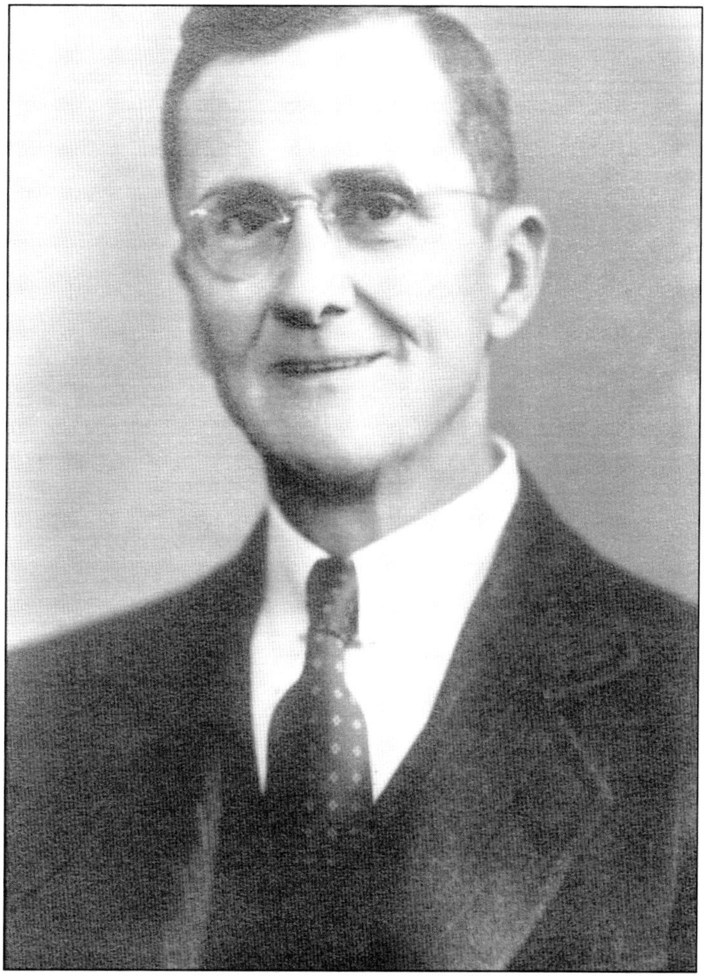

Hogan Jackson Sr. At the age of 62, Hogan Jackson recalled the Albertville of 1904: "The houses on both sides of Main Street were of frame or wood construction, with the exception of the Marshall Drug Company, which was built of rock, and the John F. Hooper private bank, which was built of brick. There were no telephones; there was no electricity, no water system, and no paved streets or sidewalks. The main event of the day was the arrival of the incoming passenger train of the North Carolina & St. Louis Railway. We would all be at the depot to see the train come and the passengers getting off and on." Actress Kate Jackson was the daughter of the late Hogan Jackson Jr.

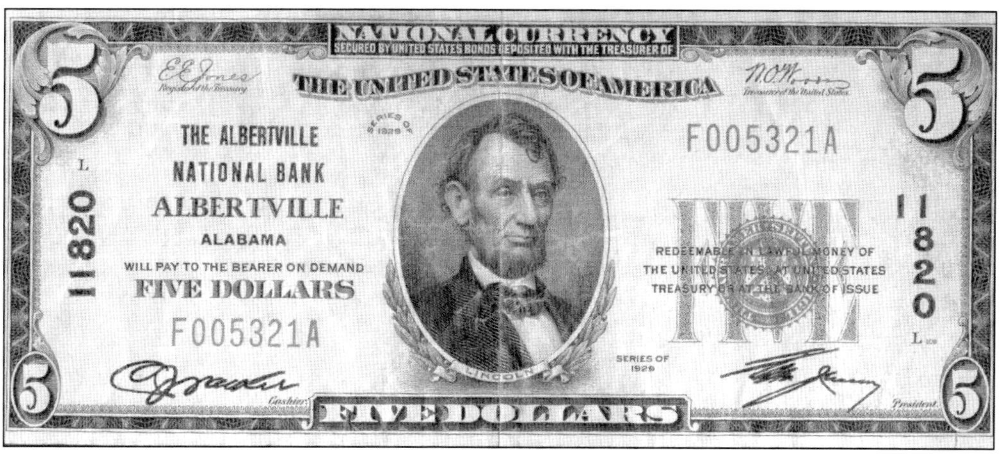

$5 Bill Issued by the Albertville National Bank. It was not unusual to receive currency bearing the name of the banking institution and signatures of bank officers 75 years ago. This $5 bill bears the name of Albertville National Bank president Hogan Jackson and bank cashier C.J. Walker.

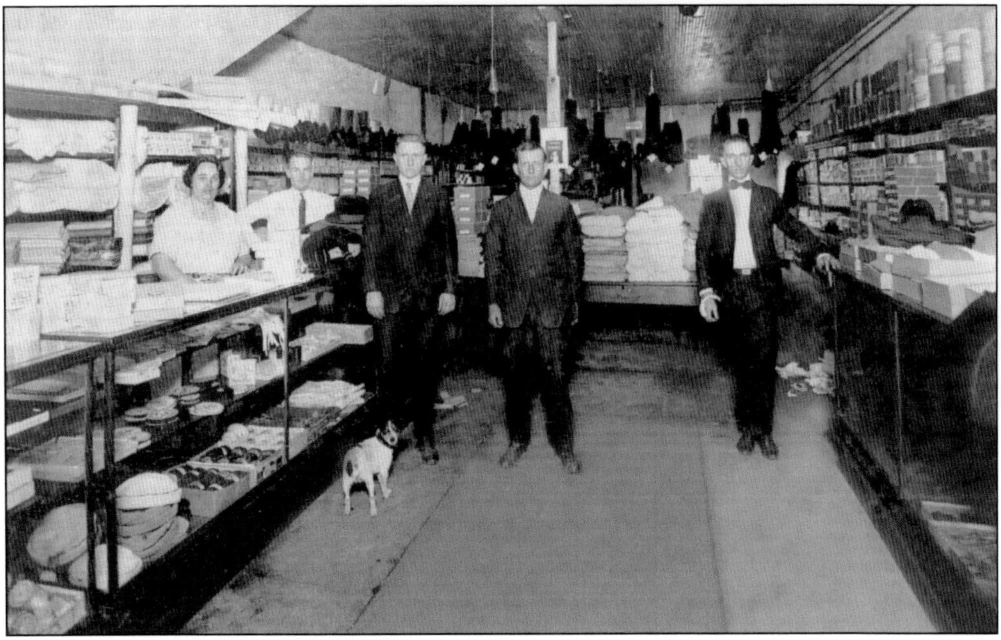

THE COLVIN AND WELLS STORE. During the summer of 1919, the firm of Colvin and Wells opened its doors in Albertville. The store, like many stores of its day, carried not only clothes, but food items, such as molasses and cured meat. A farmer needed a store that could supply all of his family's needs. As one of the partners later said, "If you didn't have some groceries in the back of the store, the farmers wouldn't trade with you."

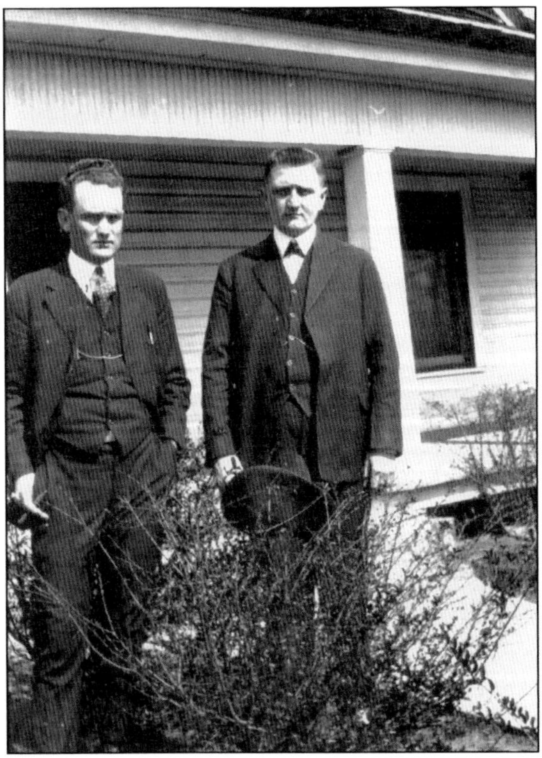

G. DEWEY WELLS AND J. PAT COLVIN. The partnership of Colvin and Wells was truly a family enterprise: J. Pat Colvin married Ethel Wells, the sister of his partner. Both businessmen brought with them valuable business experience. Colvin had operated a store in the McVille community before selling the business to H.L. Dickson and going to work for the Jefferson Standard Insurance Company. Wells had just returned from Macon, Georgia, where he had worked for 18 months in the wholesale grocery business.

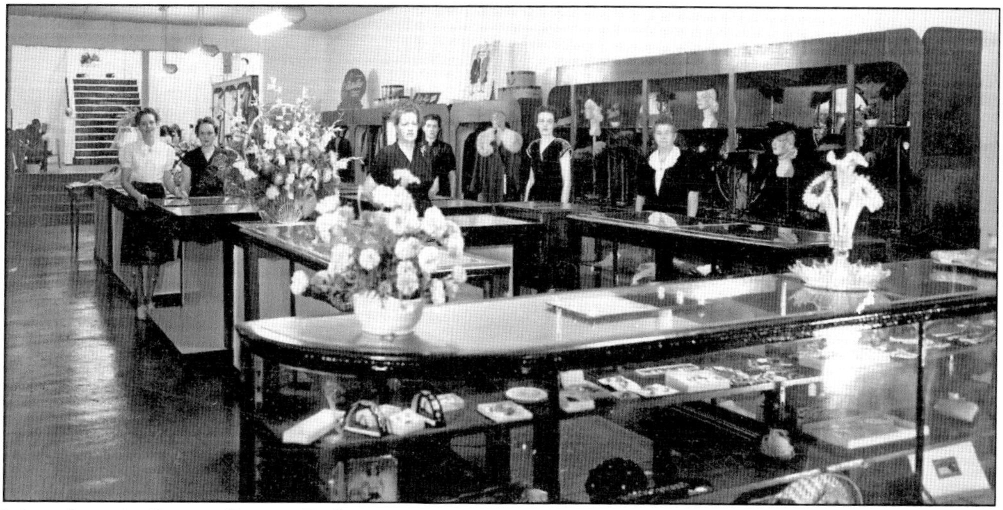

MISS JOSIE'S STYLE SHOP. Before women were even given the right to vote in the United States, Albertville's Josie Thomas was defying stereotypes for women. In 1918 she began working for the Albertville Trading Post, having already attended business courses at Athens College. After the trading post, she opened her own millinery department in another prominent store of the time, the Star Company. In 1924 she opened her own smaller store before eventually opening the store on Main Street with which she was most associated. Pictured in the center is "Miss" Josie, surrounded by her staff, including her mother, Ida Thomas, and her sister-in-law, Johnnie Thomas.

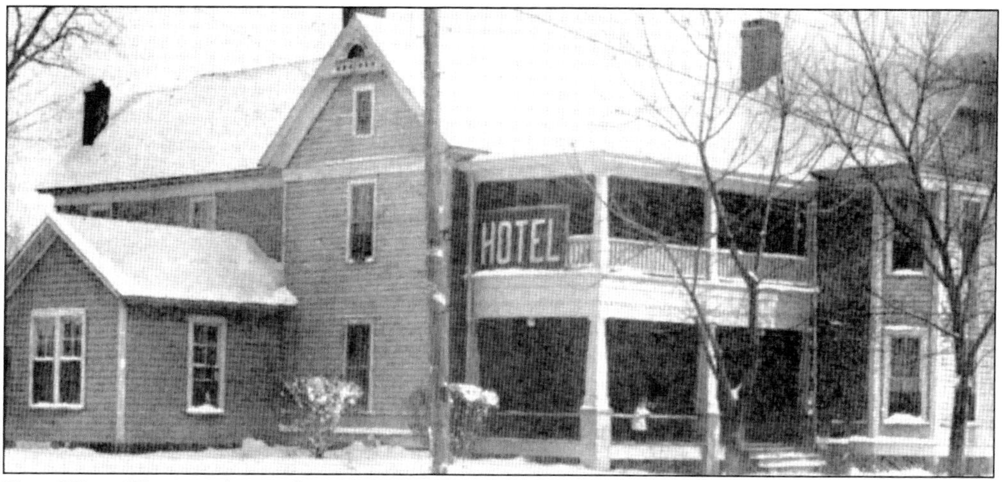

THE WITT HOTEL. Around 1907 Dr. Agrippa Scott built a hotel on Main Street across from the old wooden structure that housed the Albertville Baptist Church. About 1915 Dr. Scott announced his intentions to move to Texas. He made Birdie Saunders, who ran a boarding house in town, an offer to purchase the hotel that she could not refuse—it seemed there were a few skeletons in the Scott family closet. (Legend has it that Dr. Scott's son had murdered a man and was hiding in the attic of the old hotel. About the time the Scotts were boarding the train, a rustling was heard in the attic and a man was seen running for the train.) During the early 1930s, the grand structure burned to the ground. By this time, Mrs. Saunders had married her second husband, L.L.W. Witt, after whom the hotel was often called. It was even referred to as the New Hotel from time to time. In 1932 a new two-story brick structure was built on the old site and given the name the Saunders Hotel.

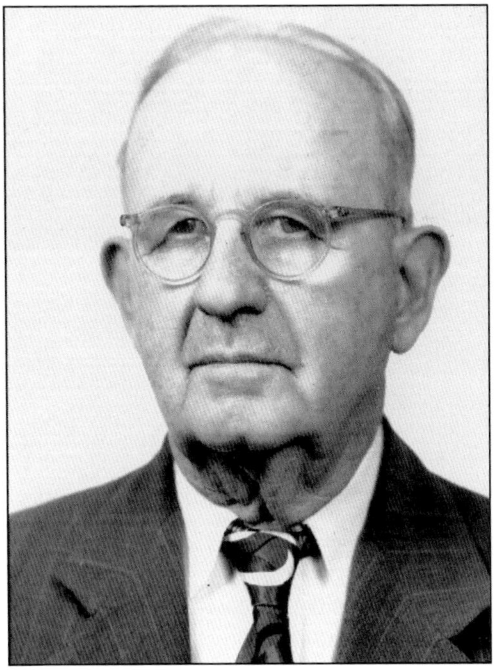

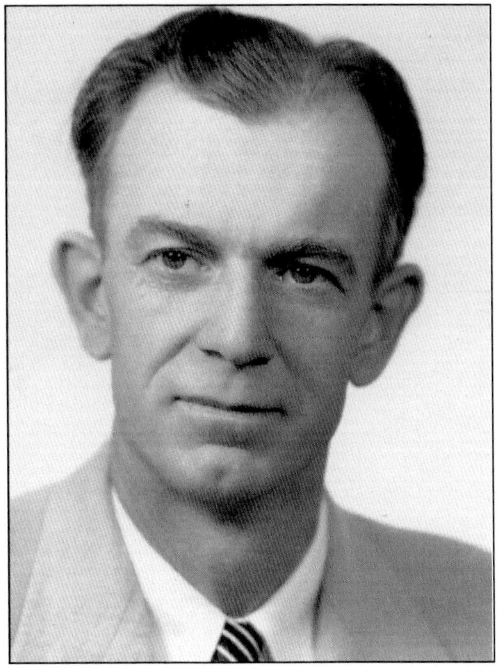

W.D. CLAYBROOKE AND NORMAN D. DARDEN. In 1912 a Kentucky attorney by the name of William Durrett Claybrooke (left) came to Albertville at the request of his father-in-law, J.E. Butler, to operate the family business, the Butler-Kyser Oil Company. After the company's assets were liquidated, Claybrooke opened a cotton gin and warehouse business. In 1929 Goodwater, Alabama native Norman Darden moved to Albertville to assume a job with the W.E. Walker Cotton Company. In 1952 he established his own business. In addition to both men being in the cotton business, they also served as deacons in the First Baptist Church of Albertville.

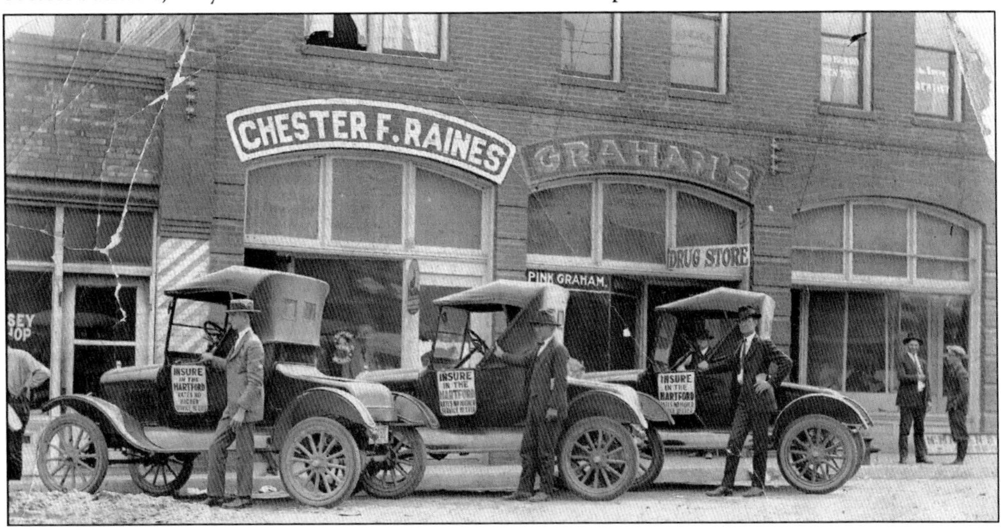

CHESTER F. RAINES INSURANCE. In 1921 Chester F. Raines added lines of insurance to his Singer Sewing Machine business. This began a 60-year span of service to the insurance needs of the citizens of Albertville. He was later honored by the Hartford Insurance Company for those many years of service. Raines is pictured standing by the vehicle on the right. Pink Graham's drug store sat beside the Chester F. Raines Insurance office.

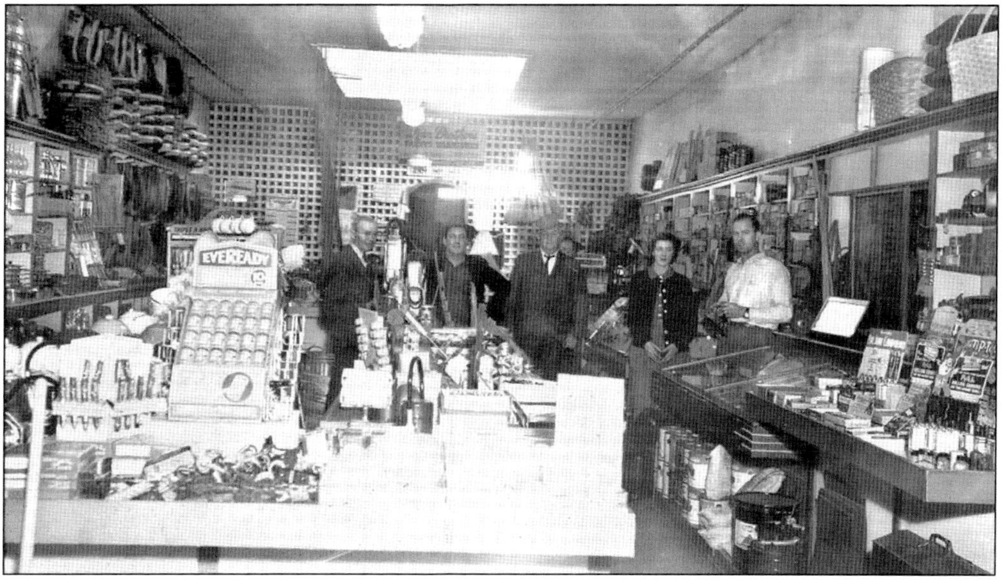

WALKER HARDWARE COMPANY. After years of serving the Albertville National Bank as cashier, Christopher J. "Christie" Walker purchased the Gipson Hardware Company. A Walker Hardware advertisement spoke of the importance of the hardware store in the life of a town: "Years ago the hardware store was the meeting place for the men folks from miles around here, around the old pot bellied stove they swapped yarns that were pretty high, wide, and handsome."

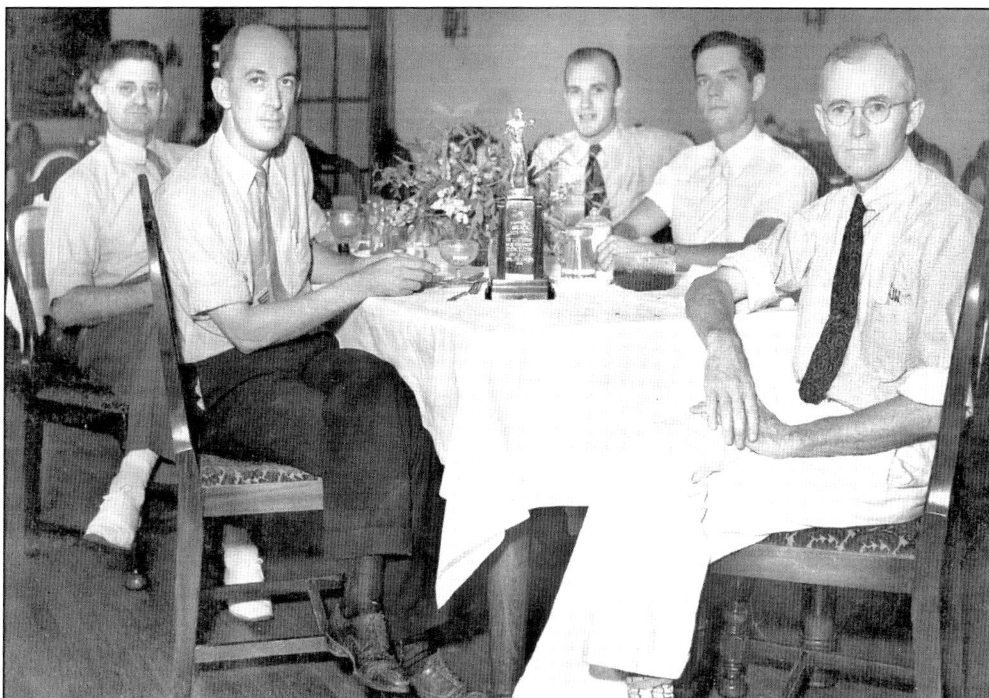

QUITE THE SALESMAN. Within a year, the Walker Hardware Company received an award from General Electric for outstanding sales. Pictured with the award from left to right are *Albertville Herald* editor J.J. Benford, salesman Ed Roberts, two unidentified persons, and Christie Walker.

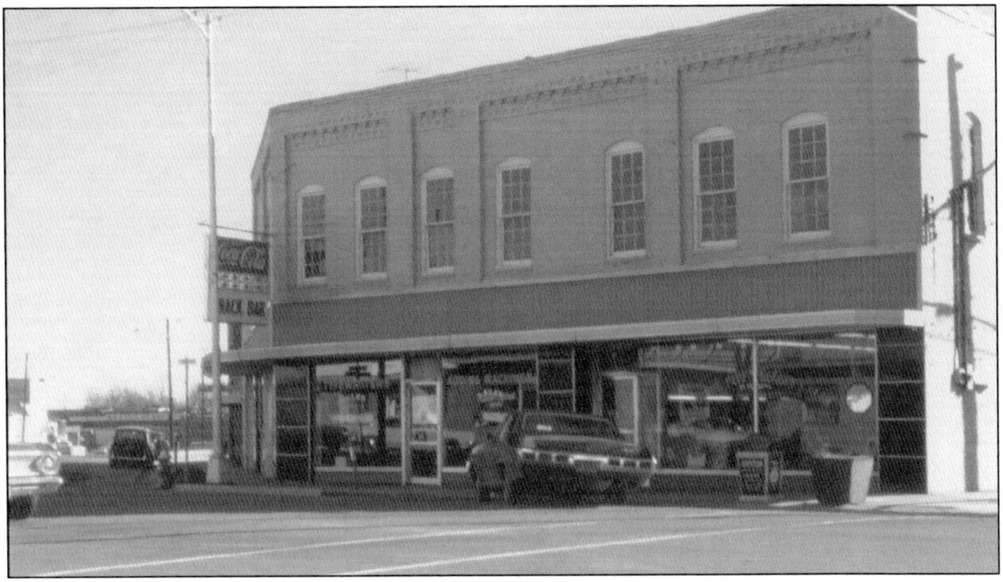

SINGLETON BUILDING. In 1917 this building was constructed by J.M. "Matt" Singleton to house his mercantile business on the ground floor and rent office space on the second. Over the life of the building, it housed a restaurant, a beauty shop, and the town's post office. The building was considered by many to be one of the best constructed in town, with the brickwork laid by the town's master mason, John Stephens.

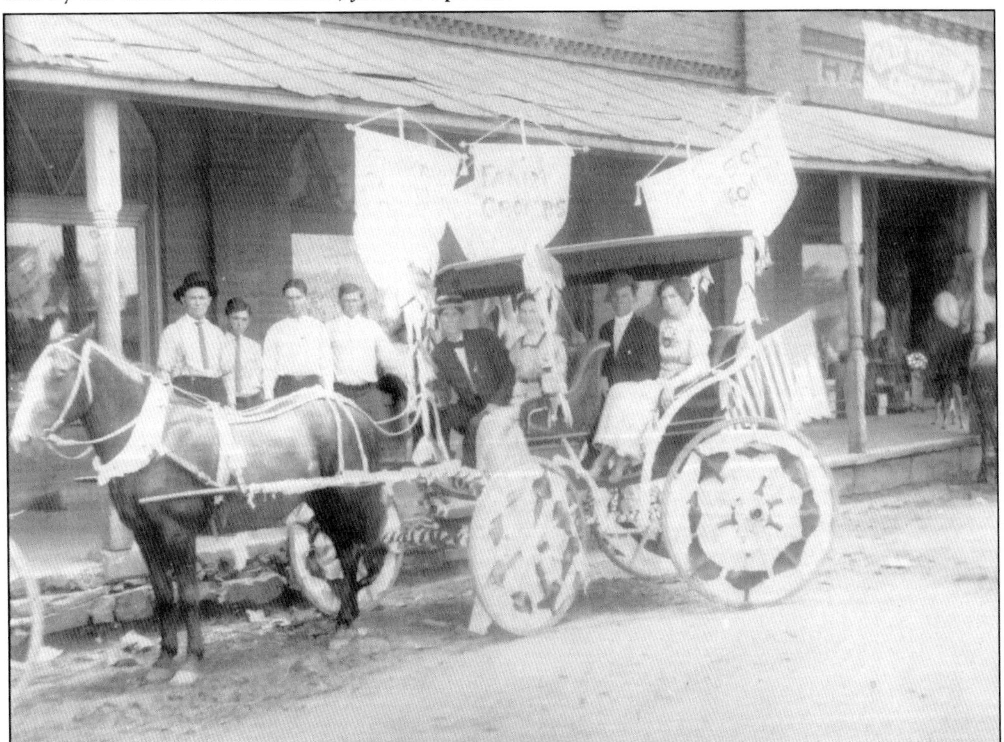

THE SINGLETON FAMILY. Shown in the town's early days are Matt Singleton and members of his family standing behind a decorative horse and buggy.

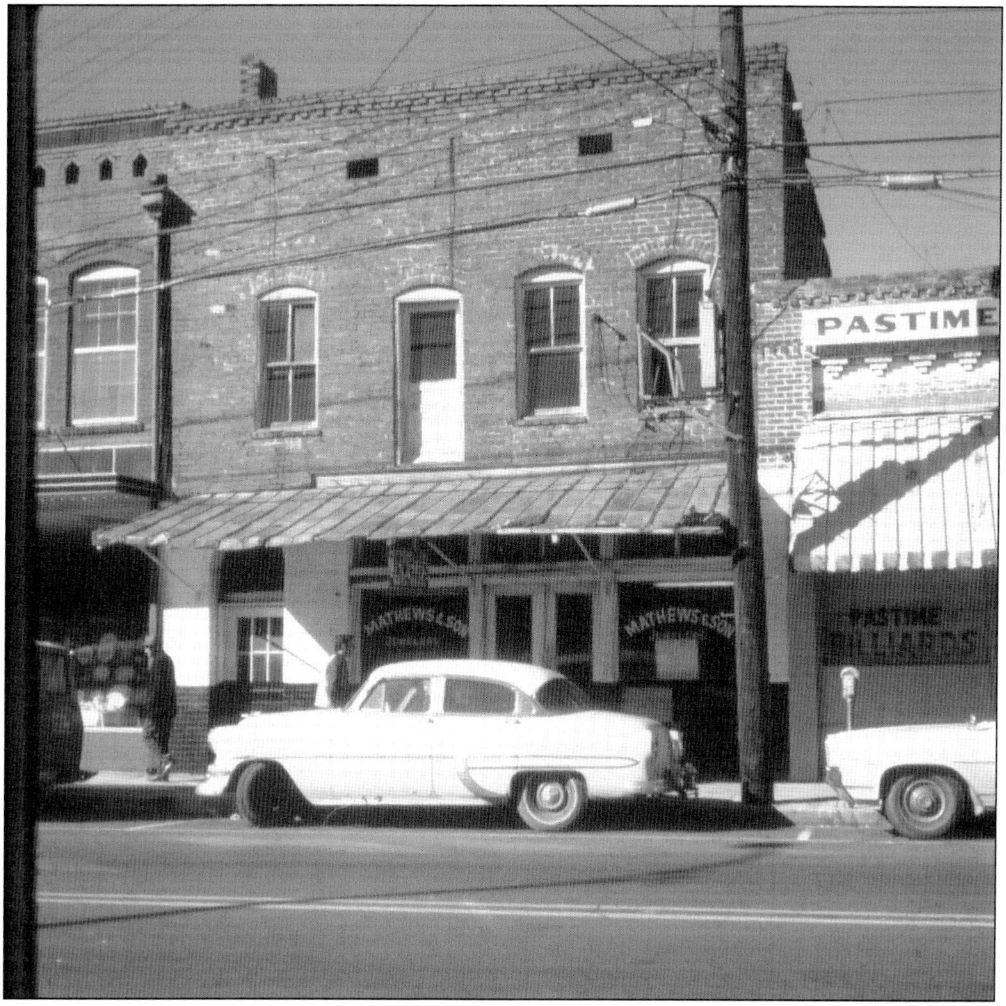

J. WILLIE JOHNSON'S EARLY STUDIO. During Albertville's era of urban renewal, one building of true legacy was razed in the name of progress; the building stood behind the current Jewel Box and was the photography studio of J. Willie Johnson. In 1908 he moved to Albertville from Fayette, Alabama, where he previously had a studio. Years later, Johnson recalled the early era of photography to newspaper reporter, Bess Williams. She wrote, "He learned to make pictures the hard way. Sunlight in those days was a must. No sunlight, no pictures. Everyday one egg must be broken and the white used to sensitize the paper, and it required seven operations to complete one picture. They must be put in strong sunlight—then dipped in a solution, and finally pasted on the fancy mat and probably sold from $1.50 to $2.50 a dozen." The Johnson family lens, first of J. Willie Johnson, and now of his son, Robert O., has captured life in Albertville for almost 100 years.

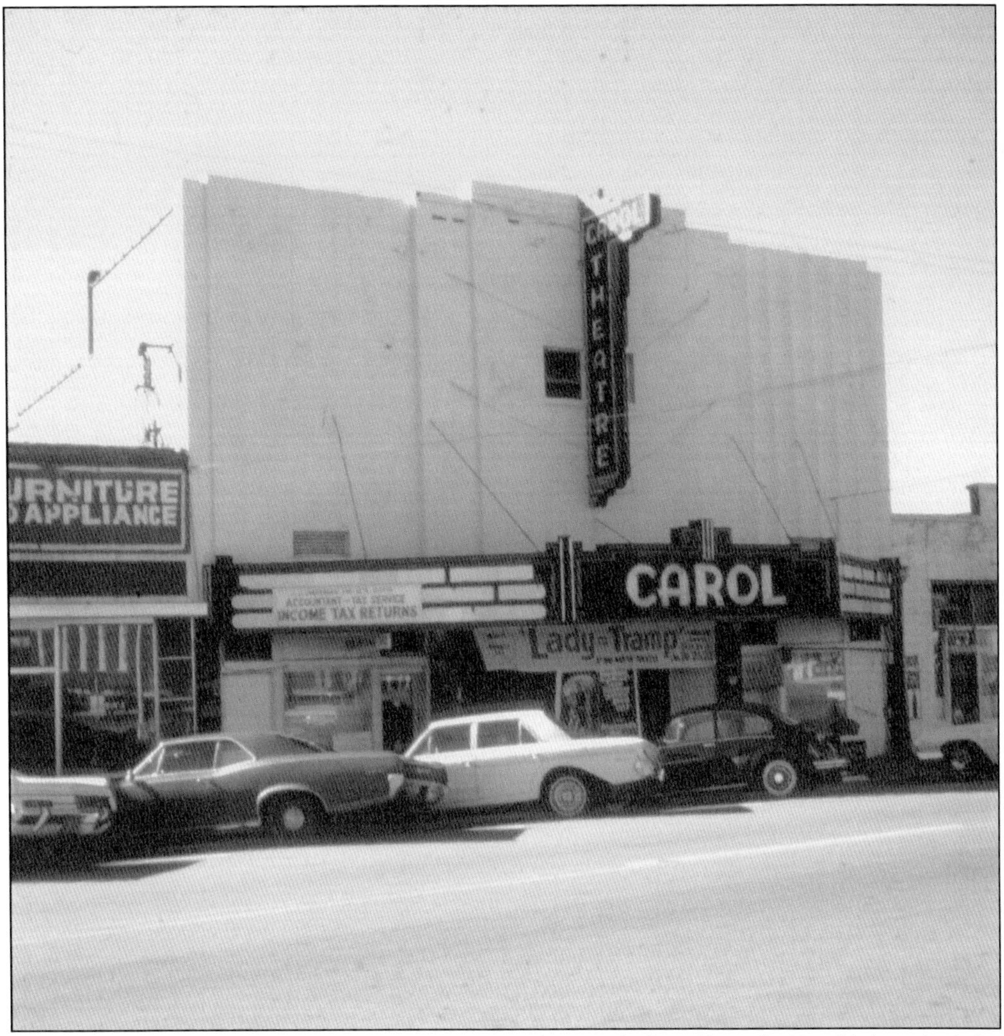

The Carol Theatre. The September 9, 1938 edition of *The Albertville Herald* described the opening of the city's newest theatre: "With the opening of the new Carol Theatre next Monday, Albertville will have one of the most up-to-the-minute, most beautiful, and most complete places of amusement to be found in the whole state." The theatre's owner, attorney Col. Thomas E. Orr, named the theatre for his daughter. His chain included a second theatre in Albertville by the name of the Princess, as well as other theatres in Boaz, Attalla, and Fort Payne. He had also opened his law office in Albertville in 1910. Orr served in the Alabama legislature by appointment after the death of Marshall County legislator and first Albertville mayor, W.M. "Bob" Coleman. In addition, he served on the state's first highway commission. The Princess Theatre opened during the glory of Hollywood. In those days, in addition to viewing great films, movie houses had another great inducement—air conditioning. Before modern methods of cooling, Colonel Orr had a system called "air washing" installed for the princely sum of $1,850. The newspaper described the system in the following manner, "When this installation is completed every bit of air that is used to ventilate the theatre will be drawn through cool fresh water and will be as fresh and pure as the sea breeze. It will lower the temperature in the theatre 8 degrees in the hottest weather than under the present arrangement."

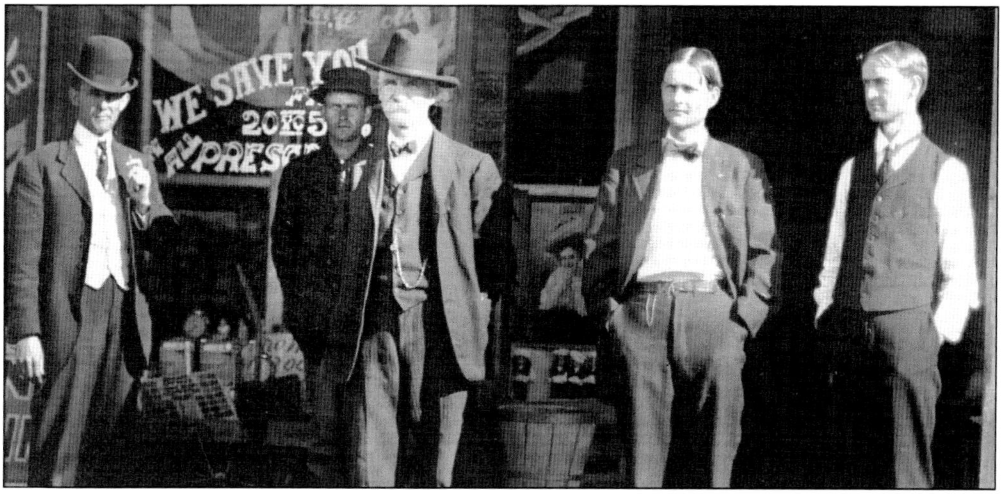

WALTER SHIPP DRUG COMPANY. One of the earliest drug stores in Albertville was that of Walter Shipp, who married the sister of Albertville mayor Bob Coleman in 1892. Billing itself as "the people's store," it carried an extensive line of products, including Prickley Ash Bitters, Moffet's Teething Powder, and Peruna. One day, the townspeople noticed an interesting announcement in the town's newspaper proclaiming "wedding announcement." It read, "Mr. Walter Shipp cordially requests your presence at the marriage of his best friends—Miss Pure Drugs to Mr. Honest Price, which takes place in their store every hour in the day, and every day in the year." In 1916 Shipp died at the young age of 45. Pictured from left to right are Shipp, town marshal R.L. "Bob" Amos, Pink Graham, and O.H. Finney Sr.

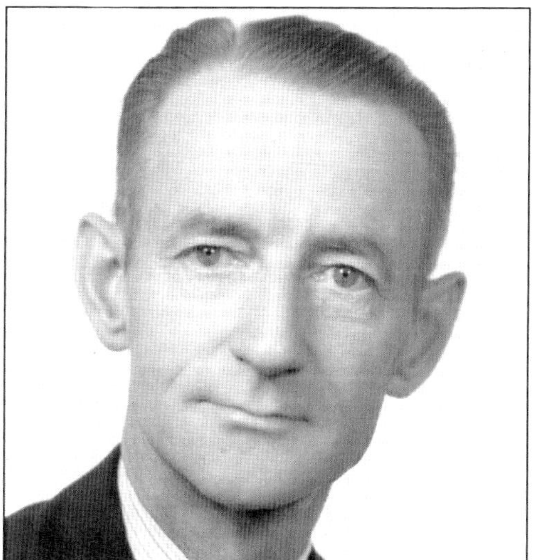

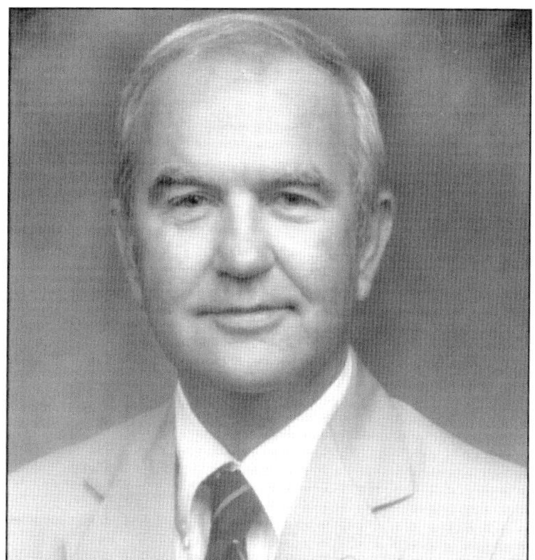

W.T. "BILL" BAINS JR. AND W.T. "BUBS" BAINS III. In January 1935 Birmingham native Bill Bains moved to Albertville and opened the Pan-Am Gas and Oil Station. That same year, Bains and his brother-in-law, Hoyt Levie, opened the Levie and Bains store, which specialized in appliances and furniture. Also in 1935 was the birth of Bill's son, William Talley "Bubs" Bains III. The Bainses also had a daughter named Mary Madeline. Just three years later, in 1938, Madeline Bell Bains died in childbirth, leaving her husband and two small children. In 1964 Bubs and Uncle Hoyt went into partnership; once again a firm by the name of Levie and Bains was a point of trade in Albertville.

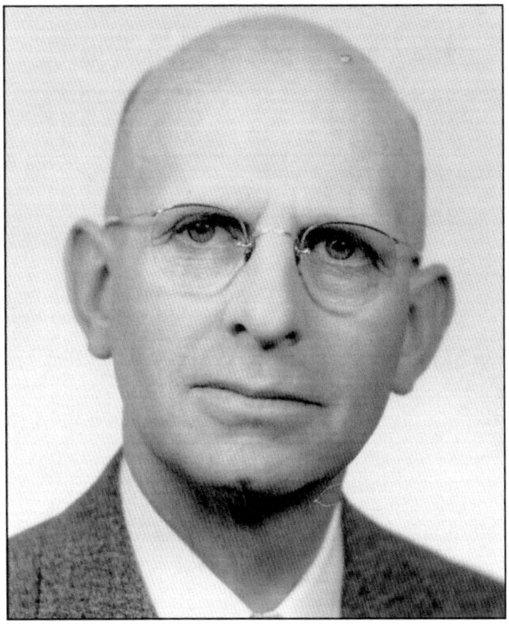

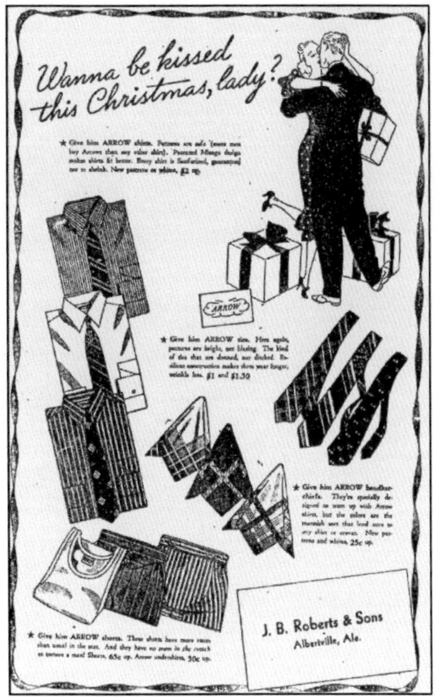

JAMES BAILEY ROBERTS JR. In 1900 J.B. Roberts Sr. and his wife, Abigail, moved to Albertville, where he operated a store until his death in 1930. After his death, his sons, Bailey and Ed, continued operating the business under the name of J.B. Roberts & Sons. On January 1, 1949, Bailey sold the business to his brother-in-law, Dee Isbell; Kelton Dendy; and O.H. Finney Jr. In 1955 Kelton Dendy and his brother, Dan, purchased the interests of Isbell and Finney and renamed the business Dendy's. At the same time, Bailey Roberts and Isbell acquired the hardware store of C.J. Walker, renaming it Roberts and Isbell Hardware. Above right is an advertisement for the Roberts & Sons store that appeared in *The Albertville Herald* in December 1937, advertising shirts for $2 and ties for as little as $1.

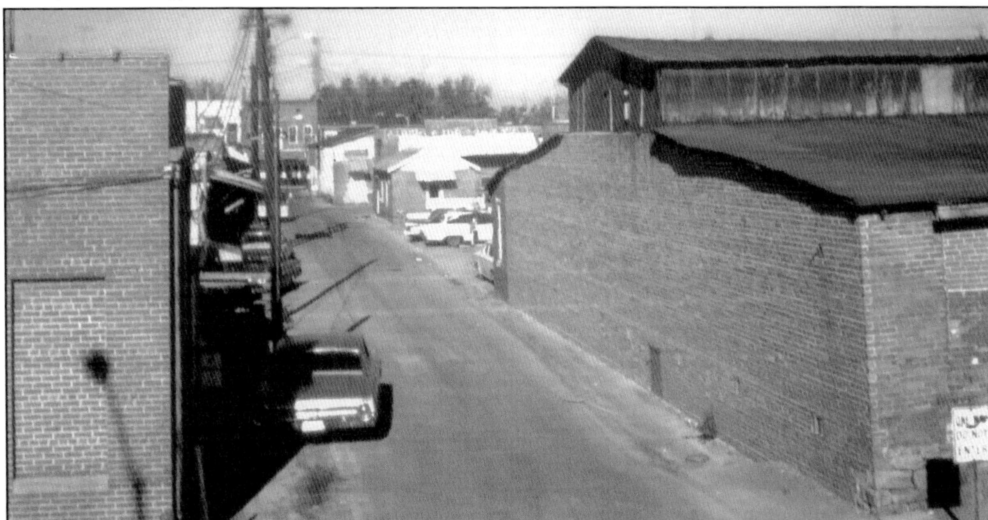

J.B. ROBERTS WAREHOUSE. For years the J.B. Roberts Warehouse building stood behind the State National Bank, one block north of the East Main Street and Simpson Street intersection. In 1975 the massive building was razed to make way for a parking lot as part of the town's urban renewal project.

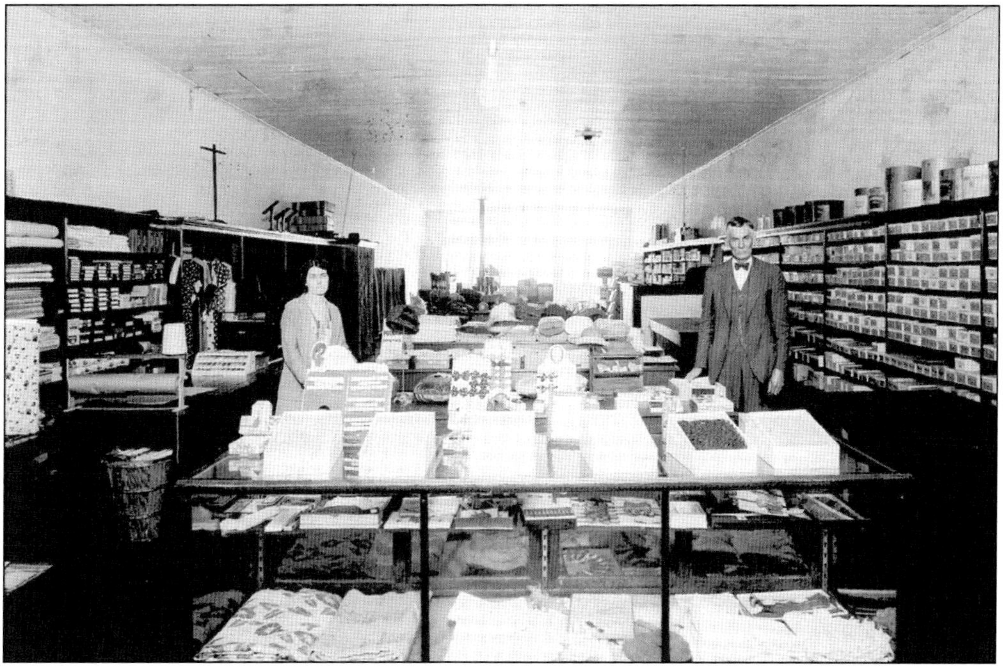

W.R. JOHNSON STORE, EARLY 1900S. For years, a coveted site for business trade has always been the northeast corner of the intersection of Main and Broad Streets, which was occupied by businessmen like Tom McNaron, R.O. Duckett, and Bobby Hammer. Pictured above on the left is the store of W.R. Johnson, set within that span of stores nearest the corner

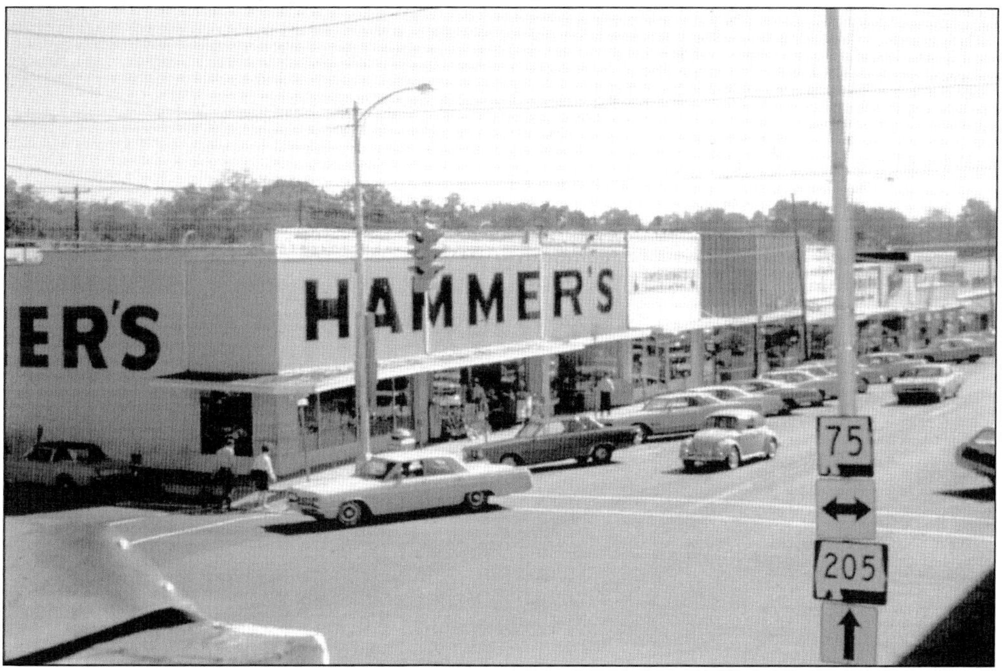

MCNARON, DUCKETTS, AND HAMMER'S. The northeast corner of Main and Broad Streets has housed downtown Albertville's anchor businesses, from the early T.B. McNaron store to the present-day's Hammer's.

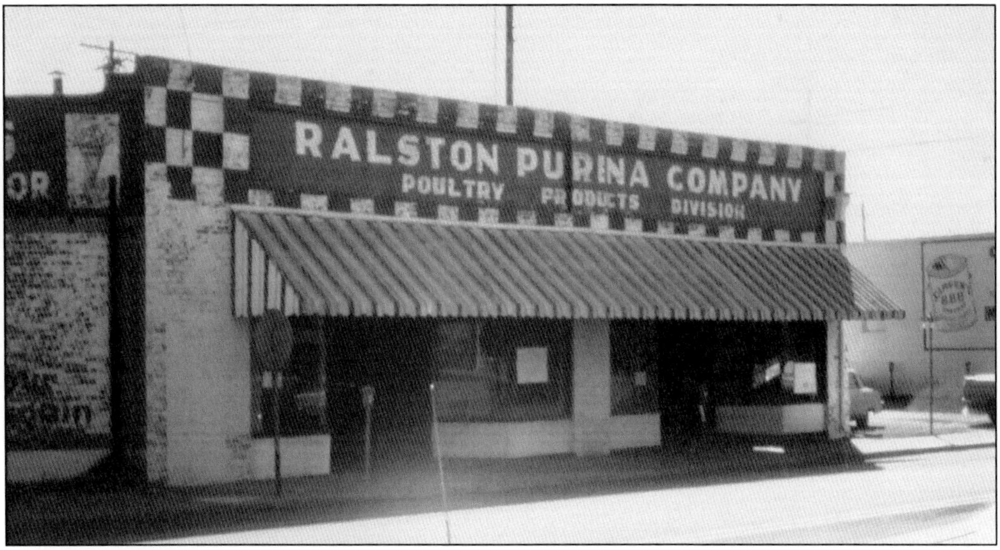

RALSTON PURINA STORE BUILDING. Known to generations of Albertville residents as the "Checkerboard" store, this building was located on the spot currently occupied by Weathers Hardware. When James P. Garvin Jr. was transferred to Albertville in 1946 as store manager, it was the smallest store in the Ralston Purina chain. During the late 1940s, the store served as the launching pad for the increasing poultry industry, offering forums with representatives from Purina Mills, proponents of a new poultry plant, and area bankers. By the late 1950s, this small link in the Ralston Purina chain had become one of its largest.

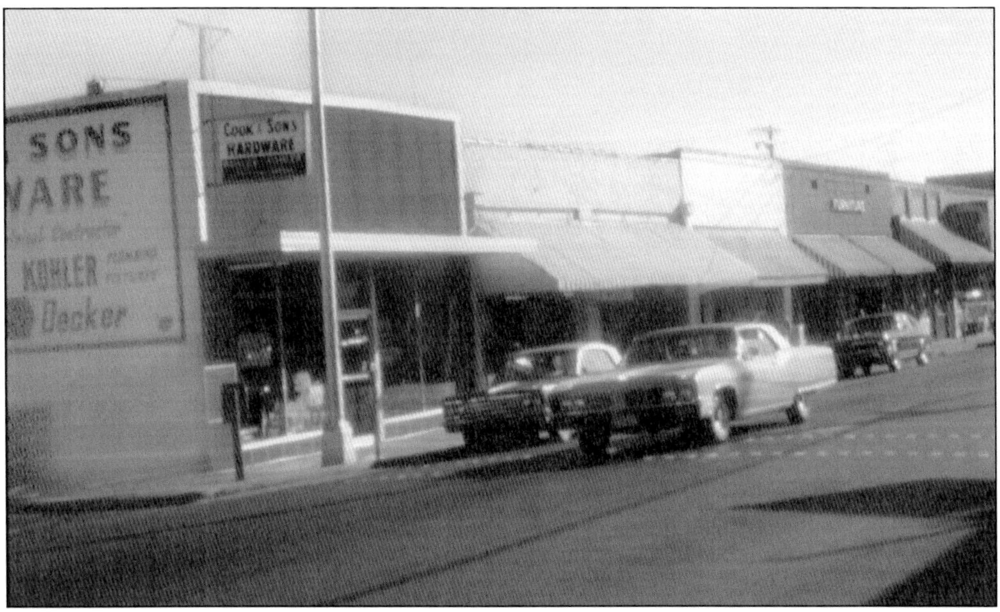

NORTH BROAD STREET BUILDINGS. In 1968 plans were formulated that would forever change the landscape of downtown Albertville. Throughout town, about 60 parcels of property were acquired at a cost of over $2 million, 75 percent of that coming from the federal government. Over the years, such stores occupied this span of buildings as Biddle Furniture, Thrasher's Western Auto, Cook's Hardware, and Driver's Café. The center building was one of the town's oldest buildings and had served as the town's first hospital under Drs. Shipp and Miller.

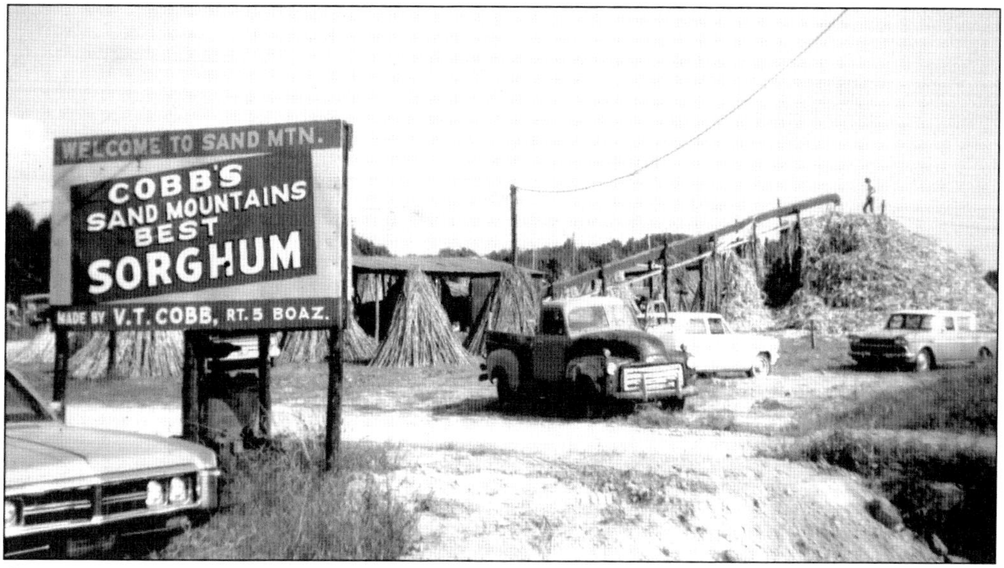

COBB'S SORGHUM SYRUP. For years, Sand Mountain was synonymous with items like car dealerships and the poultry industry. A third item was sorghum syrup production. There was no higher gift to a visiting dignitary than a can of syrup. Cobb's Sorghum Syrup in Boaz, shown above, was one the foremost processors.

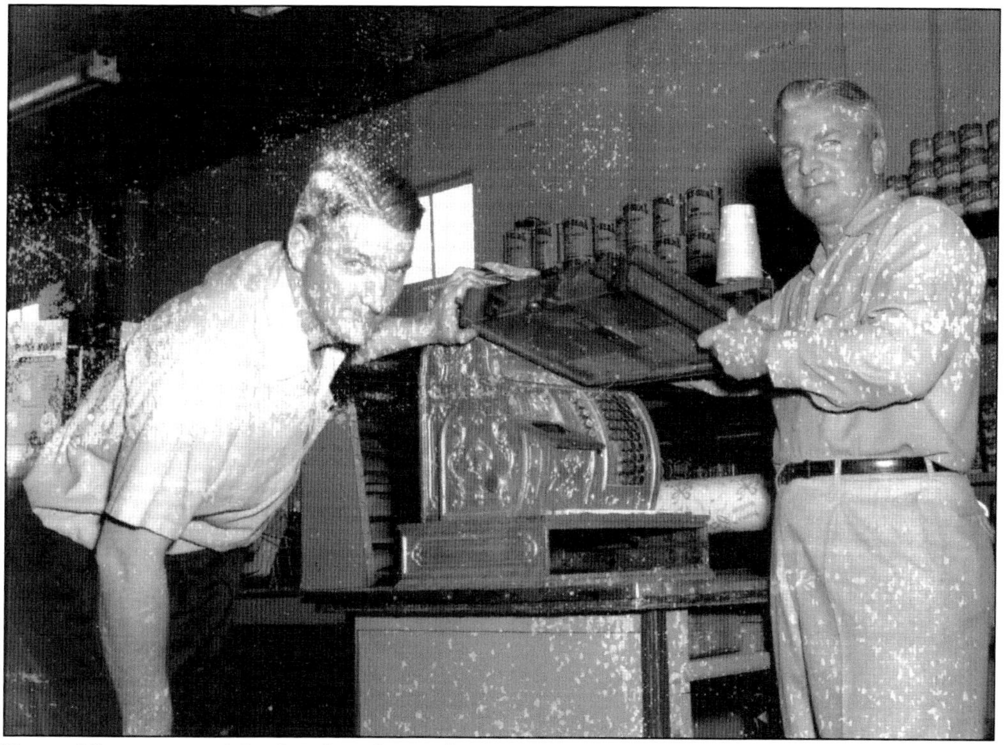

DAVIS HARDWARE. After brothers Joe and Dorsett Davis purchased Josh Sanderson Hardware, they discovered that the store's cash register was one that had been manufactured for their father, Mercer Davis, when he operated Roberts, Luther, and Company mercantile, which opened in 1914.

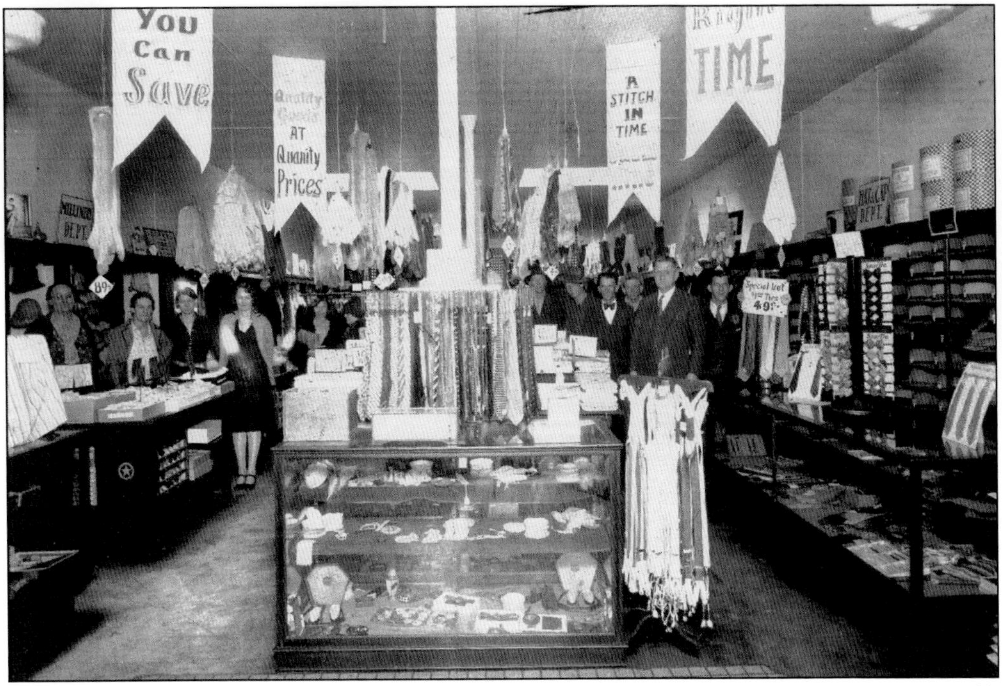

J. Pat Colvin Store. After ending his partnership with his brother-in-law, G. Dewey Wells Sr., in the Colvin and Wells store, J. Pat Colvin became involved in insurance and real estate. In 1927 Colvin once again entered Albertville's business community by establishing a small store in the King Hotel, which stood on the site of today's Courington Arcade. Two years later, he opened a store a few doors down from the hotel.

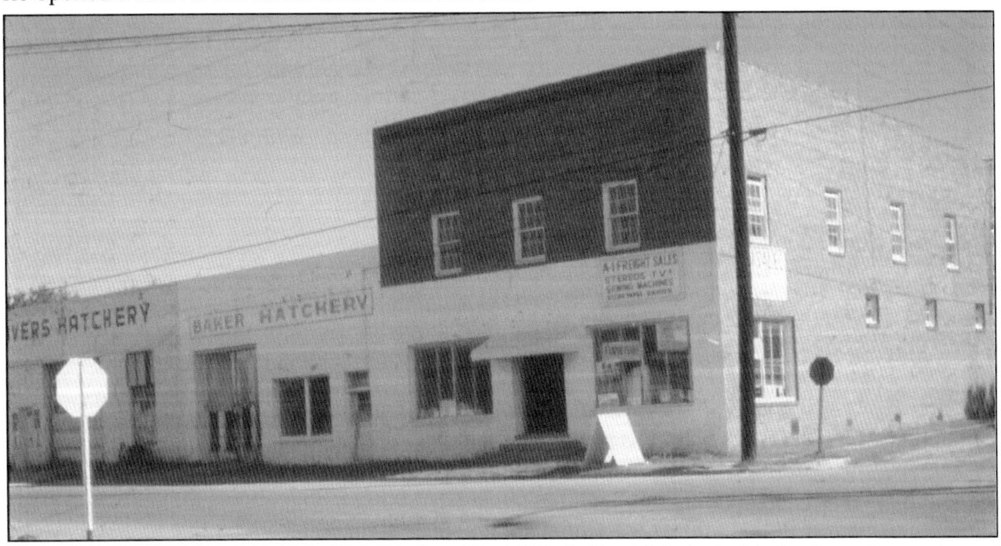

Colvin Store Building. On September 30, 1935, J. Pat Colvin held the formal opening of his business in its new location just off Main Street behind the Saunders Hotel. A mere 60 days after ground had been broken for the new location, Colvin was selling merchandise within that building. He had long believed that there was a need in the Albertville area for a wholesale house that would specialize in the needs of the smaller merchants. Just three years later, Colvin died at the young age of 43.

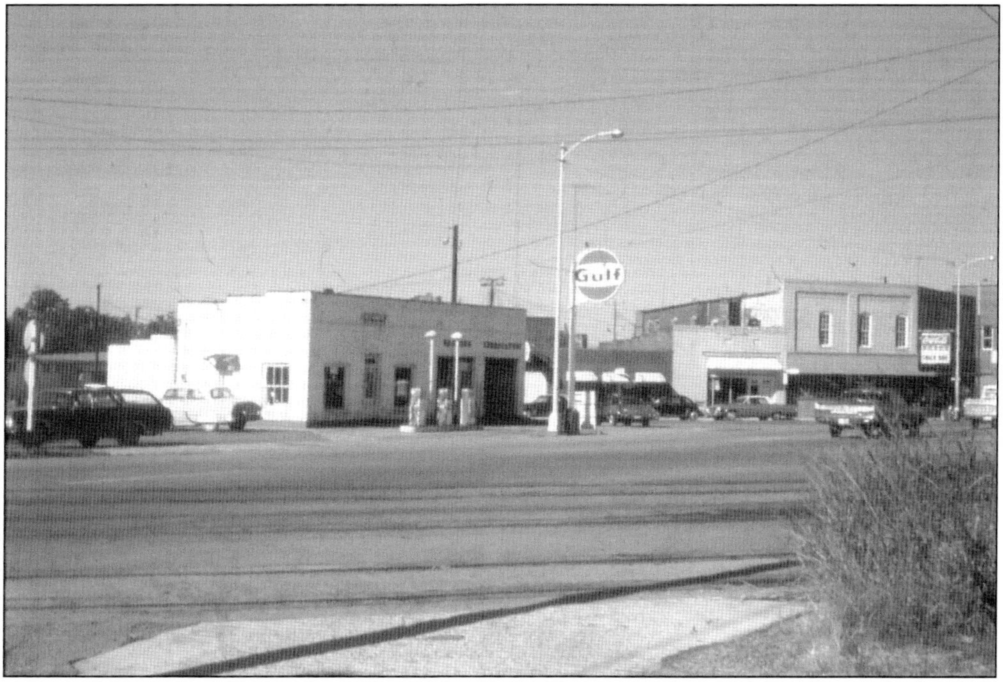

Make Way for Progress. The urban renewal project of the late 1960s and early 1970s brought about the loss of many buildings in downtown Albertville. One such loss was that of an entire block of buildings on the southeast corner of the East Main and Simpson Street intersection, shown above.

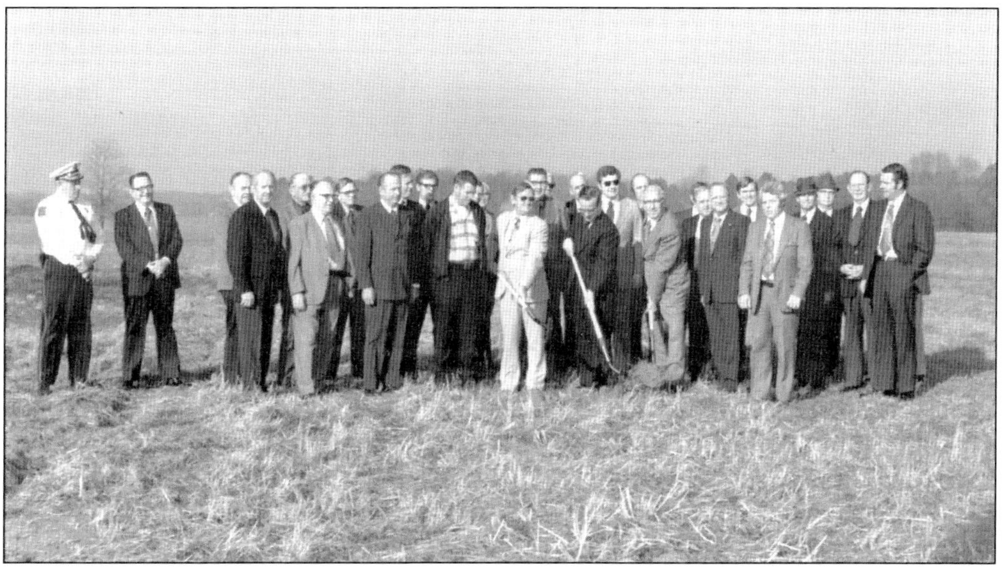

Groundbreaking for the Mueller Plant. Albertville's Mueller plant has helped to carry the name of Albertville throughout the country and overseas through its production and distribution of fire hydrants. On April 11, 1990, Mueller placed its one millionth fire hydrant manufactured in Albertville in front of the city's Chamber of Commerce building on Sand Mountain Drive. The picture shows the plant's groundbreaking, performed by Boaz mayor Billy Dyar, Mueller president Harlan White, and Albertville mayor Buford Cryar.

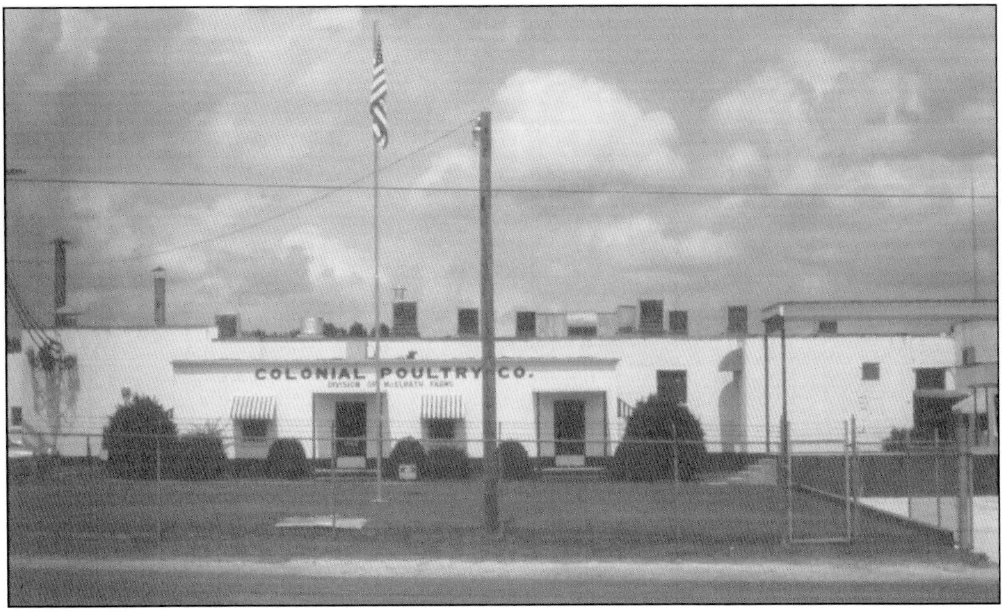

COLONIAL POULTRY. In 1953 Colonial Poultry opened in Albertville. In 1961 the plant was purchased by Ralston Purina and then by McElrath Farms. Today's plant operates at the same location, Highway 431 and West McKinney Avenue, and is owned by Tyson Poultry; however, it bears little resemblance to its predecessor.

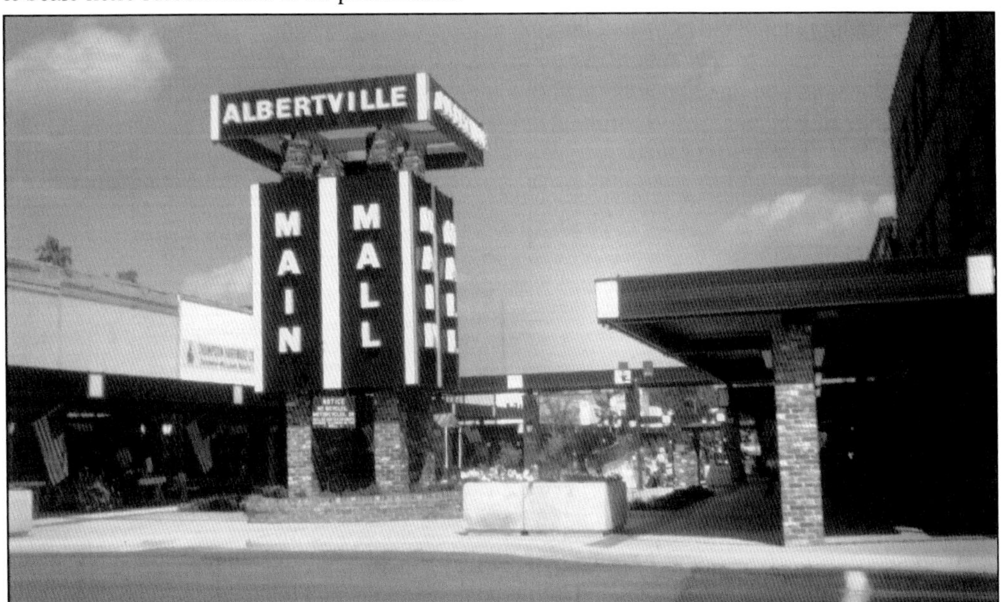

ALBERTVILLE MAIN MALL. In 1977 Albertville's new pedestrian mall, commencing on the east side of Main and Broad Streets, opened. Plans for the town's urban renewal project, the center piece of which was the mall, had begun in 1968, with the submission of an application to the Department of Housing and Urban Development. The program called for 75 percent of the project's funds to come from the federal government, with Albertville supplying the remaining 25 percent .Years later, that particular section of East Main Street was re-opened, and through the cooperation of city leaders and merchants the grandeur of the street was restored.

Three

EDUCATION

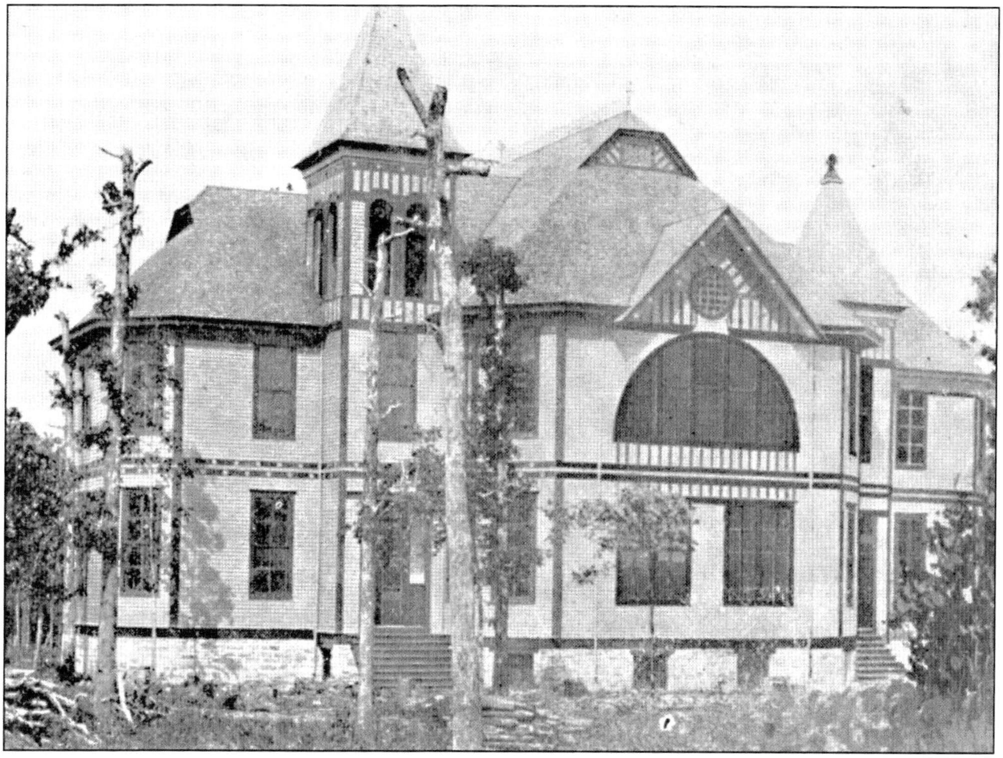

THE SEVENTH DISTRICT AGRICULTURAL SCHOOL. On February 21, 1893, the Alabama legislature passed an act calling for the construction of an agricultural school in each of the state's congressional districts. In the seventh district, the choice came down to Lebanon, in DeKalb County; Springville, in St. Clair County; and Albertville. To the townspeople's delight, Albertville was awarded the school. Pending the construction of a building, classes were held at the old Jones Chapel School building. As an inducement, Albertville Land and Improvement, which possessed several tracts of land, offered a large area at Jackson and McDonald Streets. On February 20, 1894, the cornerstone for the school was laid with much pomp and circumstance. Early that Tuesday morning, vehicles converged on Albertville. The railroad brought people from both directions, even offering reduced fairs. At 10 a.m. a procession formed at the Masonic Hall. The Masonic brethren were to oversee the laying of the cornerstone. A brass band from Collinsville led the procession, followed by over 100 Masons and over 170 students. It was estimated at the time that 2,000 spectators watched the impressive march. After remarks at the church, the procession led everyone to the future school grounds.

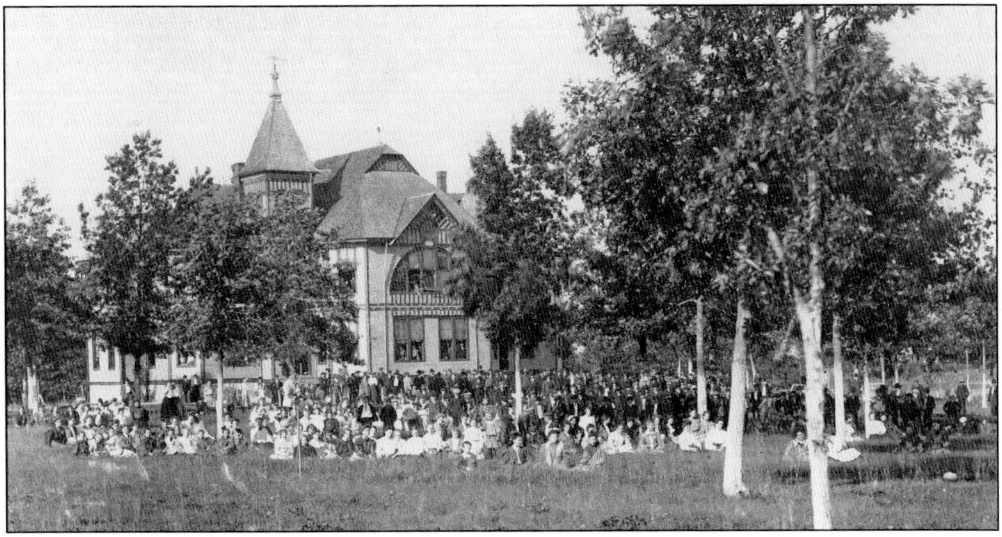

The Loss of the Agricultural School. On Saturday, January 12, 1912, the grand structure that had caused pride in every Albertville resident burned to the ground. About 6:15 p.m., fire was spotted coming out of the west side of the building and, before help could arrive, it was a mass of flames. The fire was devastating, but the town's resolve about the school was unwavering; as the newspaper put it, "embers had not burned out before plans were made to continue school." However, money was an issue. The $10,000 earmarked by the legislature for campus dormitories was redirected, and there was a payment from the insurance funds; unfortunately, that still left $6,061, which the townspeople would ultimately have to provide to keep the school; one neighboring town was offering inducements to the state to lure it away. The citizens of Albertville swore that they would retain their school, and they did.

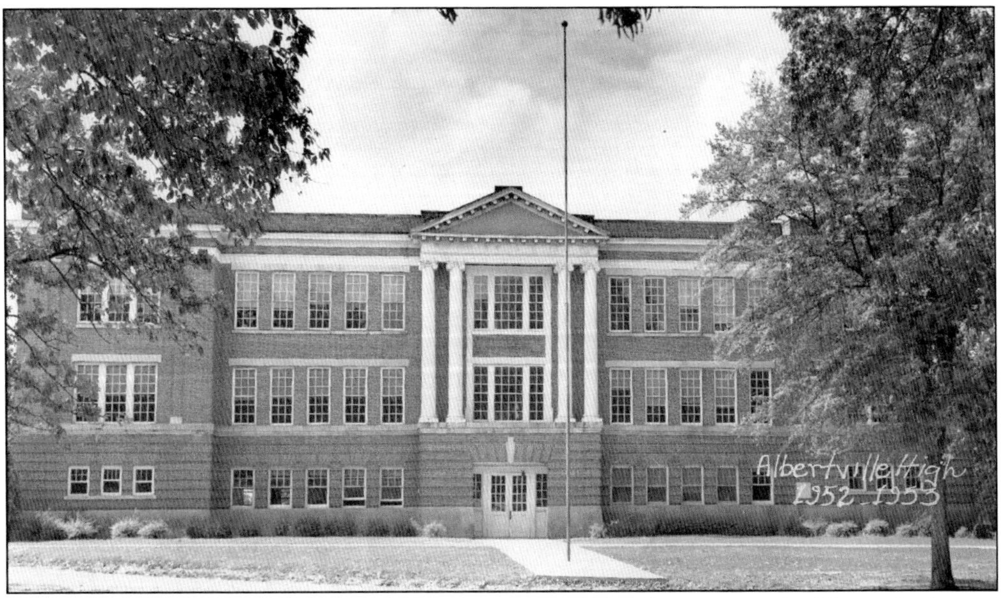

The New School. By fall 1912, a new three-story brick structure had been built and classes were beginning. For nearly a century, this building has been a source of pride to the residents of Albertville, in much the same way that the original Victorian structure had been to earlier generations.

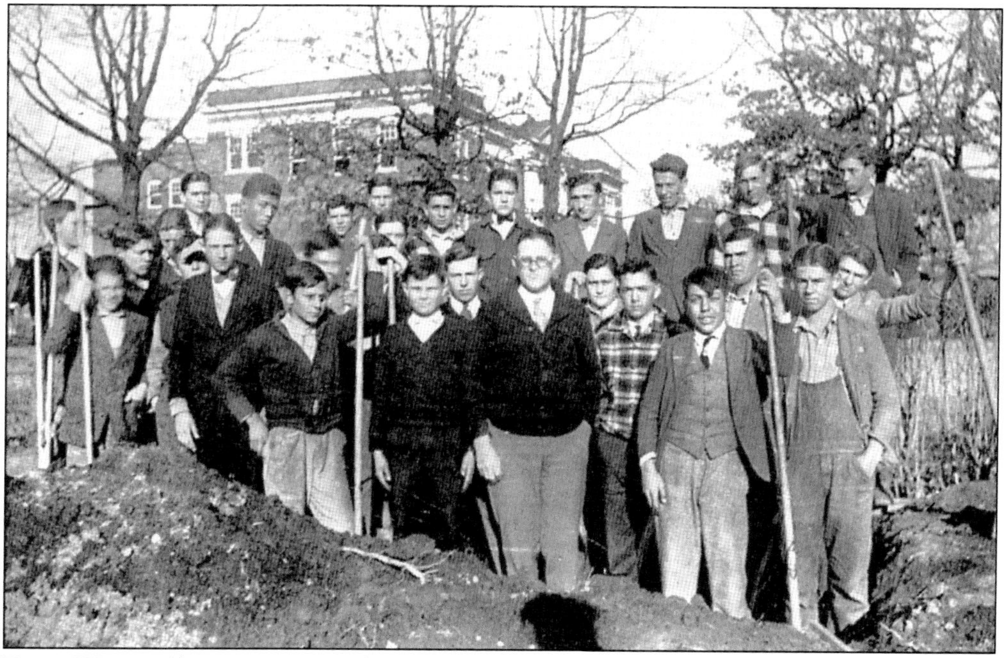

FIELD WORK. Above is a 1927 photograph of members of the agricultural department. The department, under the direction of J.W. Milner and J.J. Benford, taught four different classes of agricultural study dependent upon the student's grade in school. The 1927–1928 yearbook recorded the different classifications: "In the freshman years the study of crops and soils, fertilizers, and the planting and cultivation of the farm crops of this section of the state is made. In the sophomore year the students study live stock and poultry. They take up stock judging, feeds, and the improvement of breeds. In the Junior class horticulture is the subject that is studied. The diseases of plants, pruning, spraying, and planting of trees and truck crops are studied. The Seniors study farm management which deals with the problems of farmers and the upkeep of the farm."

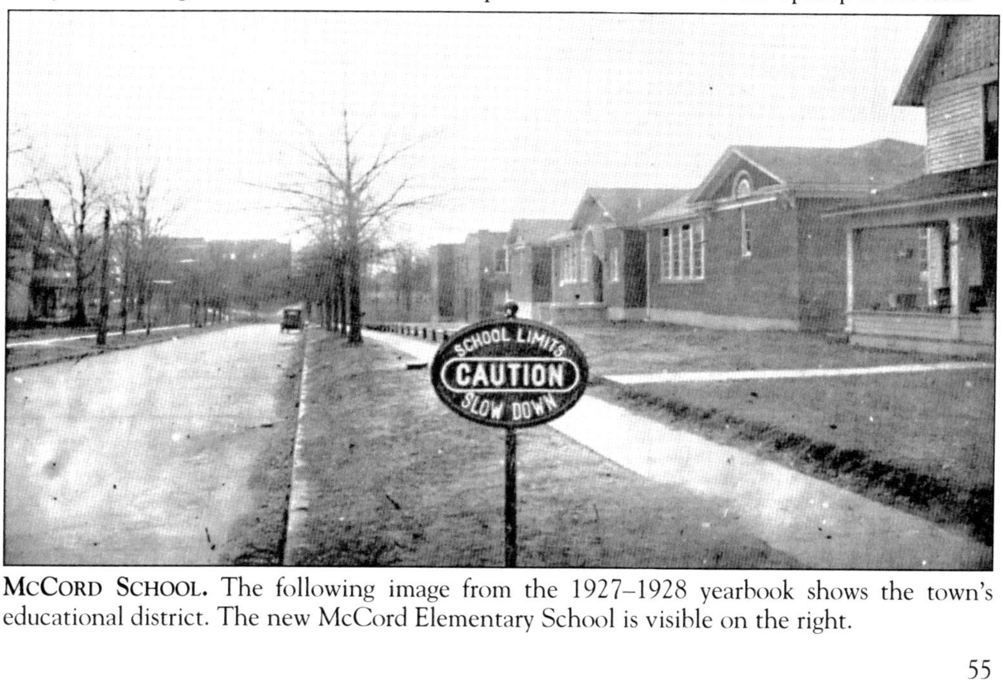

MCCORD SCHOOL. The following image from the 1927–1928 yearbook shows the town's educational district. The new McCord Elementary School is visible on the right.

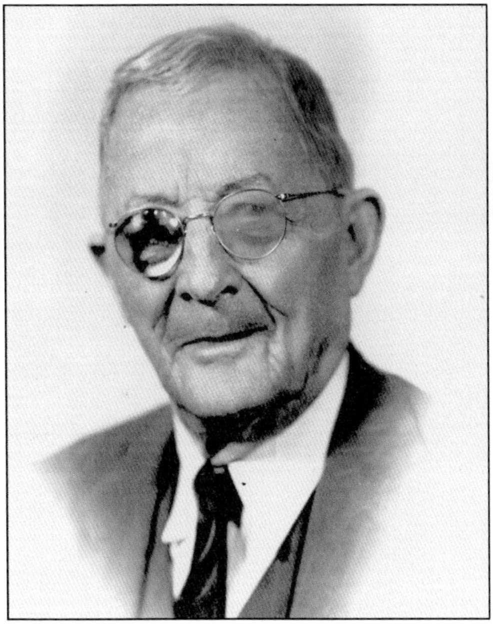

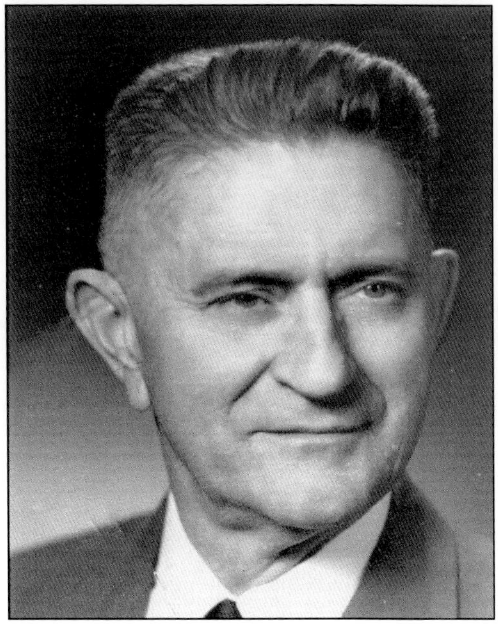

W.P. GOODWIN AND J.J. BENFORD. In March 1948 W.P. Goodwin (left) passed away at his home in Albertville. In addition to serving as a teacher in the Albertville school system and operating a real estate and insurance business for almost 40 years, he served as mayor in the first decade of the 20th century. On July 1, 1926, J.J. Benford (right) became principal of the State Secondary Agricultural School; he served the school as principal for eight years. During the last 18 months of his service, times were the leanest and he received no money. The state paid its educators in scrip, the worth of which was dubious at best. Most teachers usually traded the scrip for food. On August 1, 1934, Benford left the school system and founded the town's newest newspaper, *The Albertville Herald.*

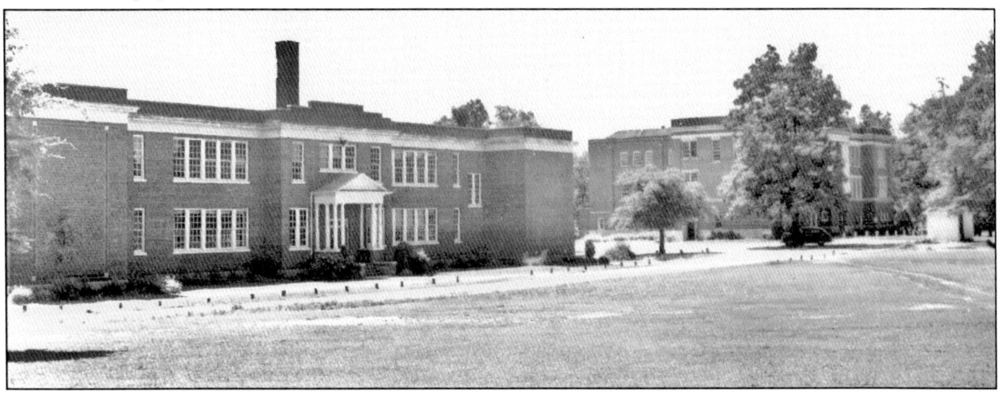

ALBERTVILLE HIGH SCHOOL CAMPUS. The year 1936 saw the demise of the Seventh District Agricultural School and its successor, the State Secondary Agricultural School, when the school became Albertville High School. The new Board of Education decided that with the school's new direction, the old agricultural school needed a new name. Board of Education chairman S.B. Hooper even proposed a contest; the person who suggested the most appropriate name won a prize of $5. In October names for the school buildings were announced. The senior high building, formerly the agricultural school building constructed in 1912, was named after early school president J.B. Hobdy. The junior high building, shown on the left in the picture above, was named for the Hooper family, which had contributed greatly to the overall growth of the town.

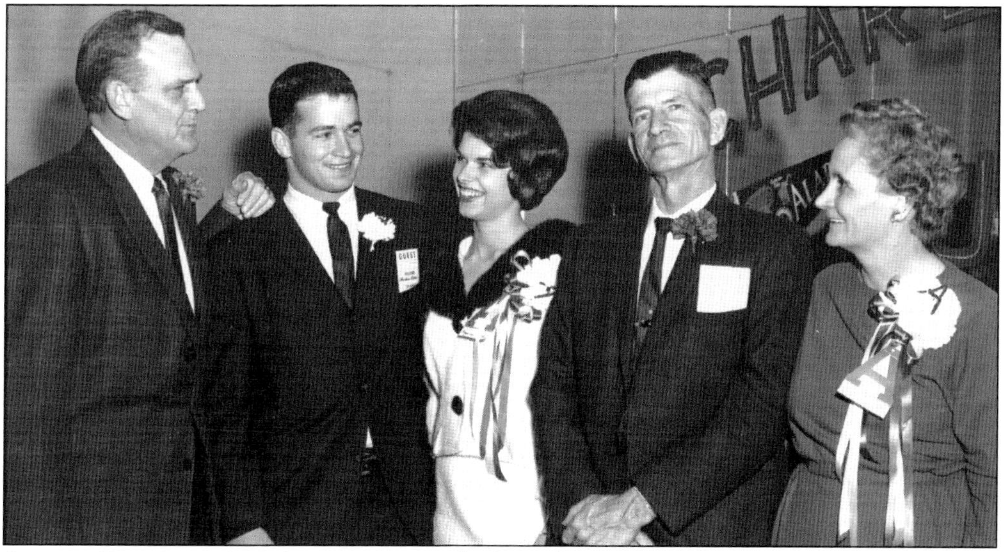

CHARLIE PELL DAY. On February 9, 1963, Charlie Pell Day was held at the Albertville Coliseum; it honored the University of Alabama's standout lineman, Charlie Pell, and other members of the 1962 Albertville High School Aggie football team. Principal speaker for the evening was the University of Alabama's head football coach, Paul "Bear" Bryant. Pictured from left to right are Coach Bryant; Charlie Pell; Pell's wife, the former Roxanne Thrasher; and Pell's parents, Mr. and Mrs. M.L. Pell. Approximately 600 people attended the event; among those were Alabama's All-American, Lee Roy Jordan, and an undergraduate player by the name of Joe Namath.

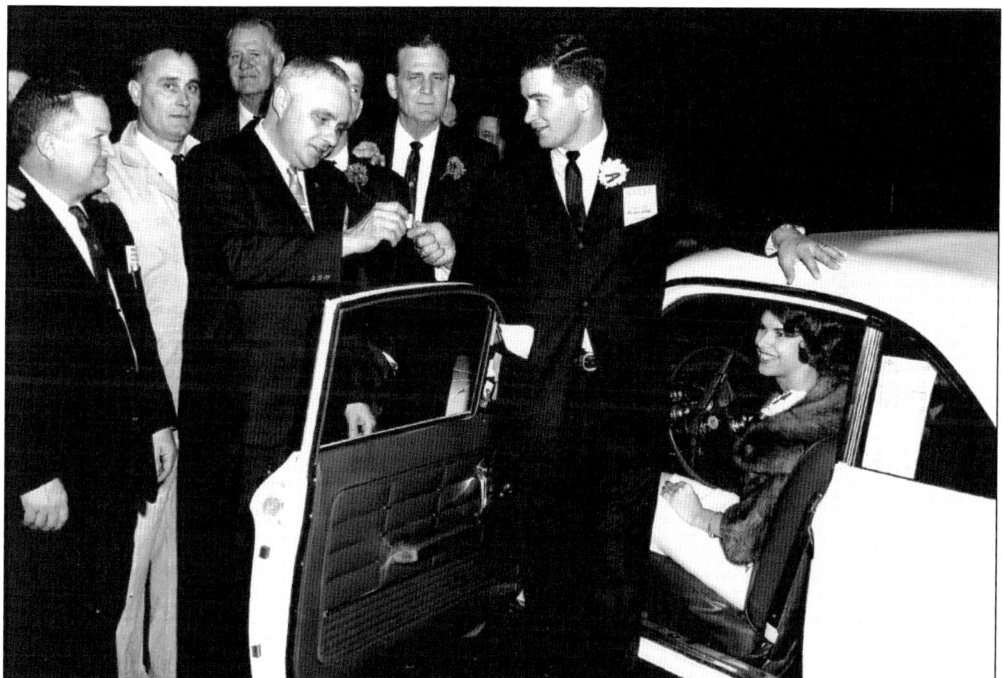

PELL RECEIVES CAR FROM THE AGGIE QUARTERBACK CLUB. The conclusion of Pell Day was the presentation of keys for a new 1963 Monza to Charlie Pell by the Quarterback Club. Shown presenting the keys is Ralph Hart; he is joined by R.G. "Pug" Moore.

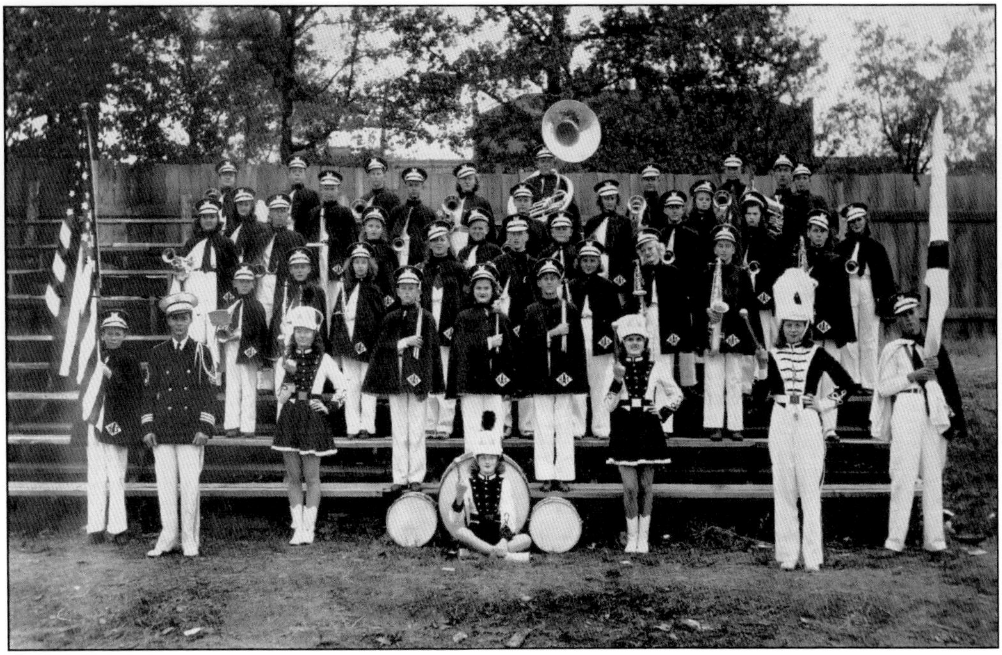

EARLY ALBERTVILLE BAND. The Albertville High School band was founded in the early 1920s by Montford Marion Cole. In addition to Albertville, Cole taught band at Guntersville and Gadsden. After a long bout of declining health, Cole died in 1929, leaving his wife, the former Mable Stevens, and three small children.

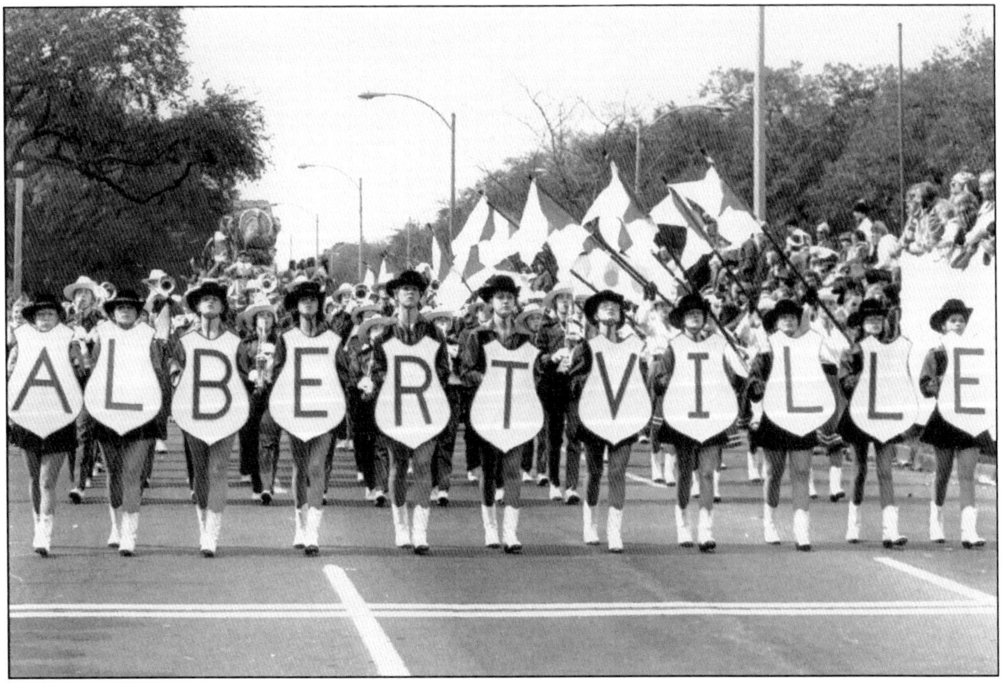

ALBERTVILLE BAND IN THE MACY'S PARADE. Through the years, Albertville High School's band has continued to distinguish itself, such as this performance in the annual Macy's Thanksgiving Day parade in New York.

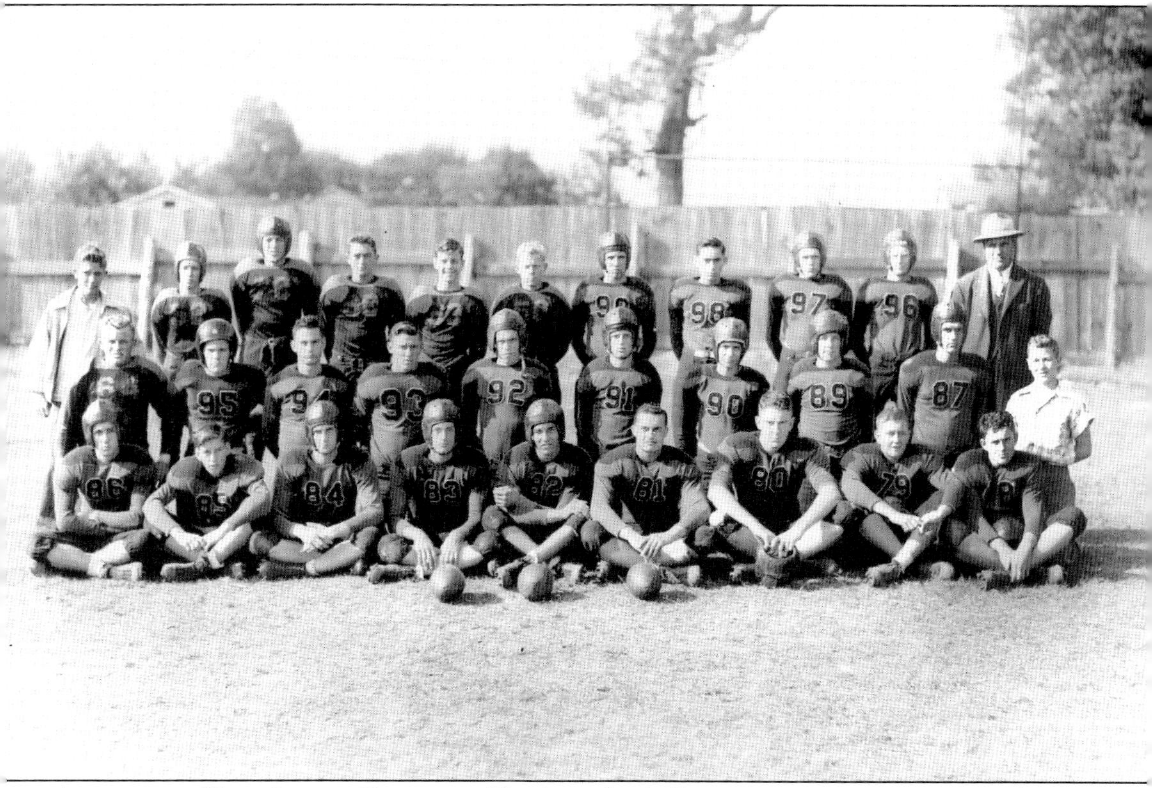

ALBERTVILLE HIGH SCHOOL FOOTBALL. The Aggie football team traces its origins to 1907, the year the first team was organized. Early teams had to contend with scarcity of equipment; this picture illustrates that there were not enough helmets to go around. That first season resulted in one of the first football fatalities in the state of Alabama. In a game held at Albertville between the "Aggies" and the visiting Anniston Presbyterian College team, Anniston player Will Norwood was tackled by Bill Keeling, who in addition to being a player and coach for the team was a full-blooded Cherokee Indian. The team's young mascot, S. Bowie Hooper, always remembered the force of the tackle, which broke Norwood's neck. Norwood was carried on a cot to the Albertville depot, where he was put on the train for the hospital in Gadsden. While this was transpiring, Marshall County's first registered nurse, Elgie Bradford, whose family had moved to Albertville that same year, was just about to leave the Gadsden hospital when she heard about the emergency coming in from Albertville. Doctors advised the family that there was no hope—Norwood was paralyzed from the neck down. The doctors recommended that they take their son home, where his last days could be more meaningful. Young Will had one request: he wanted his new friend, Elgie Bradford, to accompany him. Two to three days before he died his teammates came to see him. He asked that they take his hand and shake it for him, since he was unable to extend it himself. On the tenth day after the accident, Will died, and as Elgie always remembered, "With a smile on his face."

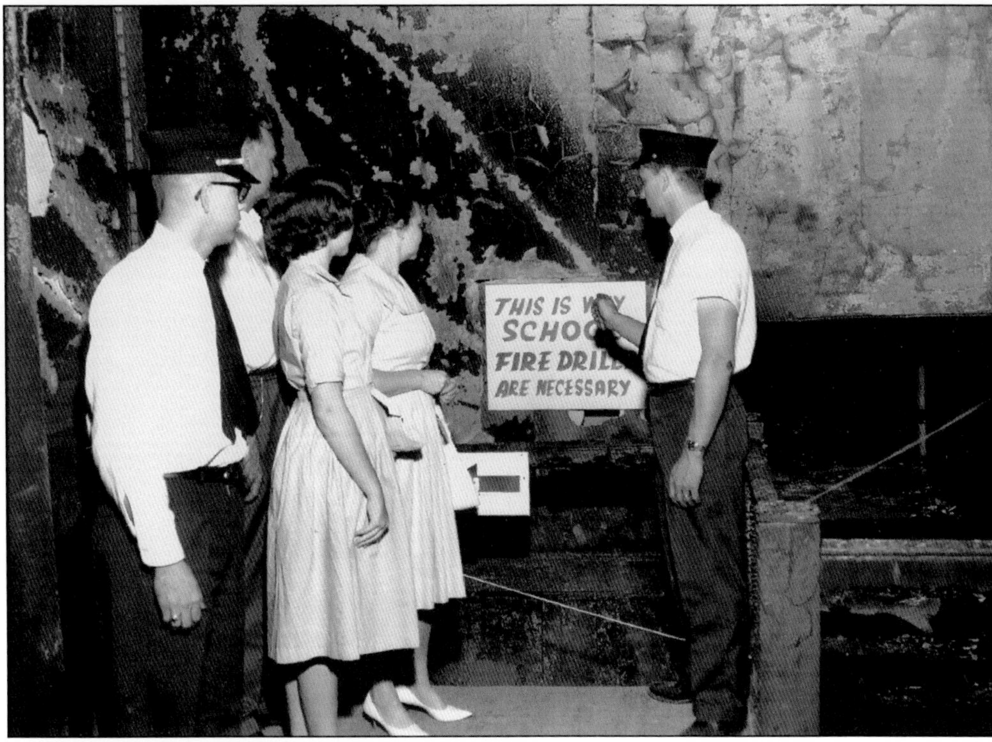

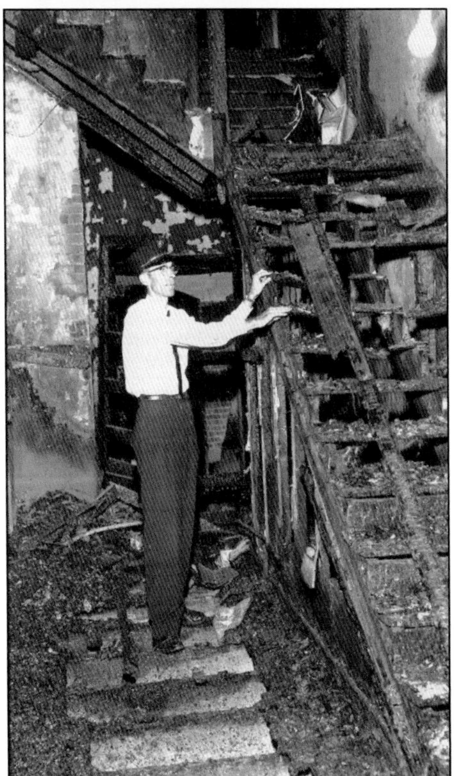

Fire at the Old Elementary School. On June 5, 1961, fire destroyed the town's oldest elementary school building. The building named for an early Albertville principal, S.J. Chandler, had been constructed to answer the needs of a previous school fire that had occurred in 1916. Ironically, just hours before the 1961 fire, the Albertville City Council had discussed a fire plan for that building. A week after the fire, members of the Albertville Fire Department, under the leadership of longtime fire chief Johnny Mack Rollings, arranged an evening of tours at the old school. The tours were conducted to show the townspeople how the fire had started and the importance of fire safety.

Stairway to Safety. Fireman Coy Williams is pictured by the building's staircase. He described that if the fire had happened during school hours, 75 children would have had to reach safety by way of these stairs. At the close of the evening the fire department offered praise to school leaders for holding regular fire drills and teaching children about fire safety.

Four

TRANSPORTATION

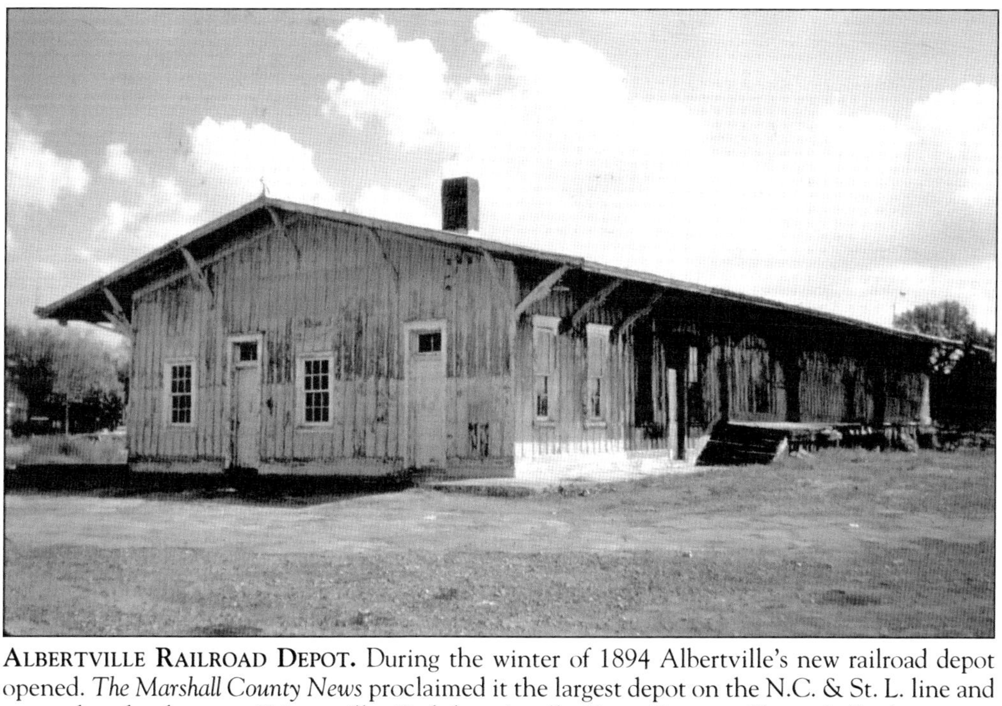

ALBERTVILLE RAILROAD DEPOT. During the winter of 1894 Albertville's new railroad depot opened. *The Marshall County News* proclaimed it the largest depot on the N.C. & St. L. line and wrote that the depots at "Huntsville, Gadsden, Attalla, Boaz, Guntersville, and all other points are laid completely in the shade." Just 14 years later, the depot attained its historical significance in Albertville; it was the only building to come through the cyclone of 1908 unscathed.

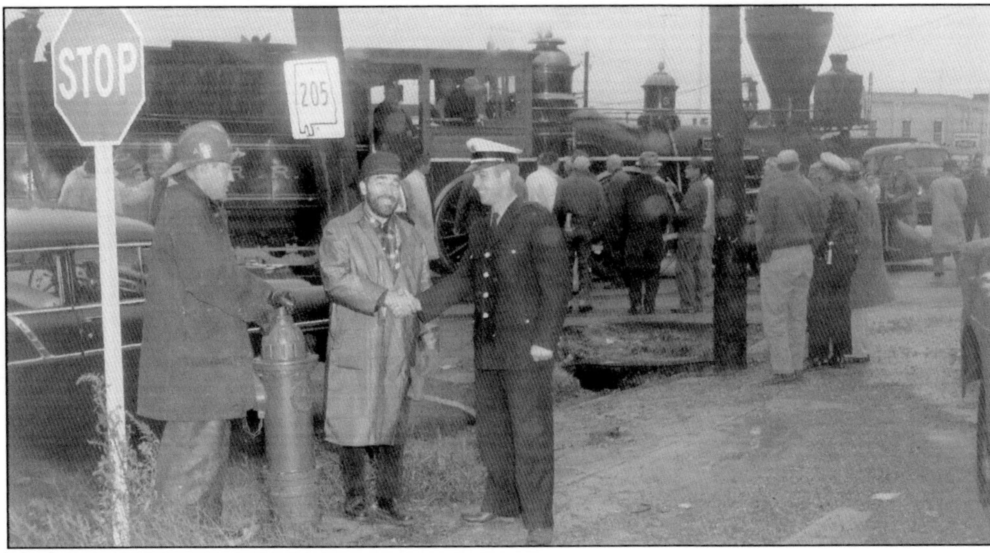

THE GENERAL. In November 1962 Albertville hosted the arrival of *The General*, the 107-year-old train made famous by the Andrews Raiders. This group of Union raiders, led by James Andrews, stole the train in April 1862 to disrupt railroad lines between Chattanooga and Atlanta. Hotly pursued by the Confederates, the raiders were eventually apprehended when *The General* finally gave out near the Tennessee line. Ultimately, Andrews, as well as seven additional raiders, were convicted of espionage and hanged. Almost 100 years later, the great relic of history was refitted and once again traveled the lines, bringing a chapter of history to life for new generations.

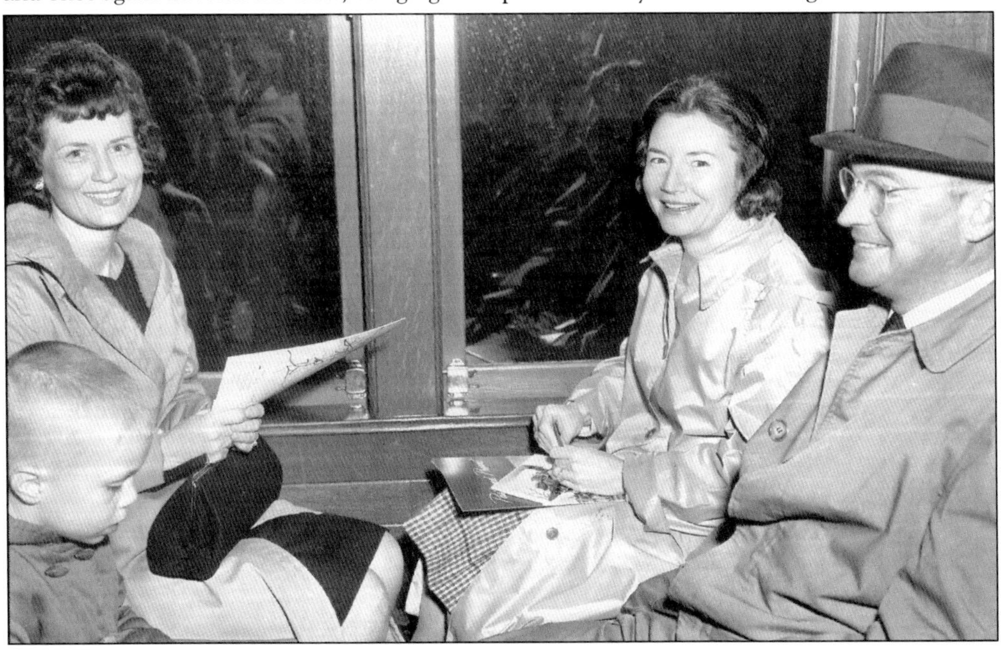

HISTORY COMES TO ALBERTVILLE. Among the townspeople visiting and riding *The General* that day was Albertville mayor E.B. Adams; others pictured include Virginia Johnson and her son, Bob (left) and Winston Walker Jr. and his wife, Cora "Corky" Helen, (right). The photograph was taken by Albertville's foremost photographer of the era, Robert O. Johnson, Virginia's husband and Bob's father.

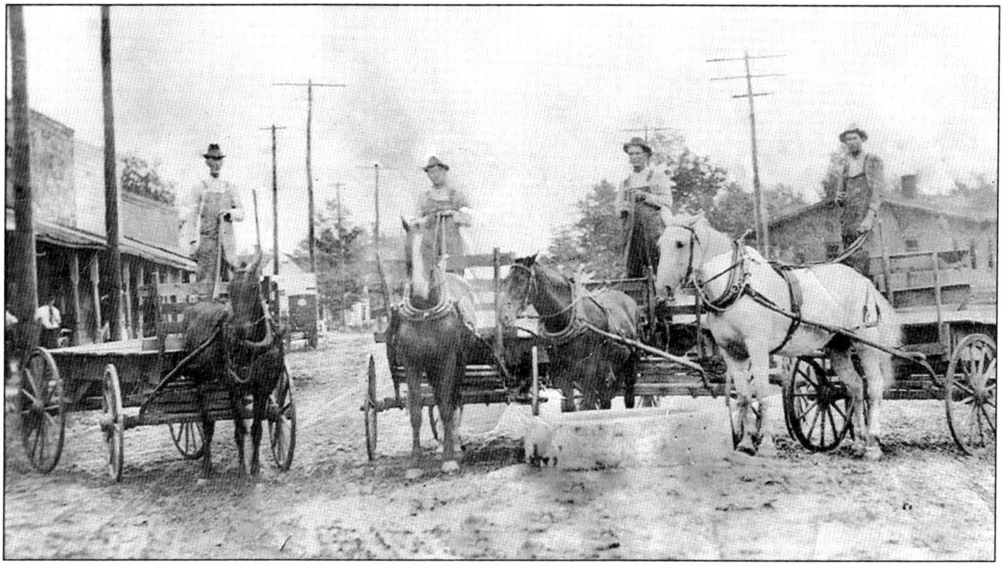

EAST MAIN STREET IN AN EARLIER TIME. Pictured from left to right are Jim Masters, J.M. Waddell, Bud Frasier, and Grady Carroll. They are standing near the intersection of Simpson and Main Streets. By 1914 horses had begun sharing the roads with "mechanized carriages." During that year a city ordinance stipulated the following: "driving vehicles should pull off to the side when meeting a horse until it passes, and if requested, turn the engine off." In April 1927 city alderman T.L. Mann made a motion that was approved by the council to install "stop and go" signals at that intersection, as well as the Main Street and Broad Street intersection.

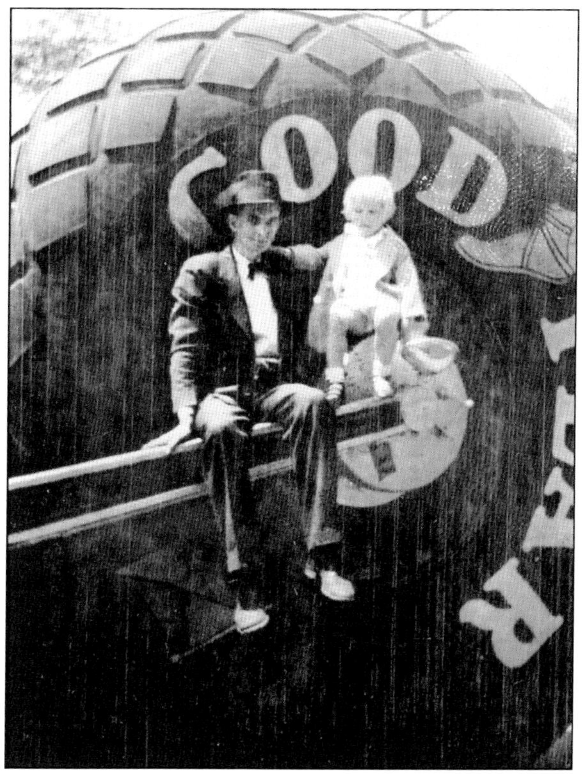

J.N. JOHNSON MOTOR COMPANY. In 1919 J.N. Johnson, son of W.R., established the J.N. Johnson Motor Company at the intersection of East Main Street and Baltimore Avenue. Initially a much smaller store, by 1935 it had grown to include not only a service station, but parts, tires, batteries, and glass works. Customers were even invited to call them at phone 93-F on the Albertville circuit and order what they needed. They offered Willard Batteries for $5.55 each, and they arranged easy terms for that amount. J.N. Johnson and an unidentified child are pictured above with a large promotional tire.

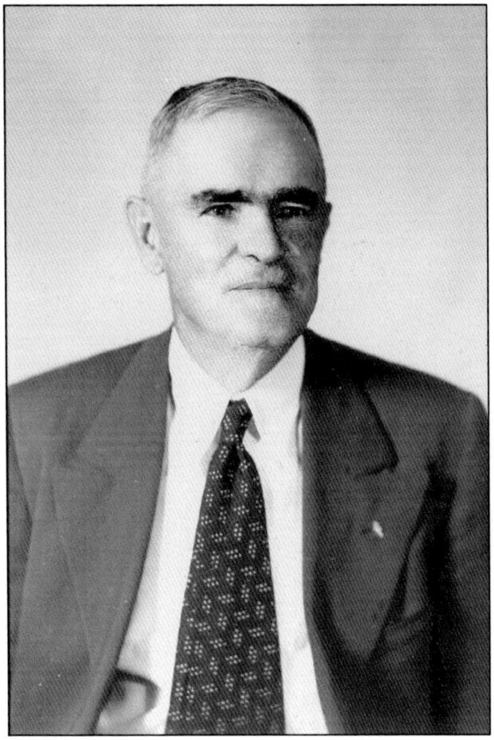

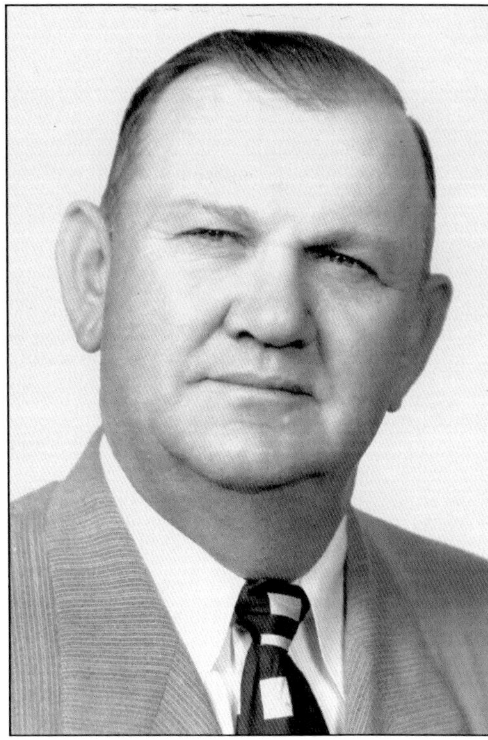

J. VAN WALDROP AND J. COLEMAN CLEMONS. In 1911 J. Van Waldrop (above left) secured the Ford Motor Company franchise for DeKalb, Jackson, and Marshall Counties operating out of Collinsville. The first year he did not sell a single Ford. The next year, he sold two or three. By his third year, demand was increasing and vehicles were backordered. In 1915 the Waldrops moved to Albertville, where he established his longstanding Ford agency. In 1928 third-generation Albertville resident John Coleman Clemons (above right) established the Albertville Wrecking Company, a forerunner of the modern auto parts stores. The Clemons ancestors had settled in Albertville in about 1871. His grandmother once served as postmaster of the town.

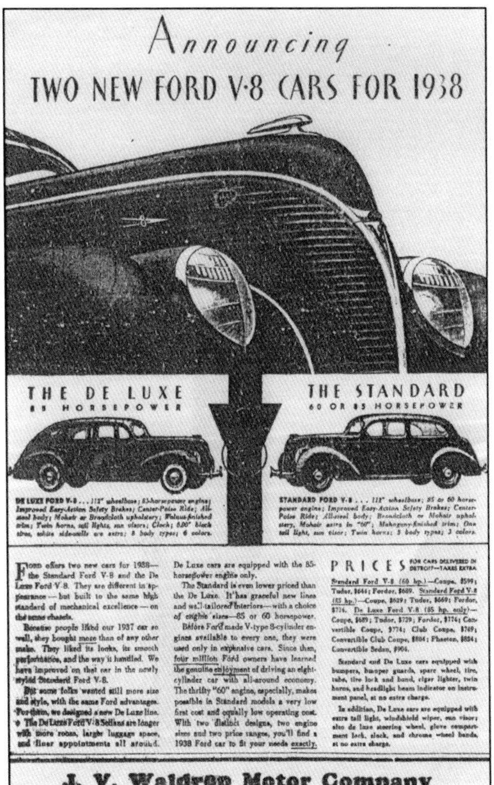

ADVERTISEMENT FOR J. VAN WALDROP FORD DEALERSHIP, 1938. One could acquire the standard V-8 on the right of this advertisement for $599, or one could "shoot the moon" and get the De Luxe in a convertible sedan for $904.

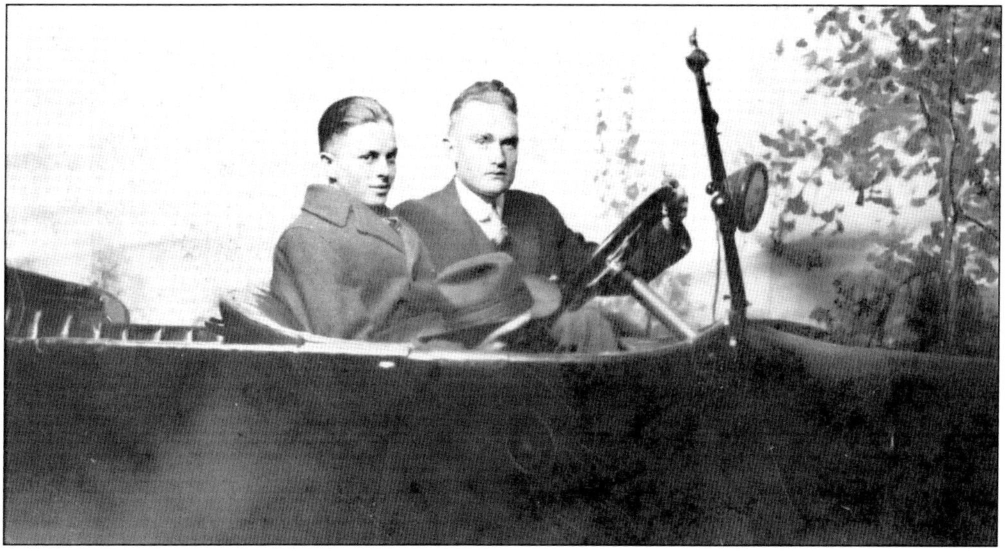

DAWNING OF THE AUTOMOTIVE AGE. The first automobile in Albertville belonged to Tom McNaron, son-in-law of business pioneer L.S. Emmett. During the earliest days of the automobile, primary ownership was by professional people such as doctors, businessmen, or the clergy. Pictured in the driver's seat of the above photograph is one of the town's business pioneers, Dewey Wells.

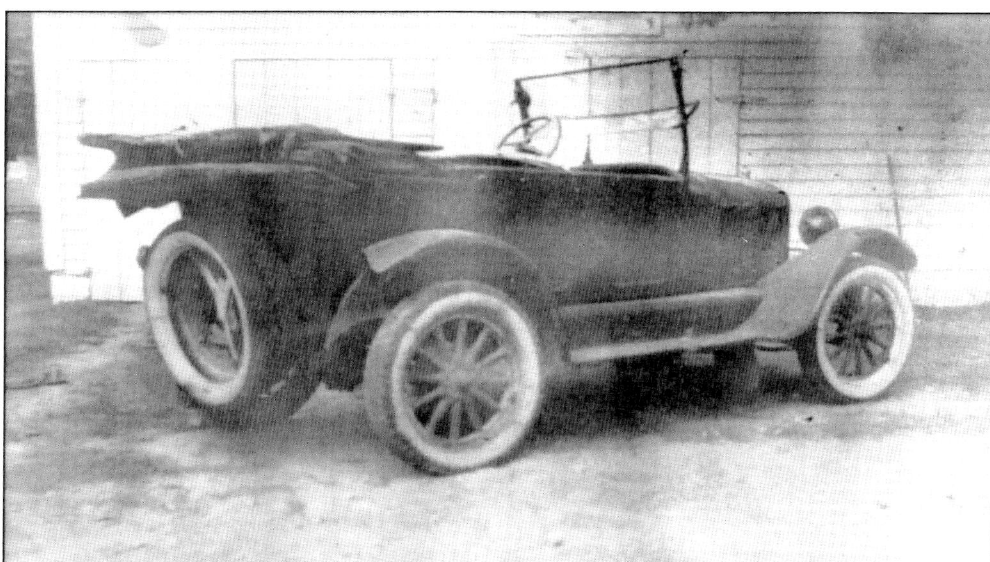

FIRST CAR. Shown is the first car of brothers Joe and Dorsett Davis—a 1926 Model-T.

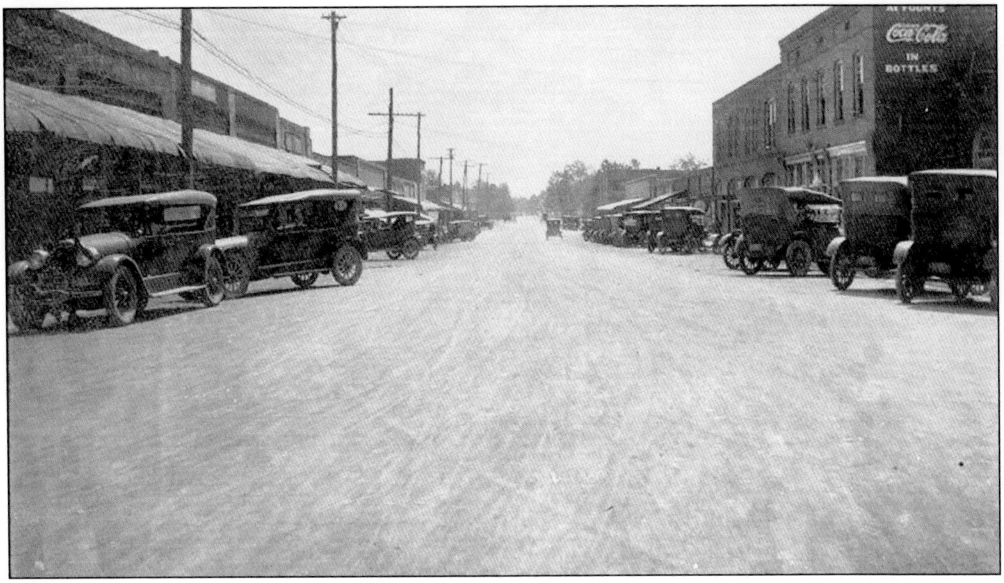

ALBERTVILLE'S MAIN STREET, 1920S. Albertville's Main Street is photographed just prior to being paved. The paving of Main Street had been a long-held dream of the town's merchants. For years, dust from the street played havoc with business inventories. In 1913 the local newspaper even put forth the idea of oiling the street. (Another idea on the editor's wish list was the placing of cuspidors at Albertville's branch courthouse; as he put it in his article, the "floors were unpleasant.")

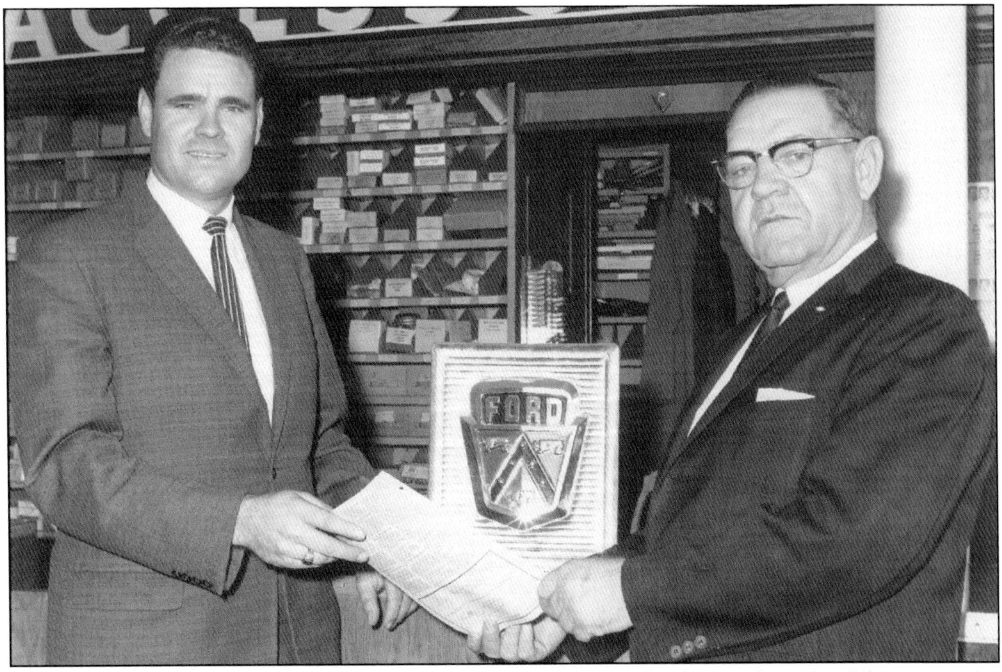

RALPH COLLINS FORD. In 1963 Ralph Collins (right), who had served as chief deputy in the Marshall County Sheriff's office, acquired Albertville's Ford dealership. Olin C. Hearn, former Ford dealer, is pictured with Collins. In 1969 Collins hired architect W.S. "Bill" Roden to design and construct a new location for the business on Highway 431.

Five

CALAMITY

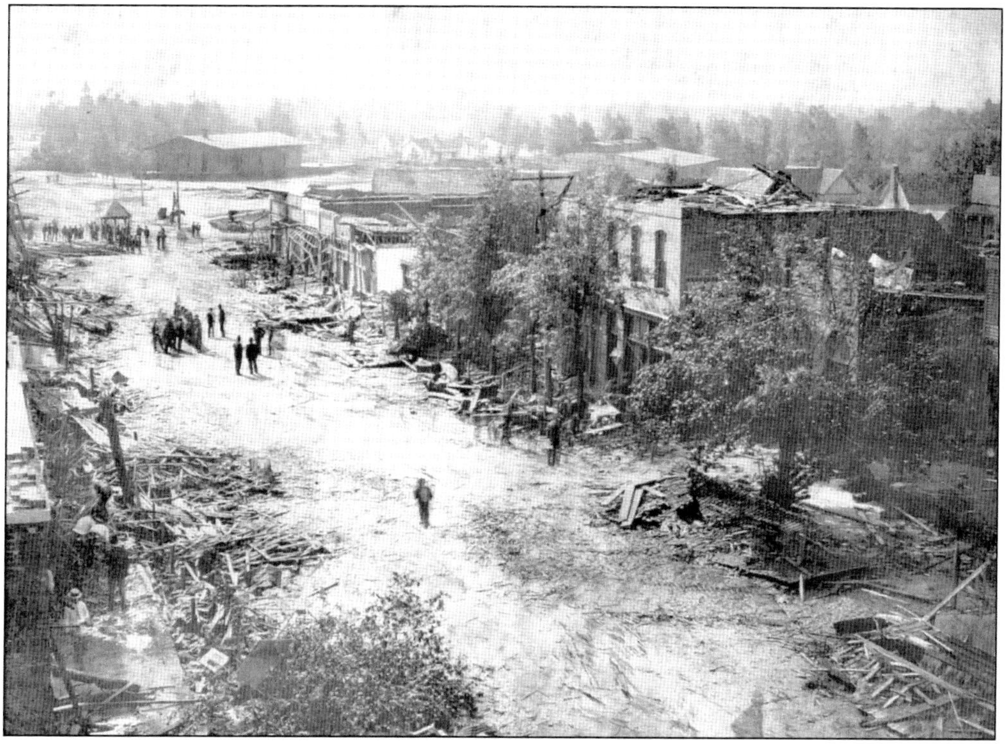

FRIDAY AFTERNOON, APRIL 24, 1908. The morning of April 24, 1908, began with the thermometer at 60 degrees. The sidewalks of Albertville that day were made up of people with different purposes; some probably dropped by the Butler-Kyser Oil Company to see its new 18,000-gallon tank, while others possibly stopped by the Marshall Drug Company to buy some chocolate-covered cold tablets advertised in the previous day's paper. By noon, temperatures had climbed into the 90s, which was followed an hour later by heavy thunder rumblings in the west. At 4:10 p.m., a cyclone of massive proportions struck the town just north of the depot. In the destruction's wake came torrential downpour, followed closely by the darkness of night. Throughout the night, search parties sifted through the debris, finding many fatalities, but remarkably, given the storm's fury, they found survivors as well. One such survivor was Christopher Walker, who retained scars from the incident for the remainder of his life. Little did anyone in Albertville realize that they had been part of a storm that had stretched from Louisiana, across Mississippi, and into Alabama. The storm left 287 dead and 1,091 injured in the combined area.

GADSDEN HURRIED RELIEF LAST NIGHT

First Details of the Frightful Disaster Brought to This City on Early Morning Train---List of Dead and Injured---Relief Train With Corps of Physicians and Nurses Sent From Gadsden.

THE DEAD

ERIC McCORD, aged 13.
MRS. G. O. BARNETT, aged 65.
T. J. SADLER, aged 70.
MRS. JOHN DECKER.
Two children of JOHN DECKER.
ARNOLD BIRDSONG, aged 14.
IDA DORSETT, aged 4.
NEGRO GIRL, name unknown.

FATALLY INJURED.

John Decker.
Two children of John Decker.
Mrs. W. M. Avery.
Prof. Sylvester Greer, Assistant Superintendent Seventh District Agricultural School.
Dr. Turk.
Mrs. Turk.
Son of Mrs. Bobo.

DANGEROUSLY INJURED.

Madison Walker.
Christie Walker.
Miss Johnnie Libas.
T. R. Robertson.
Charles Dorsett.
Child of Charles Dorsett.
J. L. Scarbrough.
Mrs. R. N. Moody.
W. M. Ragsdale.
Mrs. W. M. Ragsdale.
Mrs. H. S. Wilson and baby.
Prof. C. M. Danley.
D. B. Reeves.
Mrs. D. B. Reeves.
Four children of D. B. Reeves.
Mrs. E. O. McCord and child.

THE DAY AFTER. The following day's Gadsden newspaper listed the human suffering that was so massive as to defy description.

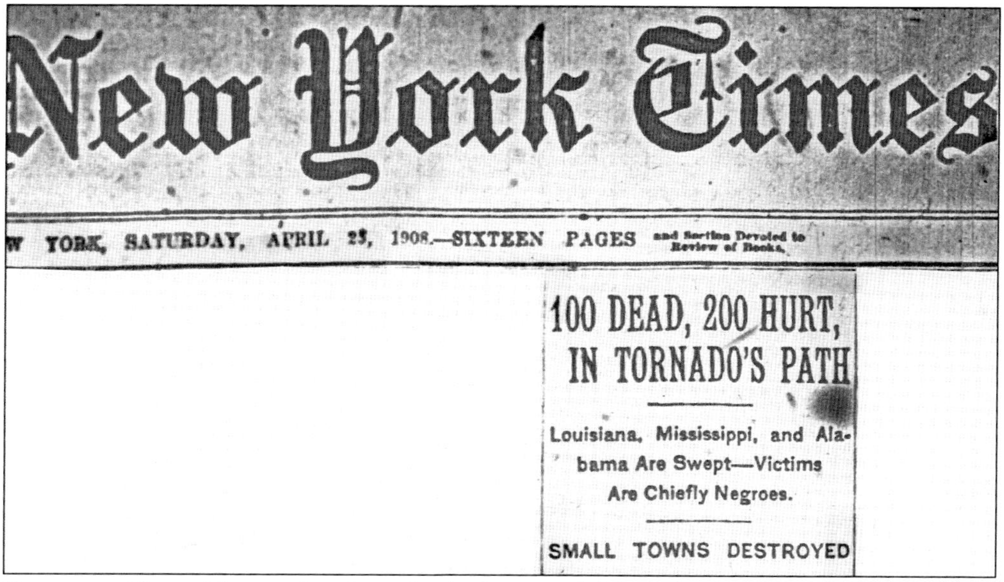

New York Times

W YORK, SATURDAY, APRIL 25, 1908.—SIXTEEN PAGES and Section Devoted to Review of Books.

100 DEAD, 200 HURT, IN TORNADO'S PATH

Louisiana, Mississippi, and Alabama Are Swept—Victims Are Chiefly Negroes.

SMALL TOWNS DESTROYED

NATIONAL NEWS. The weather front that had spawned this cyclone as well as others across the south warranted front-page coverage in the next day's edition of *The New York Times*. The article mentioned Albertville and its devastation by name.

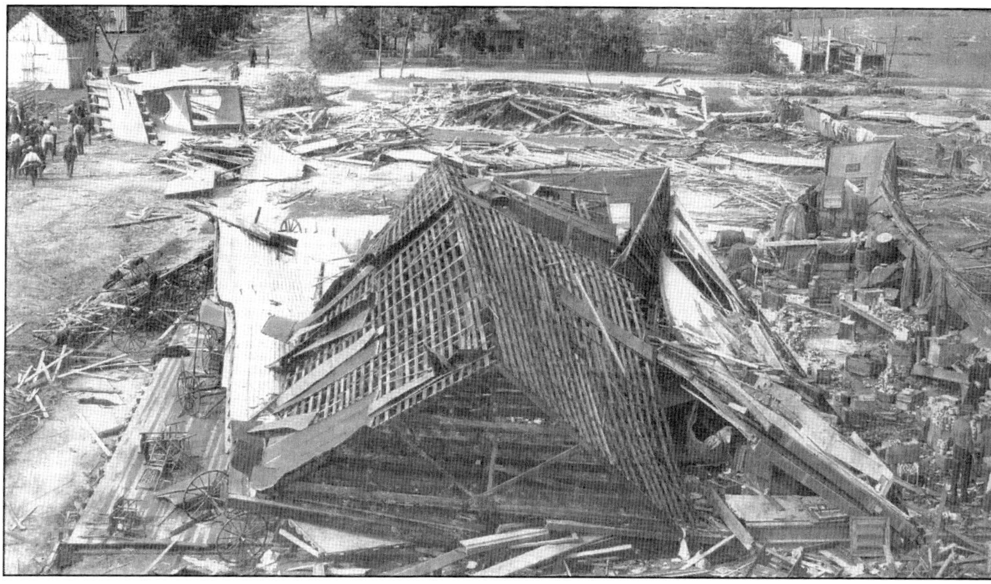

INDESCRIBABLE. Not a building downtown, except for the depot, remained unscathed. As seen in the image above, the streets and alleys were full of canned goods and clothing. At the nearby oil company, the new 18,000-gallon tank had been dislodged and hurled a quarter of a mile. Among Albertville's dead was 16-year-old Eric McCord, son of former mayor E.O. McCord, who had crawled under the family home seeking safety only to have the house collapse upon him. One of the most horrific sights beheld that day was at the home of the John Decker family. In one room lay the body of Mrs. Decker, holding the lifeless body of her one-year-old daughter. Beside them lay the body of her three-year-old daughter crushed almost beyond recognition. In the other room lay the father and four other children, all seriously injured. Fortunately, the father and the four children with him all survived.

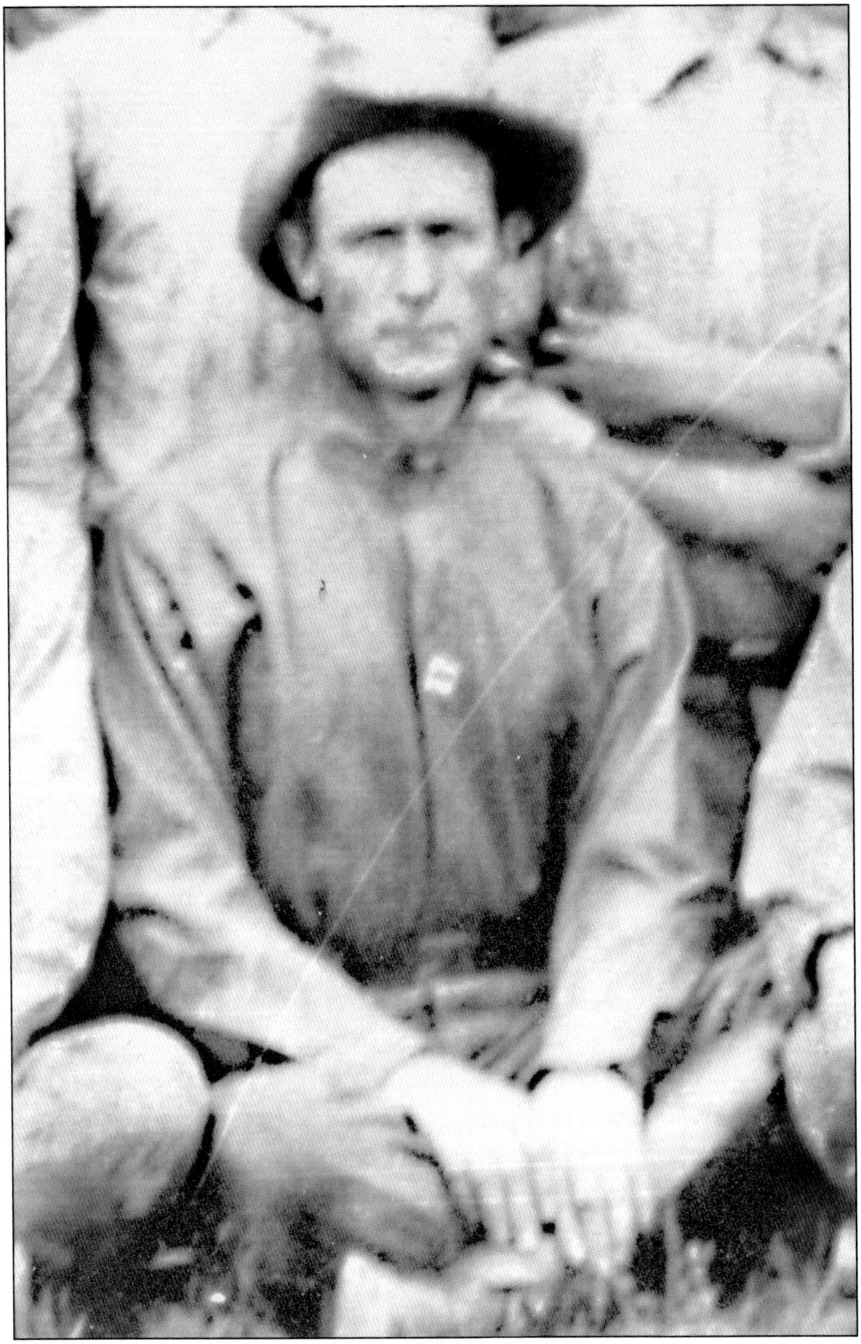

John C. Coleman. One of the true heroes of the cyclone crisis was John Crawford Coleman, who oversaw the local militia. When the Gadsden regiment returned home, its members had nothing but praise for this man who almost single-handedly established order in that most trying of times. The only time that he left his post was to bury his own mother at the West Cemetery; he returned to his position shortly after the service. John C. Coleman and his brother, W.M. "Bob" Coleman, the city's first mayor, did much to aid in the evolution of the frontier town to the city Albertville is today.

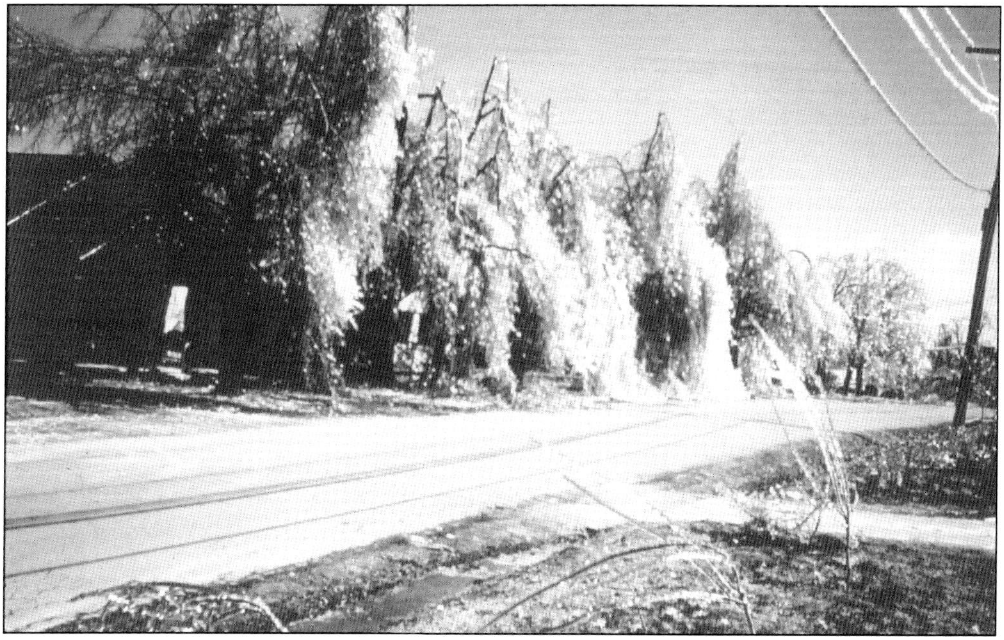

ICE STORM OF 1960. The morning of Tuesday, March 1, 1960, witnessed the falling of light snow across Sand Mountain. Even though traffic was barely hindered, school leaders exercised caution and dismissed school early. This was to be the calm before the storm. By Wednesday, a layer of ice covered everything; for a time, almost all of Sand Mountain was without power. Thus began an ordeal that would last for well over a week for some folks on Sand Mountain.

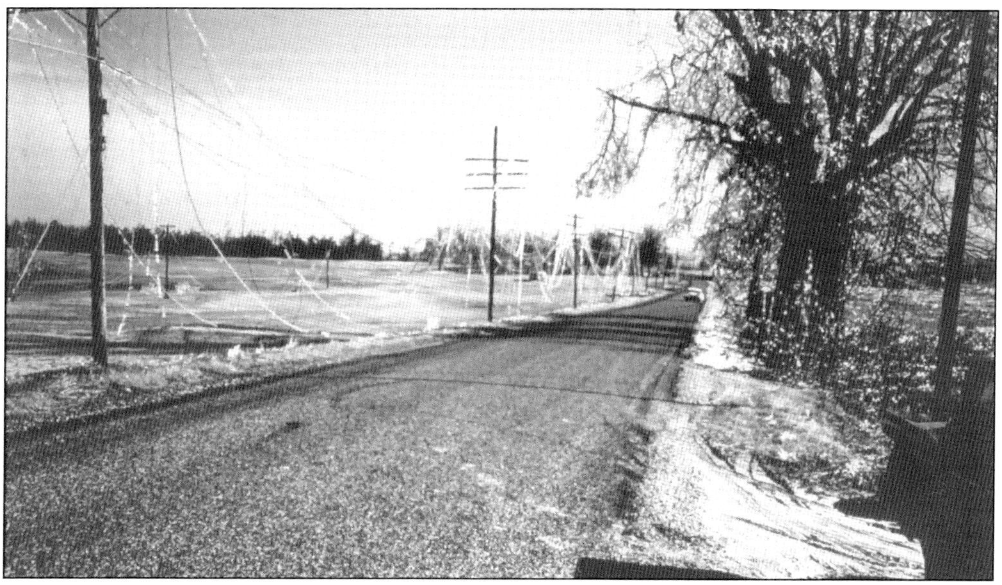

ICE STORM OF 1960. Public utilities were most affected by the ice storm. The head of Southern Bell's Albertville office, Bill Wilson, estimated the total damage to local and long distance circuits was in excess of $1.5 million. As far as electricity at medical facilities, the Sand Mountain Infirmary suffered only a brief interruption, the Albertville Clinic had to be evacuated, and the new Boaz-Albertville Hospital suffered interruption before borrowing an electric generator from Redstone Arsenal.

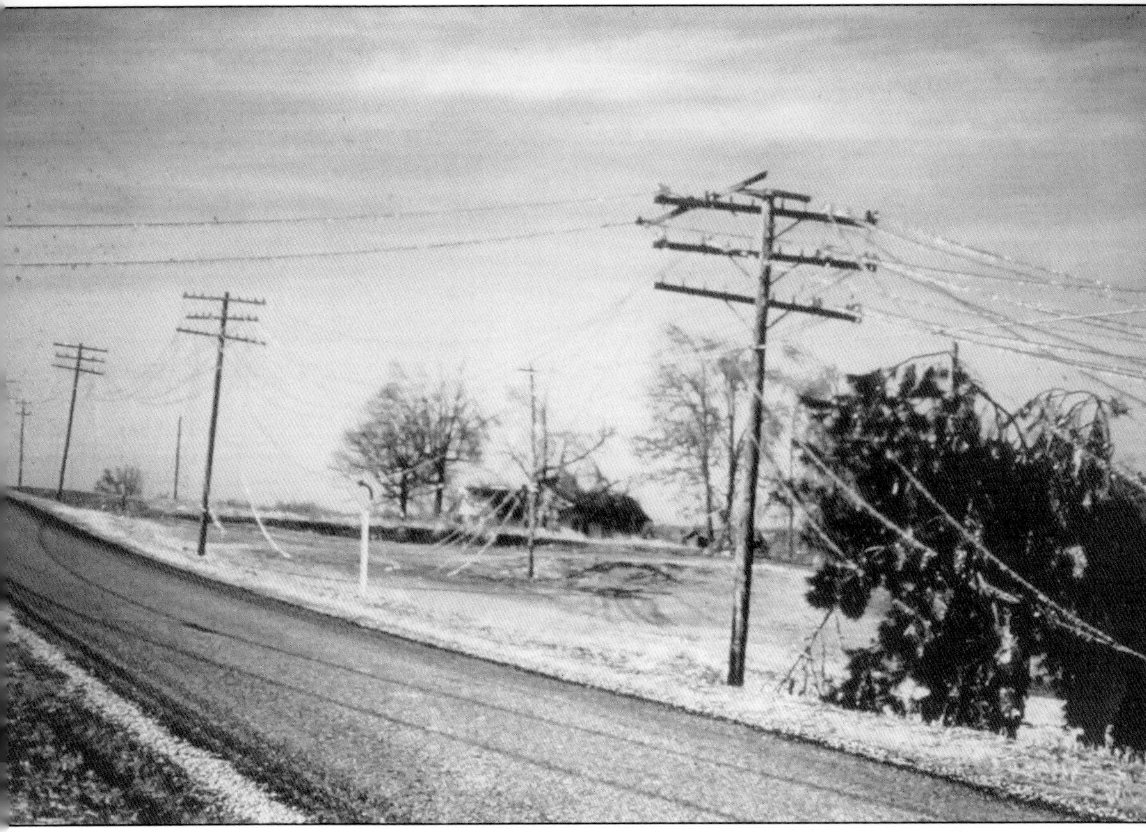

ICE STORM OF 1960. One of the most financially crucial aspects of the storm was the economic impact on the area's poultry industry. Within a short time from the onset of the crisis, the industry sustained a loss of millions of dollars. In an attempt to save the dressed chicken, Alabama governor John Patterson had a shipment of dry ice delivered to the area.

Six

Faith

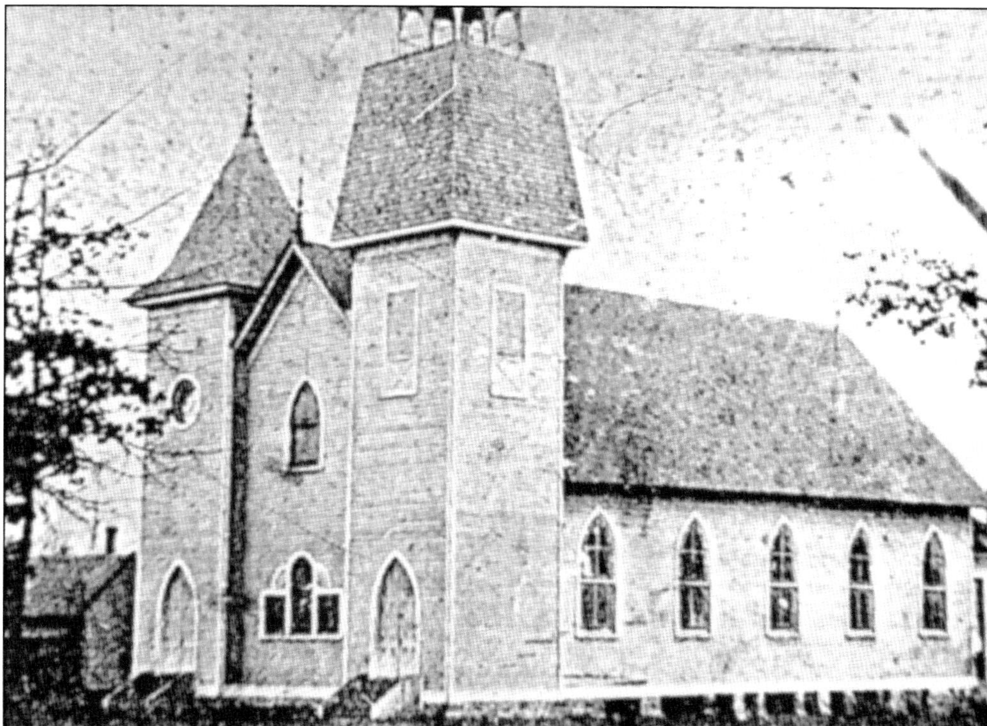

First Baptist Church of Albertville. In August 1883 the Albertville Baptist Church, forerunner of today's First Baptist Church, was organized with 16 members. Rev. S.T. Collier, the first pastor, gave the lot and led in the construction of the first building, which was located on West Main Street near the Old City Cemetery. In 1885 land was purchased on East Main Street at the church's current site. In 1900 work was begun on a new building. The building, shown above, served the church until 1924, when it was razed and a brick building was constructed. On July 19, 1910, Albertville hosted the Alabama State Baptist Convention. At 10:30 that morning, the convention was called to order in the chapel of the Seventh District Agricultural School. Albertville Baptist Church pastor Rev. A.B. Metcalfe extended a hearty welcome to the 500 delegates.

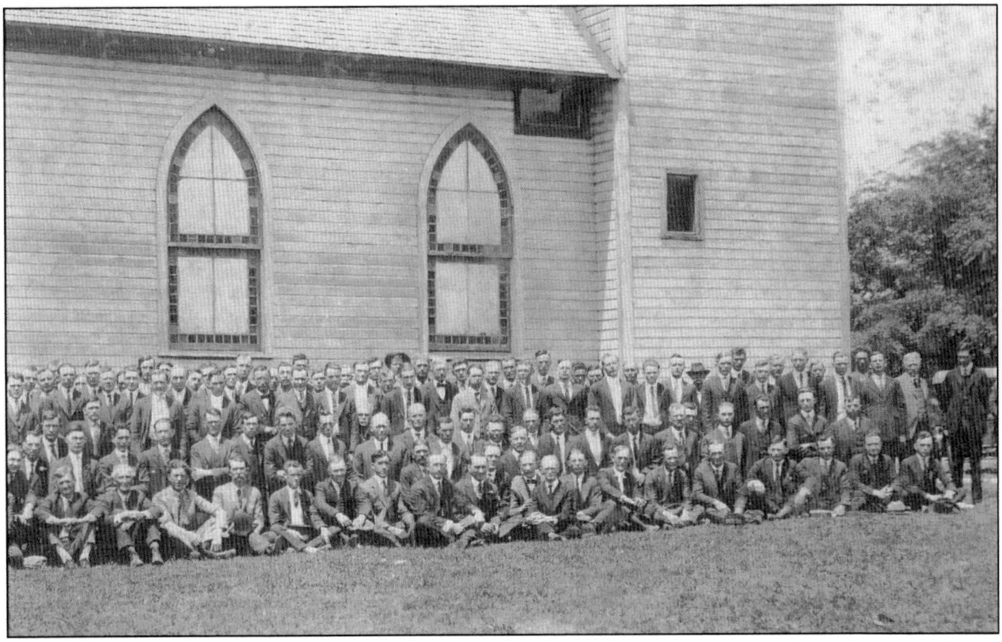

BAPTIST MEN'S GROUP, C. 1920. By the time the above photograph was taken, the attendance of the Baptist church had more than doubled. Not only was worship attendance increasing in all area churches, Sunday school attendance was showing remarkable growth. A total of 1,000 people were enrolled in classes at the three largest churches in town—Baptist, Methodist, and Christian (the current North Broad Church of Christ). There was even a contest between the Methodist Young Men's class and the Baptist Young Men's class.

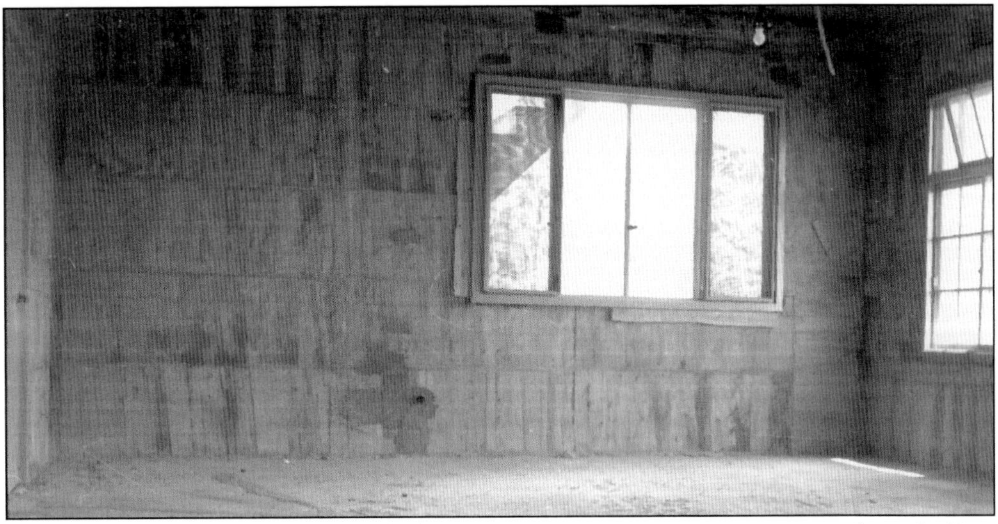

THE LIFE OF A MISSIONARY. Through the years, numerous missionaries went out from the First Baptist Church. Missionaries included Dr. T.O. Hearn, brother of C.L. Hearn; Miss Clarabell Isdell, later McDonald; and Dr. Martha Hagood. The above image is of a simple hut used by Dr. Hagood in the Orient. For many years, First Baptist Church held Martha Hagood Day to honor her and to inform the church of her missionary work. It was not until the third celebration in 1957 that she was able to attend in person. Her father, Dr. E.W. Hagood, was pastor of the church from 1931 to 1947.

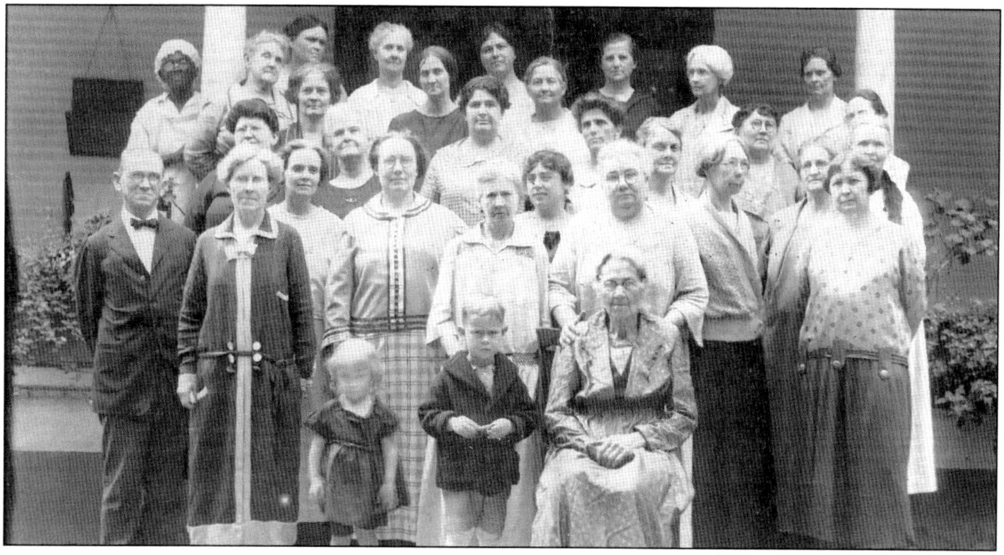

MISSIONARY SOCIETY OF THE METHODIST CHURCH, 1922. To this day, the First United Methodist Church of Albertville is the oldest continually functioning entity in Albertville. In 1856 circuit rider W.D. Nicholson established what was known at that time as the Jones Chapel Methodist Episcopal Church, South, on the site now occupied by Little Branch Primitive Baptist Church. The Old City Cemetery was established by the Jones Chapel Church. In 1895 the church members built a one-room structure on the church's present-day site; however, it was blown down in a windstorm. In 1899 a determined church rebuilt a better structure that served the church's needs until the building was enlarged in 1914. In October 1898 the church witnessed the creation of the Ladies Aid Society, pictured above.

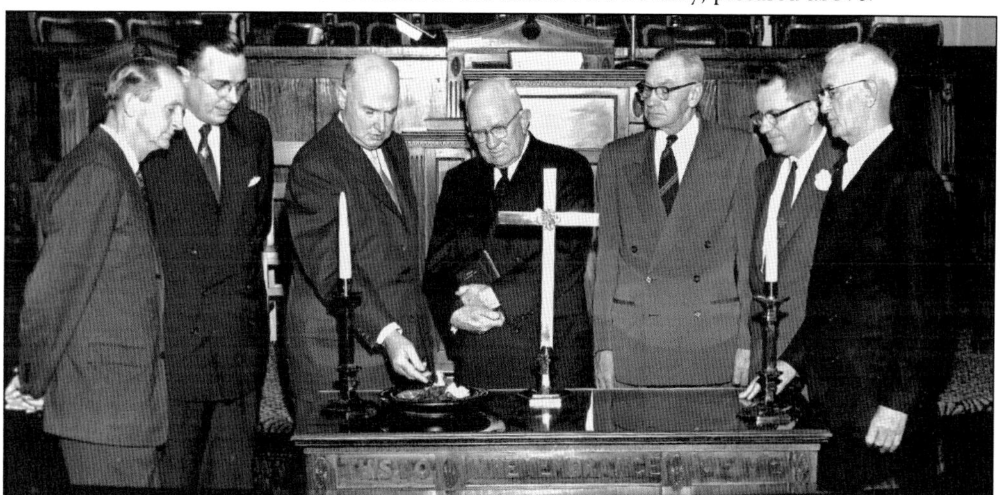

MORTGAGE BURNING AT THE FIRST METHODIST CHURCH. On Sunday night, March 11, 1956, a special service was held at the First Methodist Church of Albertville to burn the mortgage of the church's new educational building. Work had commenced on the new $80,000 structure in August 1954. Shown from left to right are Hoyt Levie, head of the building committee; Rev. Charles O. Moore, church pastor; J.R. Abney, chairman of the finance committee; Clare Purcell, Methodist bishop; Rev. W.D. Barnes, former church pastor; Rev. Harold Spradley, former church pastor; and T.J. Chitwood, Methodist district superintendent.

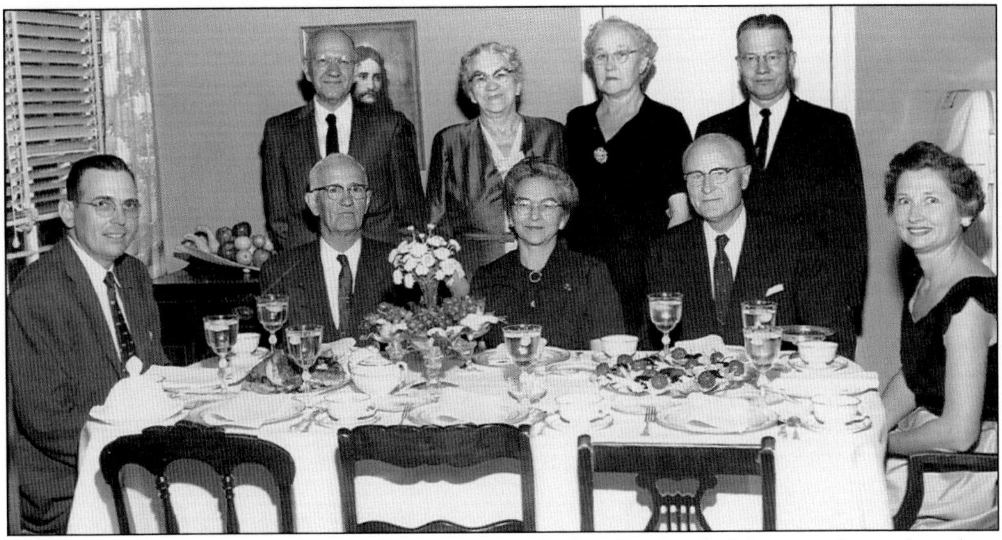

The Berckmans. During the mid-1950s, Rev. and Mrs. Charles O. Moore welcomed to their table, among others, Rev. J.H.H. (back row left) and Ruth Rice Berckman (seated center). On June 23, 1921, the Berckmans had been married by her father, Rev. W.L. Rice. Within months of their wedding, the couple departed for the Orient, where they served as missionaries for many years. Reverend Berckman continued serving as a missionary until his death in March 1963. At the time of his death, he was serving at the Christ Methodist Church in Singapore, on whose ground sits the Berckman Memorial Hall. After her husband's death, Mrs. Berckman, whose grandfather, James M. Howard, had settled in the area many years before, remained in Albertville. She became a sought after speaker at churches and clubs about her knowledge of the Far East.

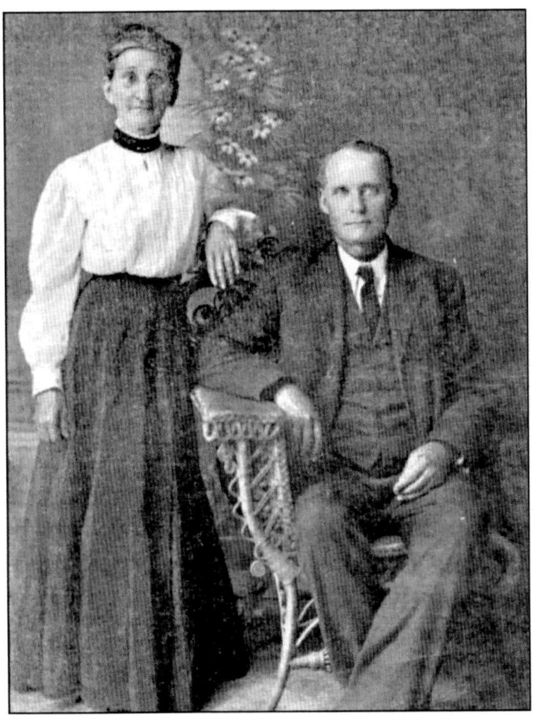

R.N. Moody. In 1889 the foundations of the current North Broad Street Church of Christ where laid when a congregation, including the families of R.N. Moody, T.J. Sadler, and John Dickson, began meeting in a small building on Beulah Road. In 1904 a building was erected for the church on the site now occupied by Hewett Drugs. This building was destroyed by the great cyclone of 1908. It was rebuilt and served the church as home until 1948, when the current church complex was begun. R.N. Moody, shown here with his wife, Eliza Ann, served as minister from its inception until his death in 1935.

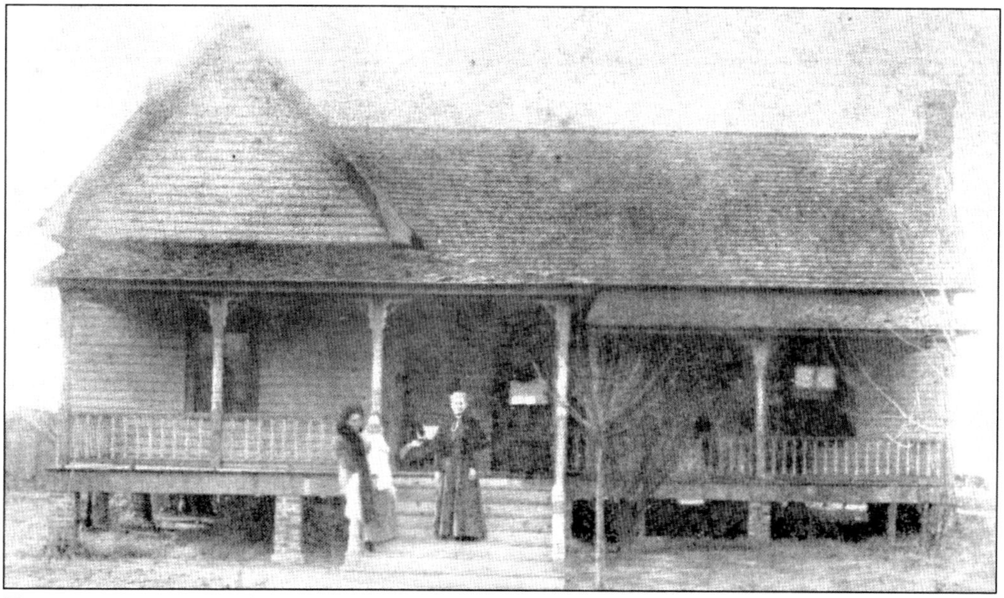

THE MOODY HOME. The R.N. Moody family home was located at the intersection of South Broad Street and Alabama Avenue. Throughout his life, R.N. Moody distinguished himself as a strong student and teacher of the Bible. In addition, he wrote extensively; one of his books, *Eunice Loyd*, can still be obtained through Amazon.

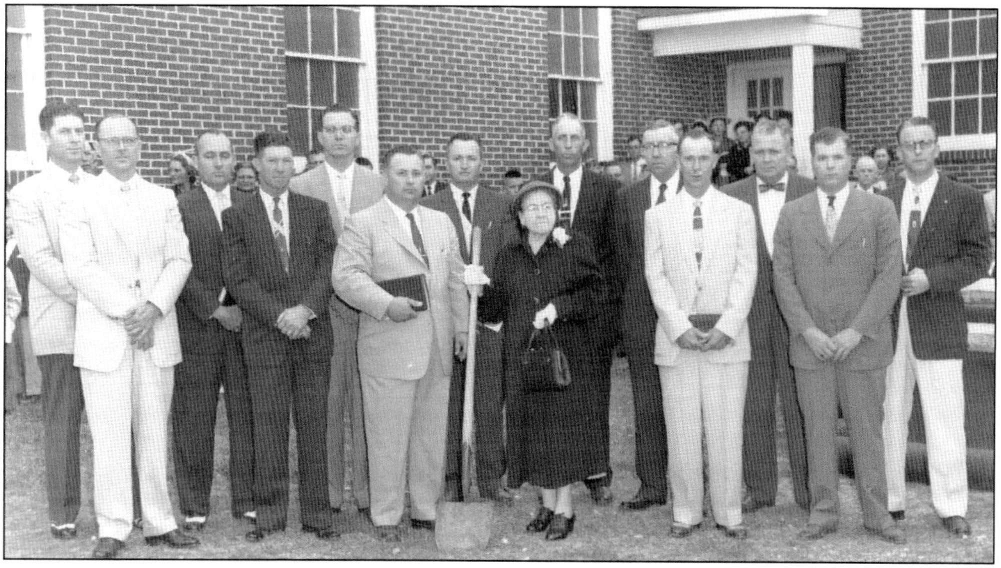

MT. CALVARY BAPTIST CHURCH. Organized after a tent revival in Albertville in 1936, Mt. Calvary Baptist Church has grown to become one of the county's largest churches. Just 20 years after its establishment, the congregation outgrew the structure that had been built. In April 1956 groundbreaking for a new building was held. Those pictured from left to right are Hollis Jolley, Berley Bishop, Ralph Barkley, Floyd Jones, B.L. Bishop, Rev. R.H. Clemons, Eugene Lang, Sara Frances Heaton, Claude McNeal, L.O. Ragsdale, Grover Robinson, Vernon York, Revell Cofield, and A.M. Smith. They were members of the board of deacons, the building committee, or the bond selling committee. Since the naming of Reverend Clemons as pastor in 1952, membership by 1956 had increased by 248 and Sunday school had increased from 280 to 440.

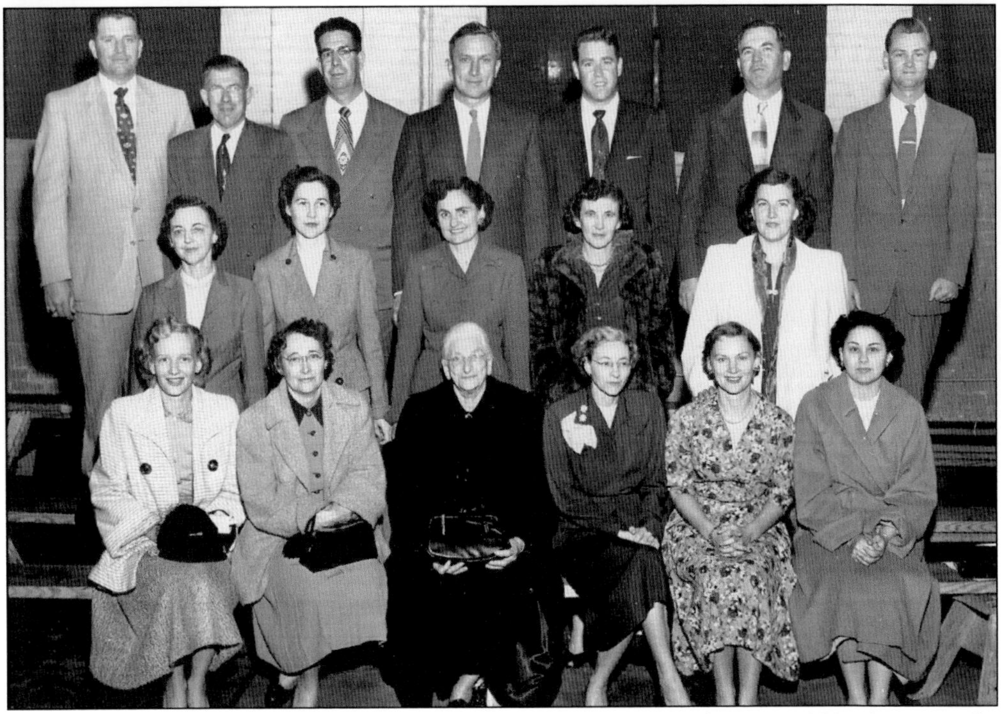

First Presbyterian Church Charter Members. On November 29, 1953, charter night services were held at the National Guard Armory for the First Presbyterian Church of Albertville. Ross Knox, Ben H. Hamby, and Forrest Crowe were elected as elders and ordained.

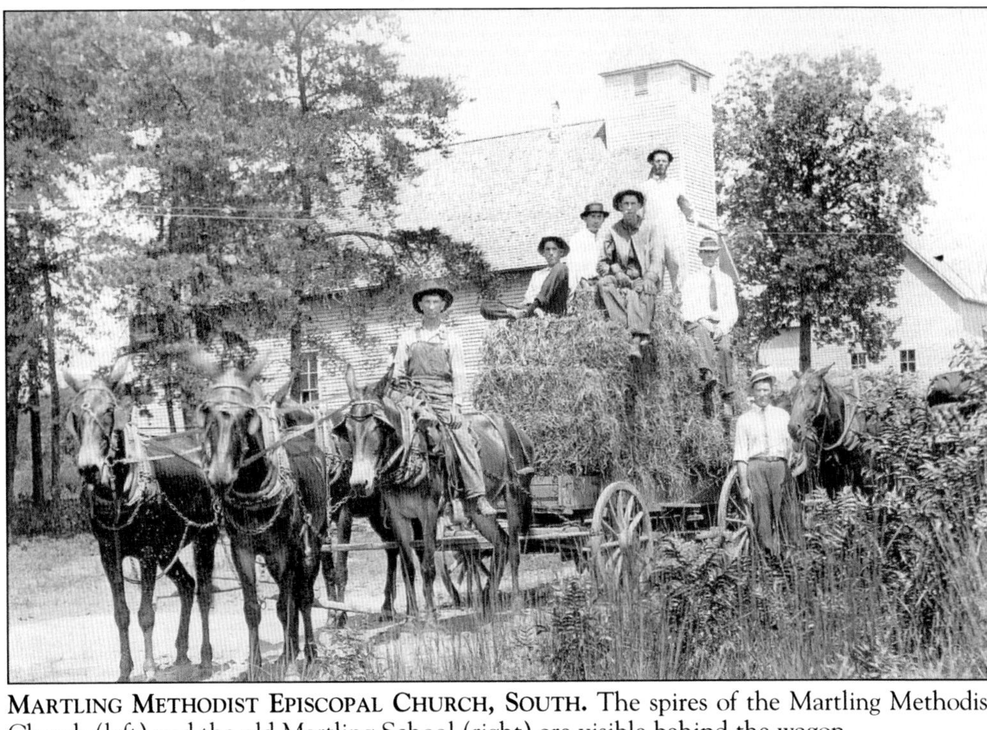

Martling Methodist Episcopal Church, South. The spires of the Martling Methodist Church (left) and the old Martling School (right) are visible behind the wagon.

Seven

HEALTH

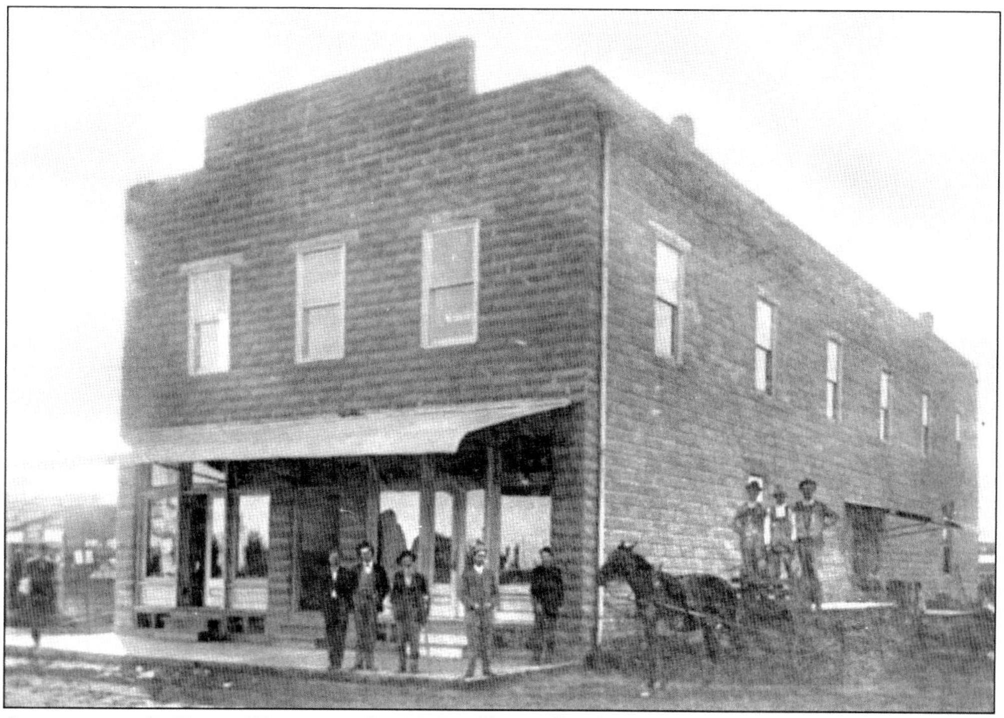

ALBERTVILLE'S FIRST HOSPITAL. In 1917 Albertville physicians Dr. Montgomery Shipp and Dr. W.T. Miller opened the town's first hospital on the second floor of the McNaron brothers' building. The ground floor served as a feed store. In addition to Shipp and Miller, other doctors of the time were John Arnold, W.A. and S.M. Elrod, W.M. Scarbrough, and W.P. Hall. William Presley Hall began his medical career at Rock Springs in 1886 after graduating from Emory University. In 1900 he moved his family and practice into a house he had built at the corner of Baltimore Avenue and Neely Graham Lane in Albertville. Years later, his son, Edwin Press Hall, who followed in his father's medical footsteps, recalled those early years of practice. He remembered how the shelves of his father's office were lined with various bottles, pills, and powders. A number of Dr. Hall's patients lived in rural areas and were unable to get to the neighborhood . Press remembered one of his father's house calls in particular. His father told the family, "Give [him] the medicine every four hours, just like I told you, and bathe him all over today." The family responded, "We're afraid to give him a bath, Doctor. He hasn't had one since he was a boy and went to the creek."

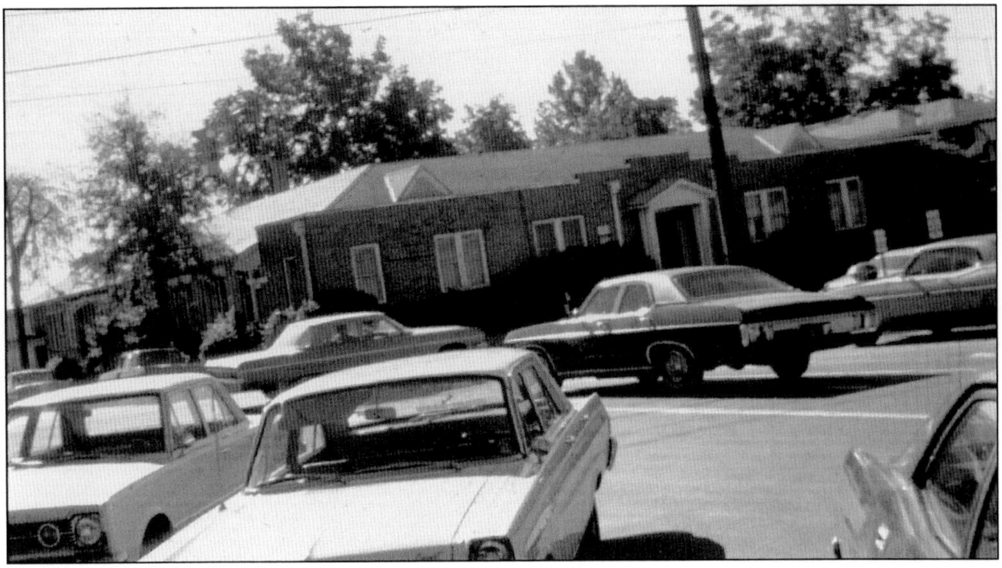

The Sand Mountain Infirmary. The close of 1927 saw the opening of a medical facility that served the citizens of Albertville and the surrounding area for many years, the Sand Mountain Infirmary. Its founder, Dr. Bemon C. Scarbrough, grew up in Albertville before relocating to Ashland. His grandfather, W.M. Scarbrough, practiced medicine in Albertville from his arrival in 1890 until his death in 1900. In 1922 Dr. B.C. Scarbrough returned to Albertville after graduating from the University of Tennessee Medical School. When he arrived in Albertville, Scarbrough open his medical office over Pink Graham's drug store on the south side of Main Street.

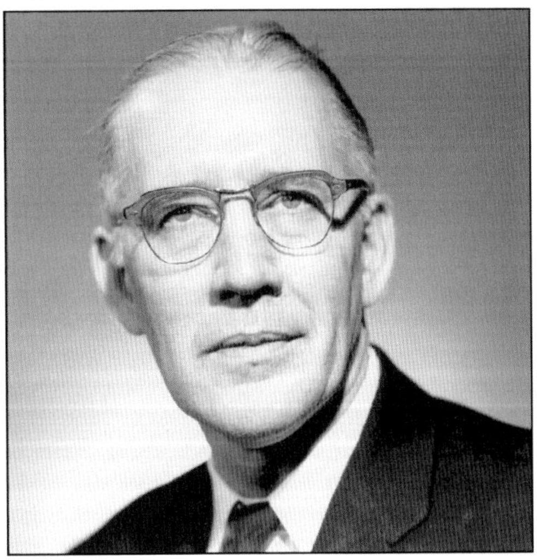

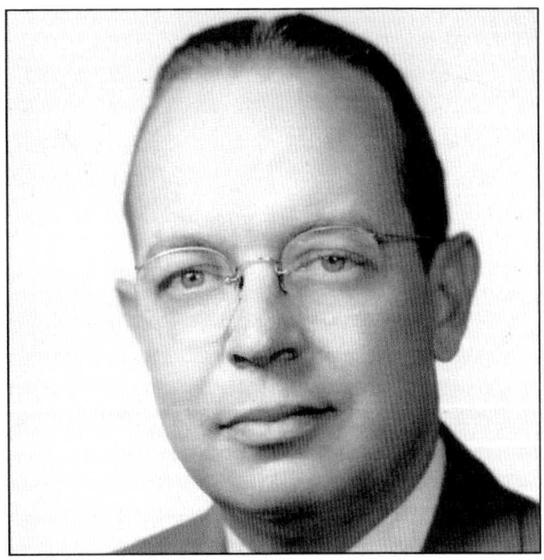

Dr. H.L. Rogers (Left) and Dr. B.N. Lavender (Right). In 1938 Dr. Harold L. Rogers of Hillman Hospital in Birmingham came to Albertville and entered into a partnership with Dr. B.C. Scarbrough of the Sand Mountain Infirmary. In 1944 he became co-owner of the infirmary and, when Dr. Scarbrough died in 1950, he bought the infirmary property from Mrs. Scarbrough. Shortly thereafter, Rogers sold an interest in the business to Dr. Kenneth Christian. Dr. Belton N. Lavender moved to Albertville in 1940, initially entering into practice with Dr. A.L. Isbell. In 1942 he established his own 15-bed facility that came to be known as the Albertville Clinic. He continued to practice until his death in 1987.

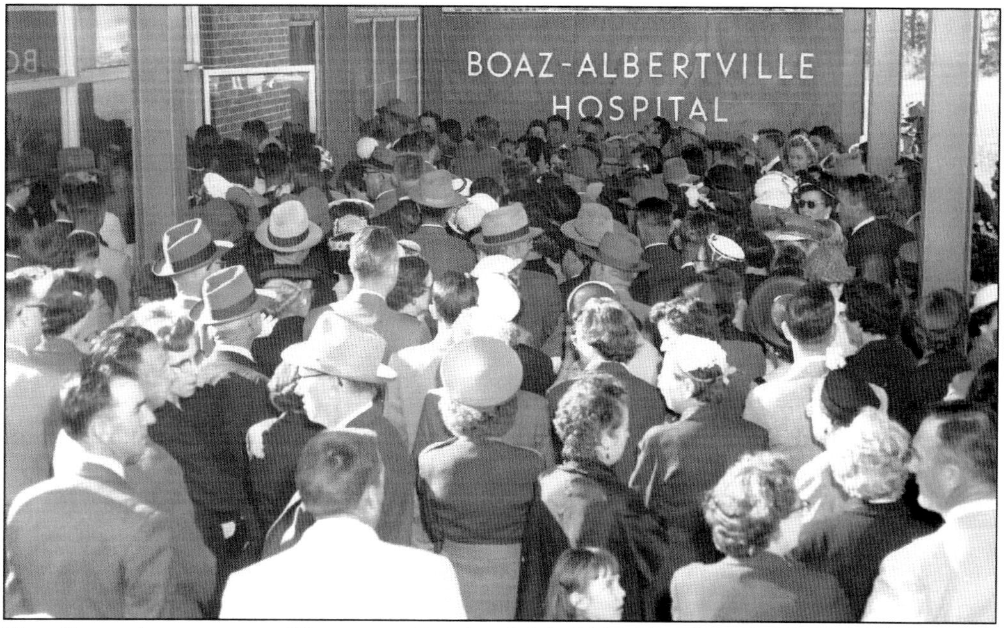

THE BOAZ-ALBERTVILLE HOSPITAL. On April 22, 1956, the formal opening of the Boaz-Albertville Hospital was held with much fanfare. An estimated 2,000 people attended the opening ceremony. Albertville and Boaz High School Bands opened the program with music. Following the dedication program, R.W. Bishop, chairman of the Marshall County Hospital Board, cut the ceremonial ribbon and welcomed the throng of people inside. The hospital's first patient, Sam T. Smith, was admitted the following Tuesday, suffering from pneumonia.

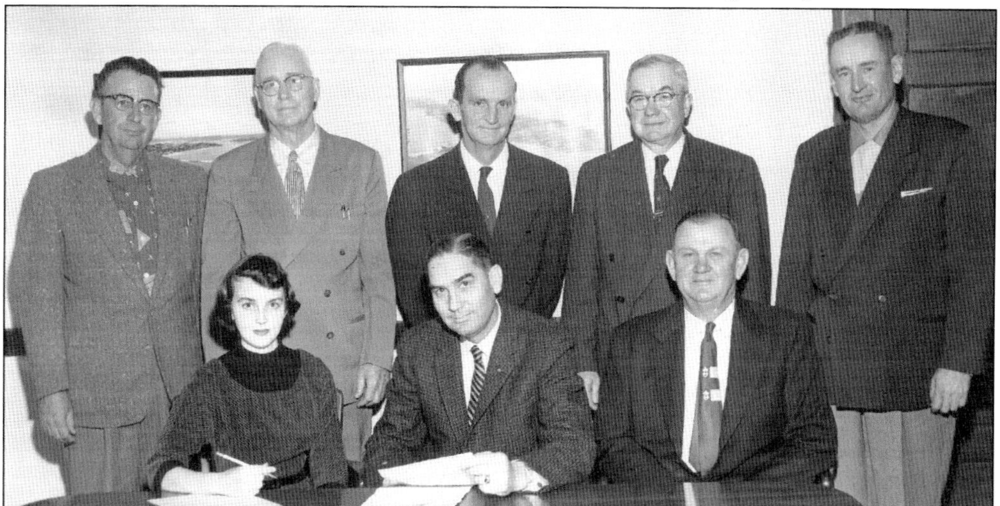

THE MARSHALL COUNTY HOSPITAL BOARD, 1956. The Marshall County Hospital board members are shown in session preparing for the opening of the Boaz-Albertville Hospital. The following members in attendance are pictured from left to right: (front row) Betty Taylor, board secretary; R.W. Bishop, chairman of the board; and J.C. Coleman, board member; (back row) Luther Gibbs, treasurer; M.O. Brock, board member; Hoyt Levie, vice-chairman; George Cox, secretary; and Doyle Medlock, member. Board members Walker Rollings and Elmer Wright are not pictured.

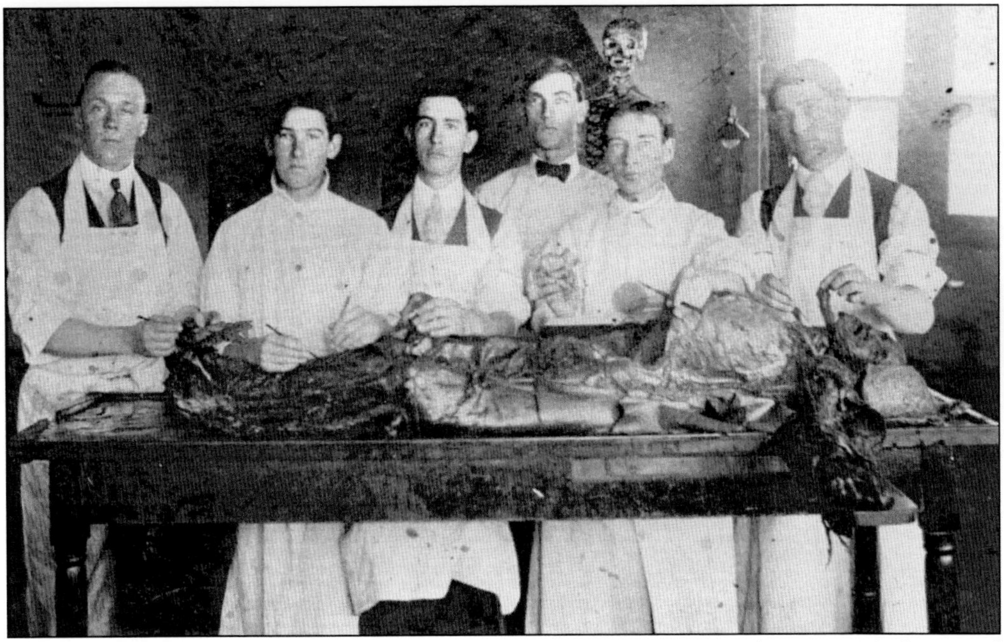

MEDICAL SCHOOL ANATOMY CLASS, THE EARLY YEARS. In 1908 Arthur Levi Isbell entered the University of Chattanooga Medical School and later the Birmingham Medical College. Isbell is pictured third from the left.

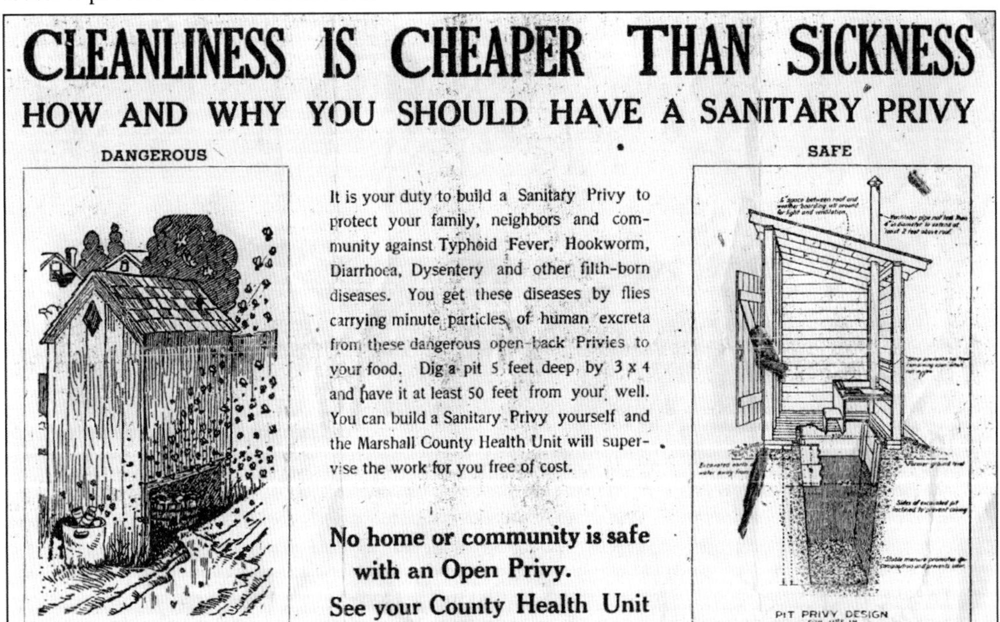

CLEANLINESS IS CHEAPER THAN SICKNESS

HOW AND WHY YOU SHOULD HAVE A SANITARY PRIVY

DANGEROUS

SAFE

It is your duty to build a Sanitary Privy to protect your family, neighbors and community against Typhoid Fever, Hookworm, Diarrhoea, Dysentery and other filth-born diseases. You get these diseases by flies carrying minute particles of human excreta from these dangerous open-back Privies to your food. Dig a pit 5 feet deep by 3 x 4 and have it at least 50 feet from your well. You can build a Sanitary Privy yourself and the Marshall County Health Unit will supervise the work for you free of cost.

No home or community is safe with an Open Privy.

See your County Health Unit for assistance.

PIT PRIVY DESIGN FOR USE IN RURAL DISTRICTS

This is an unsanitary privy. It is NOT clean, NOT fly proof, NOT odorless and is the cause of many diseases.

This is a sanitary privy. It is fly-proof, clean, odorless and inexpensive to build.

THE PROPER PRIVY. During the 1920s, the county health department published a newspaper notice to make more people aware of how to dig the proper pit for an outhouse. While we all may get a good laugh from this, an improperly dug facility was a serious health risk. In 1925 there were 234 privies inspected; 38 were at county schools.

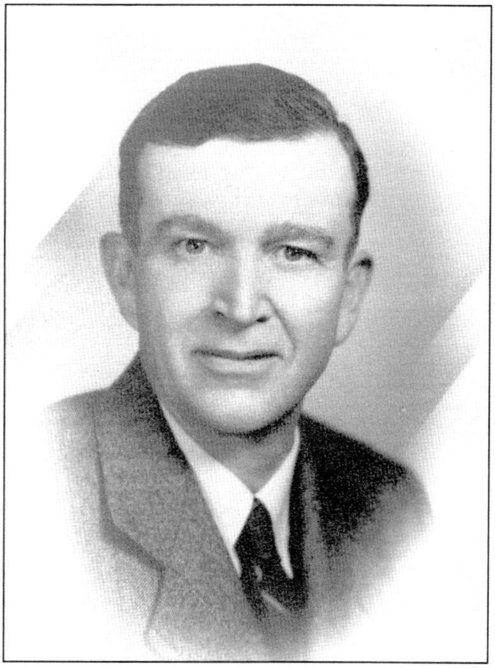

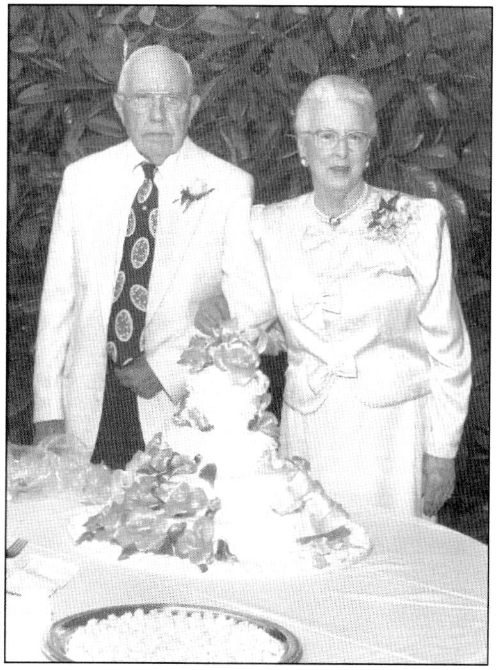

DR. SHELTON APPLETON AND DR. AND MRS. J.L. HUGHES. In 1925 a 23-year-old dental school graduate by the name of Shelton Appleton (left) arrived in Albertville. Appleton was originally from Collinsville, where his father was a medical doctor. Through the years, he distinguished himself by his professionalism and gentle good humor. Dr. J. Luther Hughes, shown with his wife, the former Frances Weatherly, moved to Albertville in 1931 and acquired the dental practice of the late Dr. Homer Gunn. For the next 60 years, he practiced in the same office.

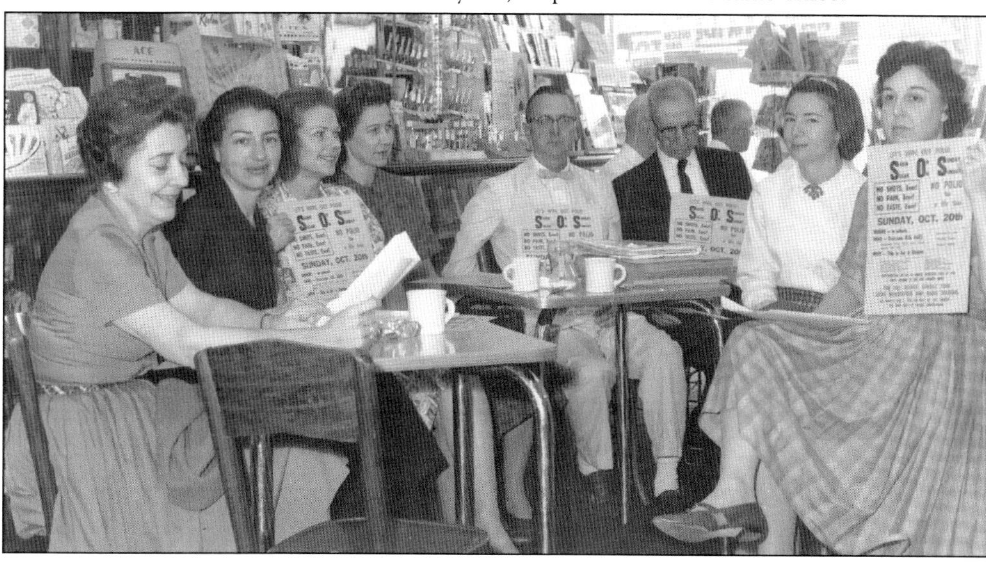

THE POLIO VACCINE. October 1963 saw the effort by doctors, health care workers, and average citizens to vaccinate the citizens of Marshall County against the scourge of the age—poliomyelitis. Under the direction of Dr. C.C. Erwin, teachers, preachers, and leaders stepped forward to set the example for others. The picture shows a planning session held at the Marshall Drug Company. Seated in the center are Dr. C.C. Erwin and Dr. A.L. Isbell.

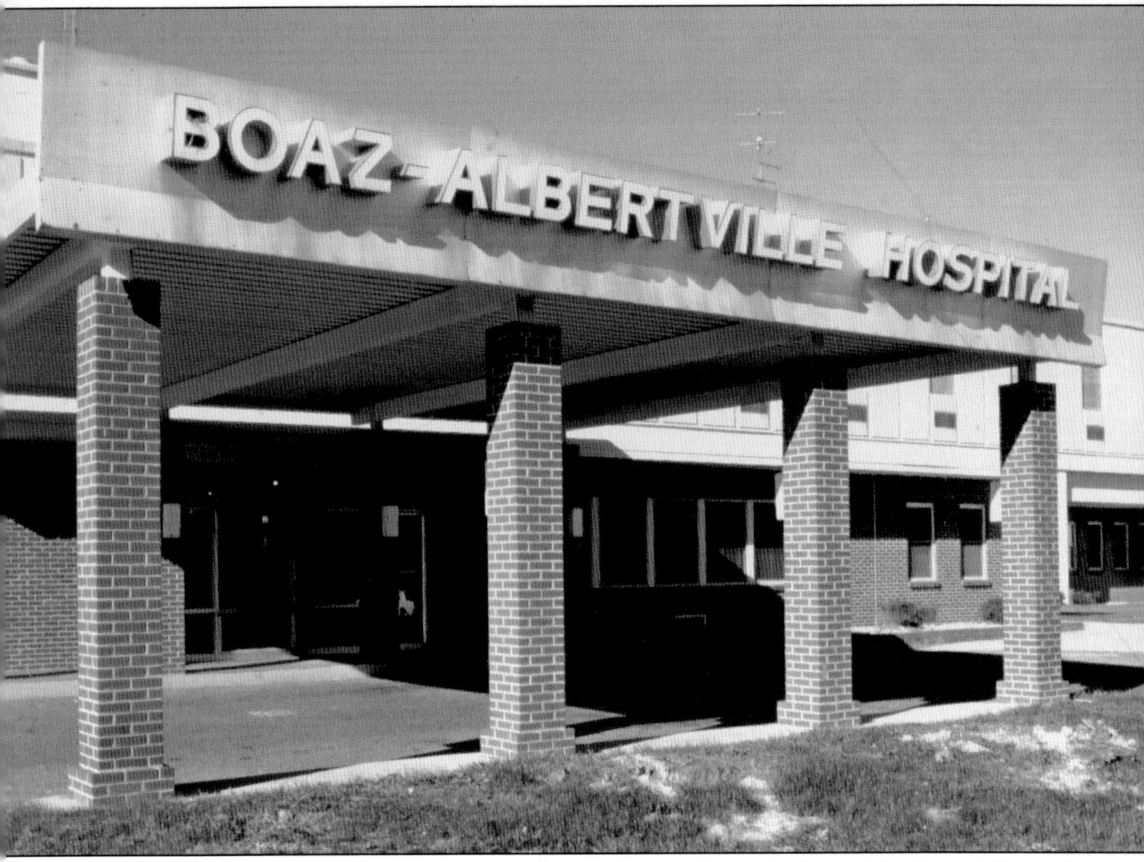

BOAZ-ALBERTVILLE HOSPITAL MEDICAL STAFF. During the early days of the Boaz-Albertville Hospital, the medical staff included such physicians as H.E. Barker, Marston T. Hunt, A.L. Isbell, Luther Corley, Harry G. Martin, Claude C. Erwin, B.N. Lavender, M.B. Bray, Kenneth G. Christian, and H.L. Rogers. The director of nursing was Jean Bohannon. A number of these physicians' portraits, as well as one of Nurse Bohannon, hang in the hallways of today's hospital.

Eight
Government and Services

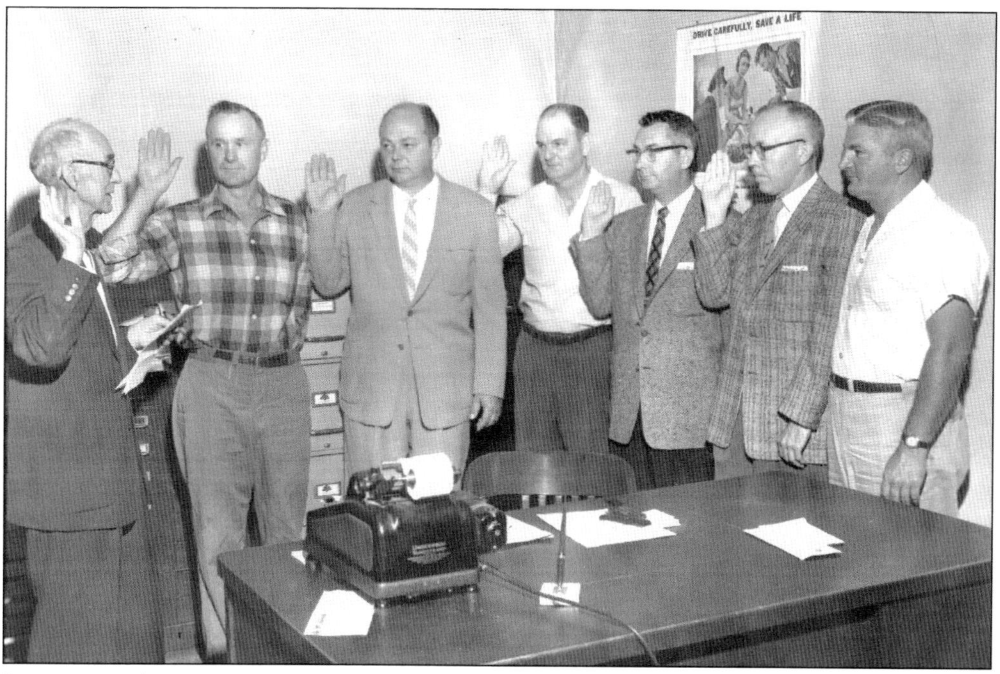

Incoming Administration. In October 1956 county judge Mack Killcrease (left) administered the oaths of office to Albertville's incoming administration. Shown with Killcrease from left to right are Russell Garrett, Ashton Denham, O.H. Williams, incoming Mayor Robert Dickson, Dr. J.L. Hughes, and Dr. Joe Davis.

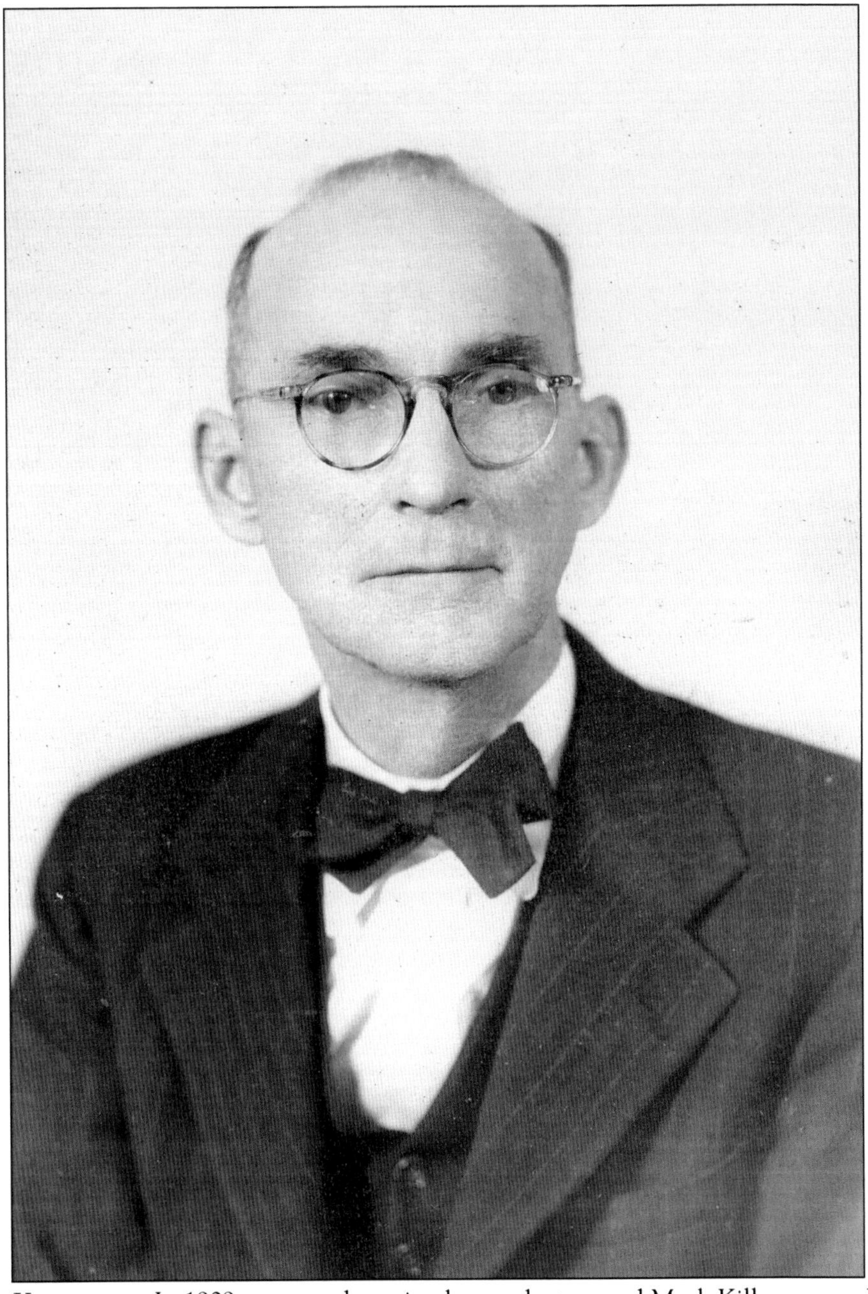

MACK KILLCREASE. In 1909 an up-and-coming law student named Mack Killcrease graduated from the University of Alabama with a Bachelor of Laws degree. Following his admission to the bar, Killcrease practiced law in Guntersville with Charles Kennamer, who later served as a federal judge. In 1913 the young lawyer was elected mayor of Guntersville and served one term. In 1920 he moved to Albertville, and in 1922 he was elected mayor of that town as well, making him possibly the only person in the state's history to have served as mayor of two different cities. In 1921 Killcrease married Eunice Letson, whose father, J.W. Letson, was president of the agricultural school. In addition to his municipal offices, Killcrease served as the county solicitor. He retired from the position of county judge on August 31, 1962.

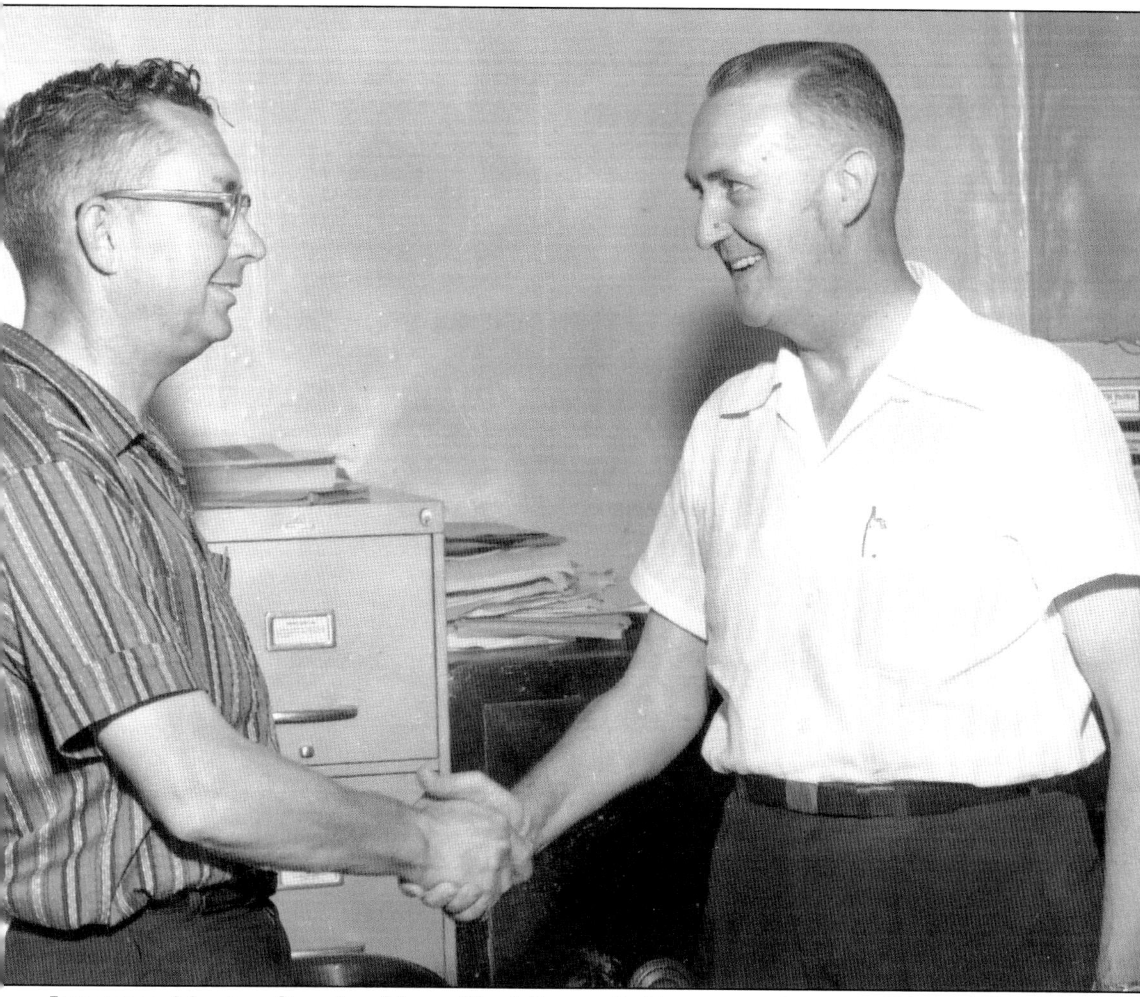

INCOMING MAYOR. Outgoing Mayor Floyd Brown (left) is pictured greeting the incoming mayor, Robert Dickson. Prior to assuming the office of mayor in 1956, Dickson served on the city council with Mayor Brown.

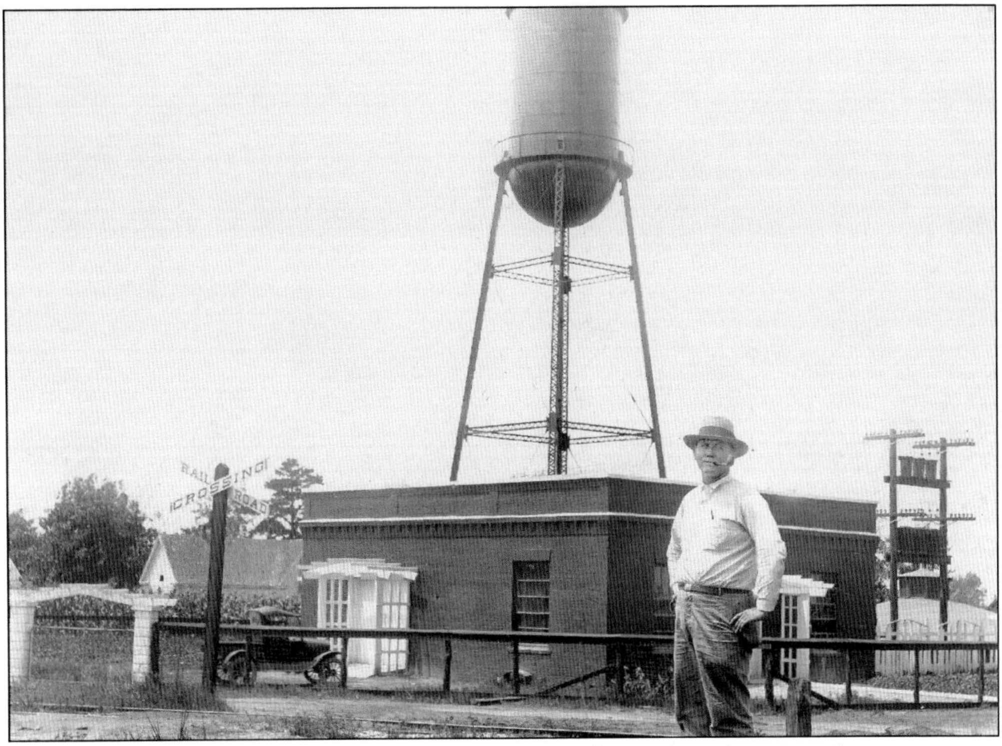

A.H. PHENY. On August 15, 1910, the City of Albertville conducted a referendum concerning a waterworks. For such a massive undertaking, bonds would have to be sold to underwrite its cost. The August 18, 1910 edition of *The Albertville Banner* records that the vote was 130 for issuing bonds and 20 against. Albertville's first water system superintendent, Amos H. Pheny (pictured above), moved to Albertville from his native Anniston as a small child. His father, Patrick Pheny, was born in Dublin, Ireland. Albertville's first water storage tank is in the background.

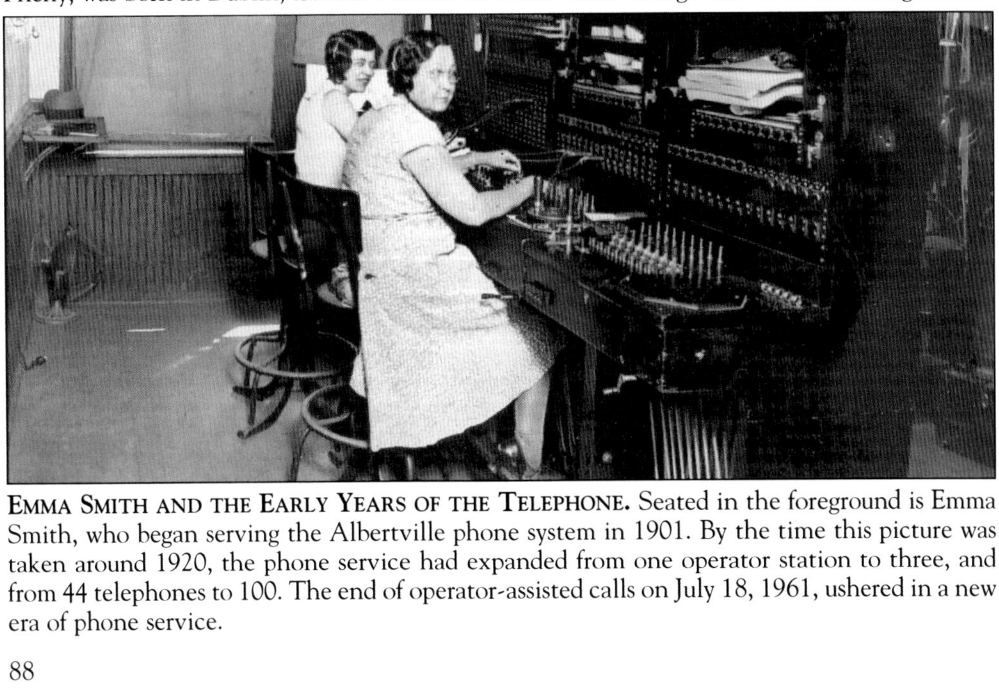

EMMA SMITH AND THE EARLY YEARS OF THE TELEPHONE. Seated in the foreground is Emma Smith, who began serving the Albertville phone system in 1901. By the time this picture was taken around 1920, the phone service had expanded from one operator station to three, and from 44 telephones to 100. The end of operator-assisted calls on July 18, 1961, ushered in a new era of phone service.

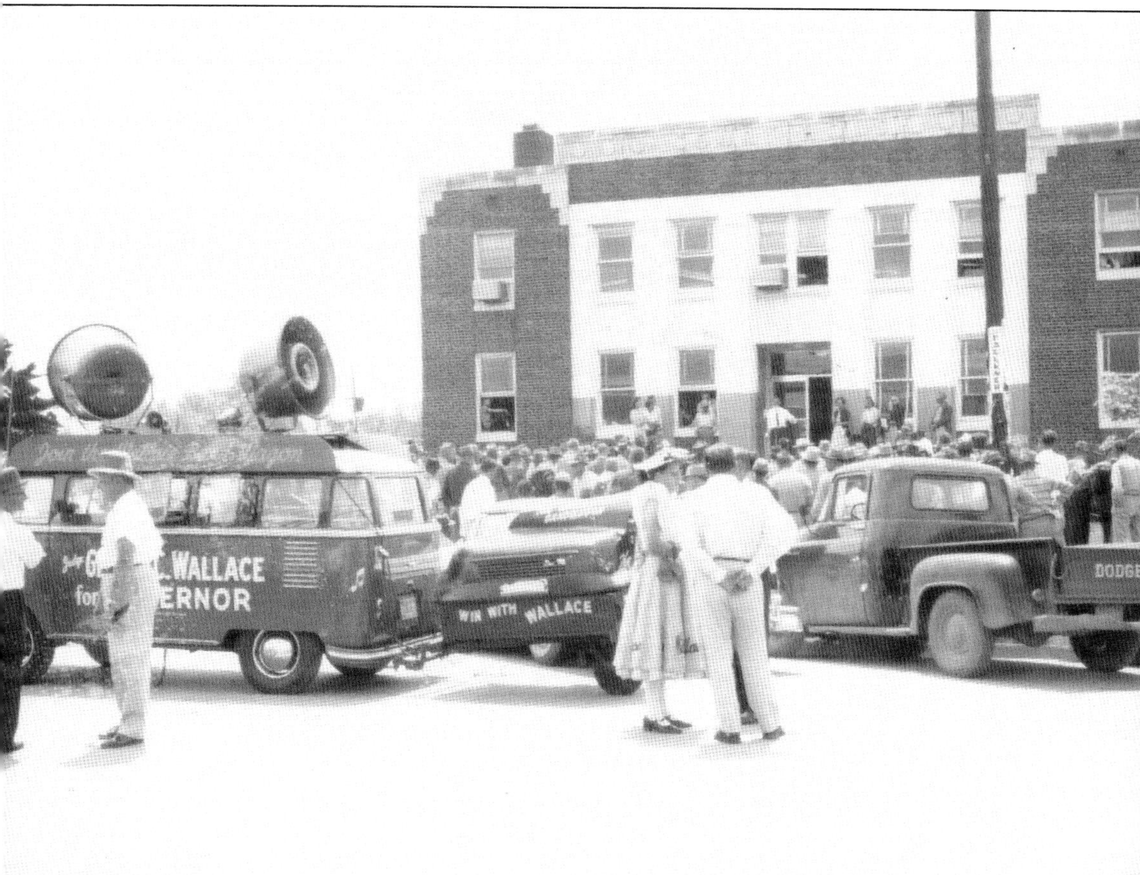

THE ALBERTVILLE COURTHOUSE. Albertville's courthouse has served its citizens primarily as a place of justice but also as a town square, from the time a wooden structure was built in 1910, to the present structure built in 1935, until today. The photograph above shows a 1960s political rally for George Wallace during one of his campaigns for the office of Alabama governor.

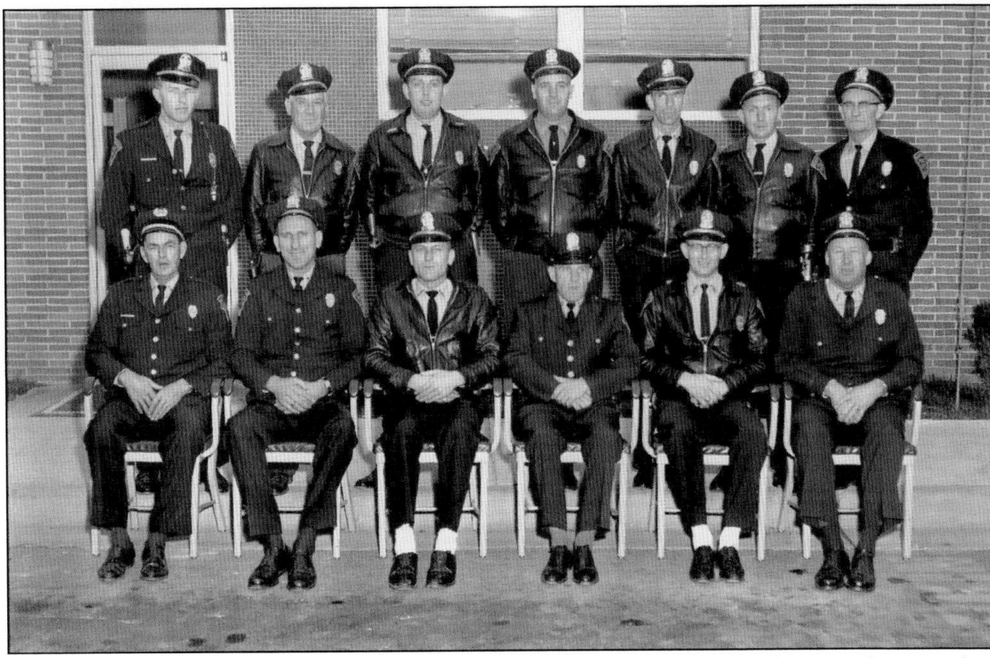

THE ALBERTVILLE POLICE DEPARTMENT, 1960S. This police group photograph was taken outside the Albertville Police Department in the early to mid-1960s. Seated at the extreme left is Bige Denham, who was appointed chief of police by Albertville mayor E.B. Adams.

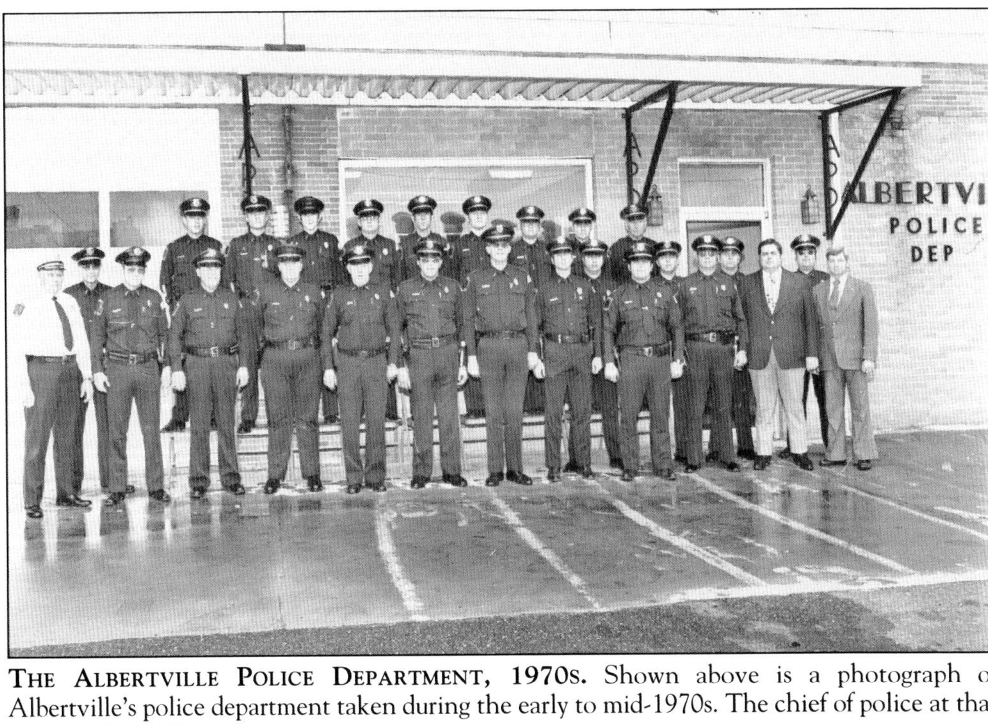

THE ALBERTVILLE POLICE DEPARTMENT, 1970S. Shown above is a photograph of Albertville's police department taken during the early to mid-1970s. The chief of police at that time was Louie Townson.

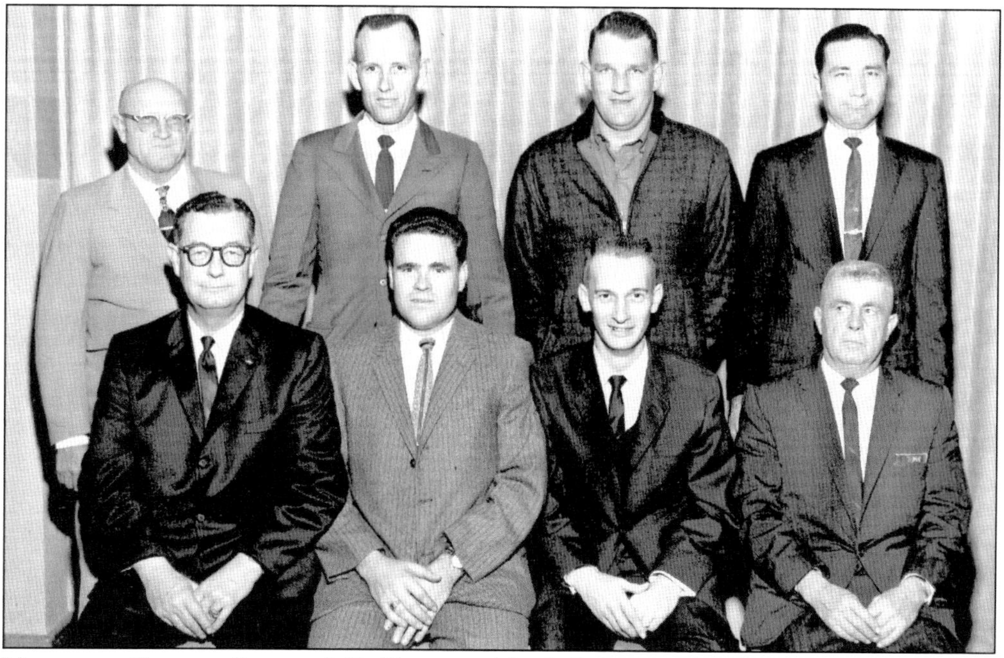

MARSHALL COUNTY SHERIFF L.P. DICKSON. Marshall County sheriff L.P. Dickson began his term in January 1963. He and his staff are pictured from left to right: (front row) Dickson, chief deputy Ralph Collins, office deputy James "Buddy" Albert, and Albertville office deputy Wofford Chambers; (back row) jailer Troy Hughes and field deputies Troy Williams, Jimmy Weir, and Lowell Alewine.

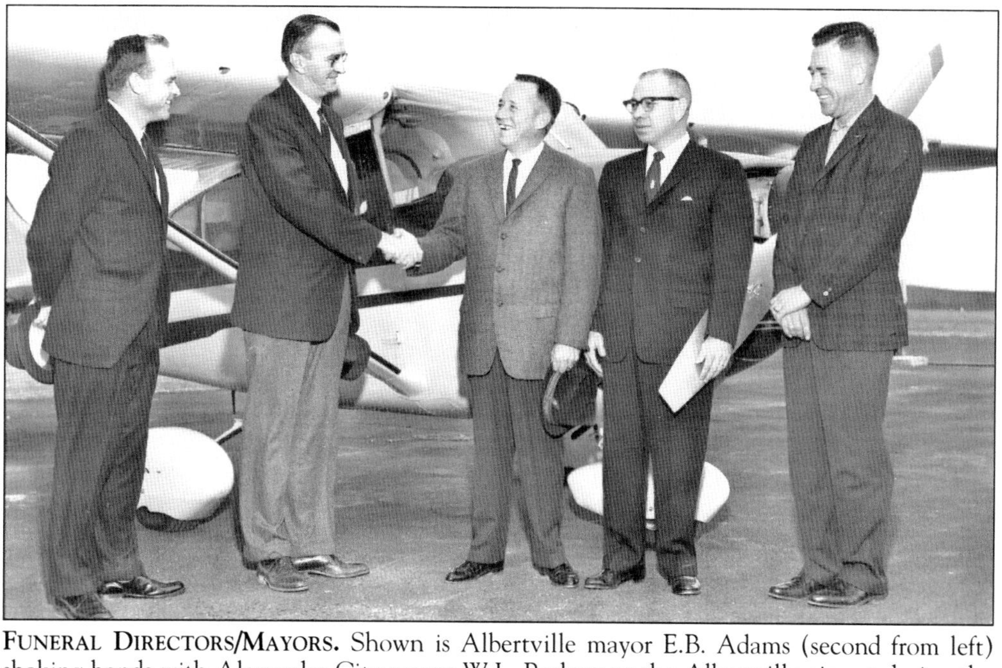

FUNERAL DIRECTORS/MAYORS. Shown is Albertville mayor E.B. Adams (second from left) shaking hands with Alexander City mayor W.L. Radney at the Albertville airport during the early 1960s. In addition to serving as mayors of their respective towns, the two were friends from years of operating funeral homes in Alabama.

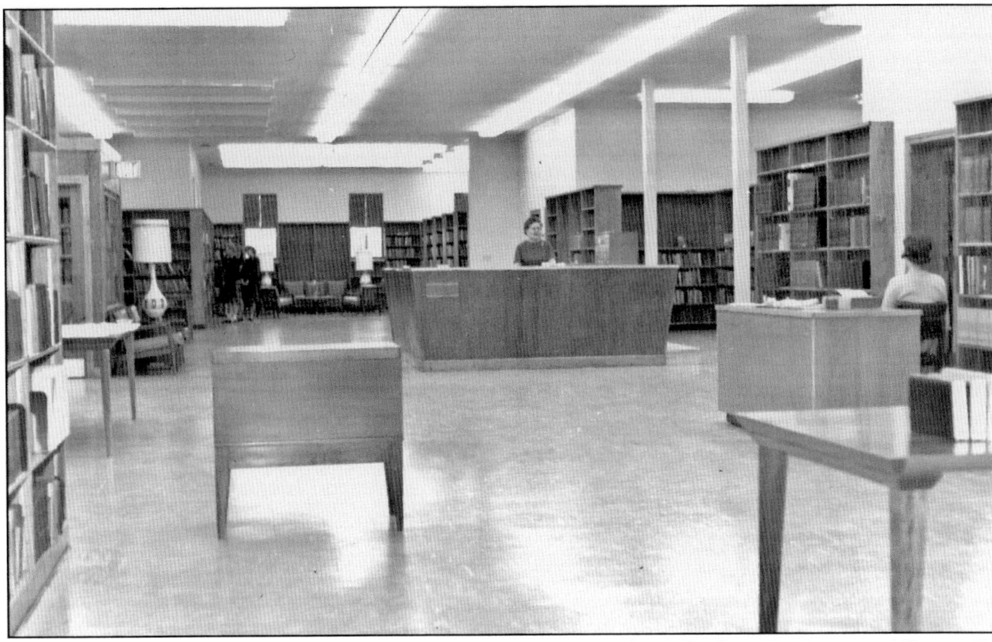

OPENING OF THE ALBERTVILLE PUBLIC LIBRARY. During the fall of 1963, the new Albertville Public Library opened at the corner of Baltimore Avenue and Jackson Street. The new $112,000 structure was an improvement from its former location on the second floor of the old city hall building. At the time of its relocation, the library possessed some 17,000 volumes (the current circulation is over 80,000 volumes).

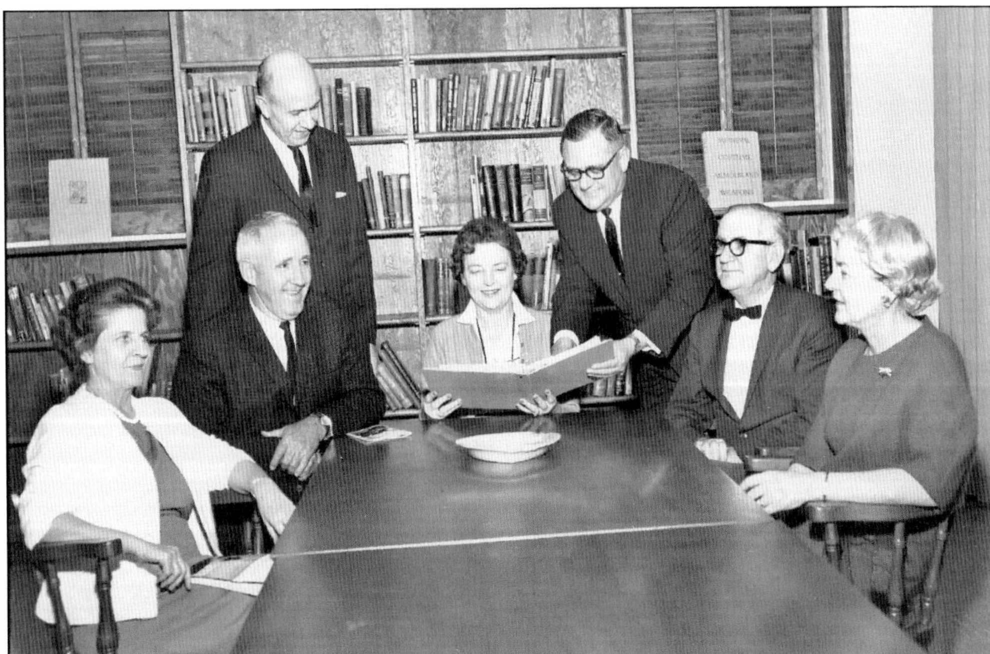

ALBERTVILLE'S FIRST LIBRARY BOARD. The following members of the first Albertville library board are pictured from left to right: (seated) Sue McBrayer, Buford L. Cryar, Frances Rogers, S. Bowie Hooper, and Jo Jackson; (standing) A.E. "Andy" Chiles and Robert "Bob" Finney.

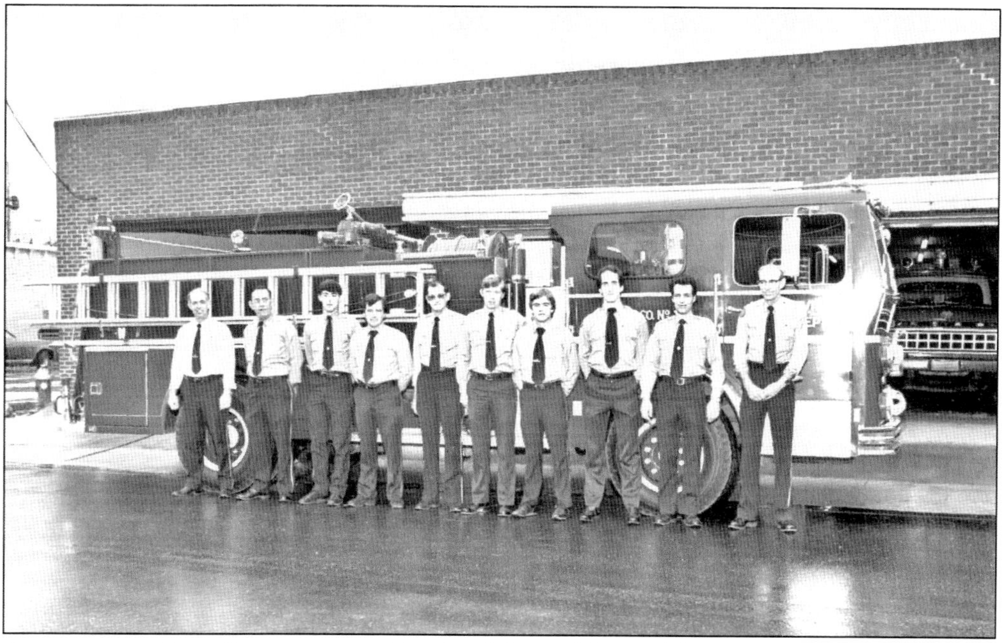

ALBERTVILLE FIRE DEPARTMENT. By the 1970s, Albertville's fire department had been relocated from the city hall complex to the former site of Frank's Grocery. The department continued at this location until Fire Station #1 was constructed on South Broad Street. The fire chief in the picture is longtime chief Johnny Mack Rollings.

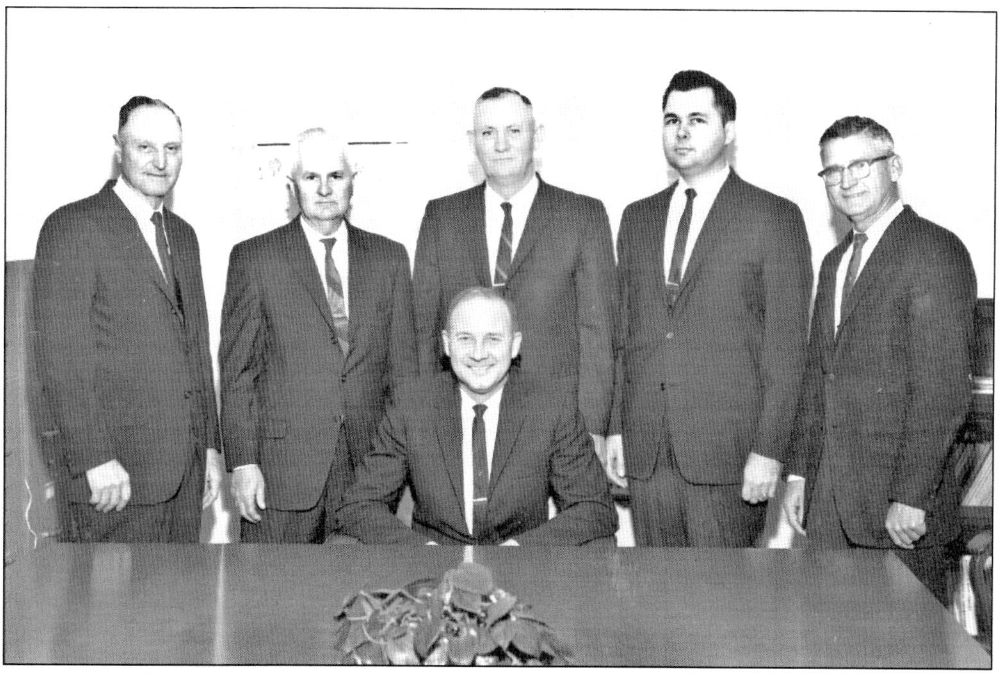

MARSHALL COUNTY BOARD OF EDUCATION. Superintendent Wayland Cooley and members of the Marshall County Board of Education are shown in this photograph taken during the 1960s.

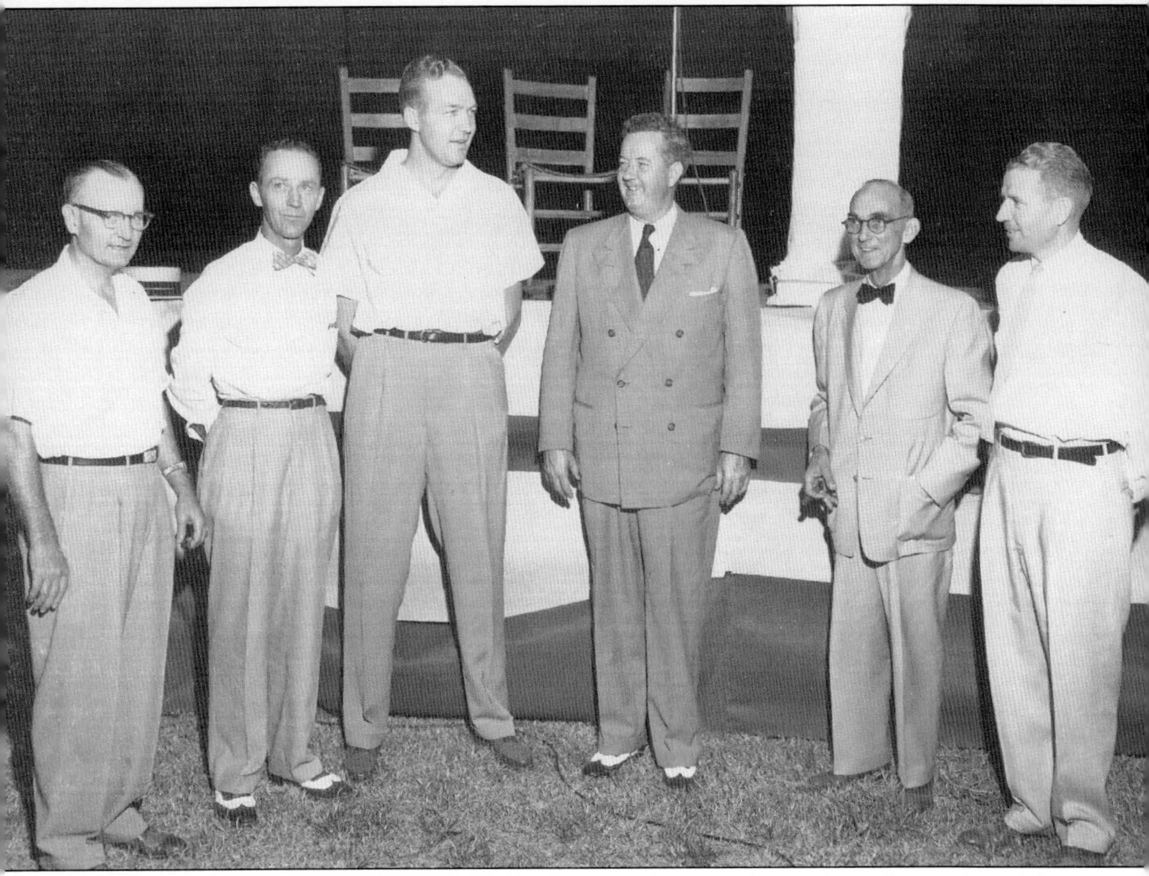

SEN. JOHN J. SPARKMAN. Sen. John J. Sparkman is shown with members of area civic clubs at a 1950s event. Though originally from Hartselle, Senator Sparkman had long ago been declared an adopted son of Marshall County because of his marriage to Ivo Hall of Albertville. In 1952 the senator was named the vice-presidential running mate of Democratic nominee Adlai Stevenson. On August 19, 1952, Albertville threw a huge celebration to honor its native daughter, Ivo, and her husband. Throughout the day, older residents remembered attending the couple's wedding at the Methodist church and accompanying the couple to the train depot for their departure. They recalled that so much rice was thrown it looked like it had snowed.

Nine

MOMENTS

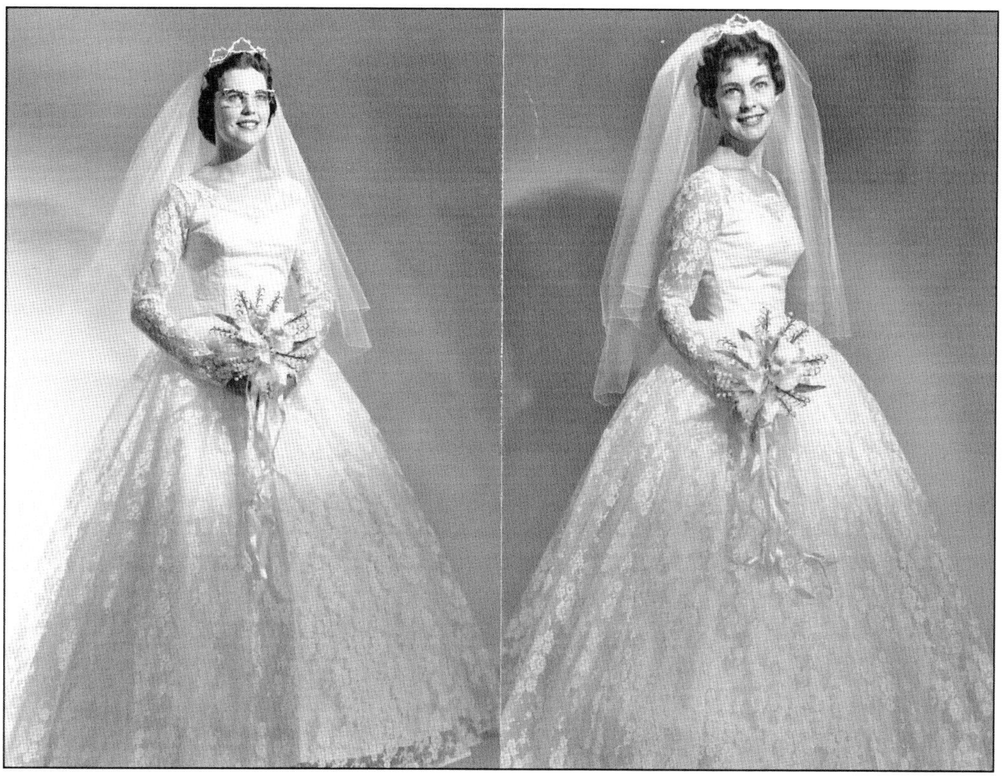

DOUBLE WEDDING. On August 1, 1961, Albertville witnessed the double wedding ceremony of the daughters of former Albertville mayor Floyd Brown and his wife, Lora. Jackie (left) married John David Hawkins, and Jean married Oran "Buddy" Adams Jr.

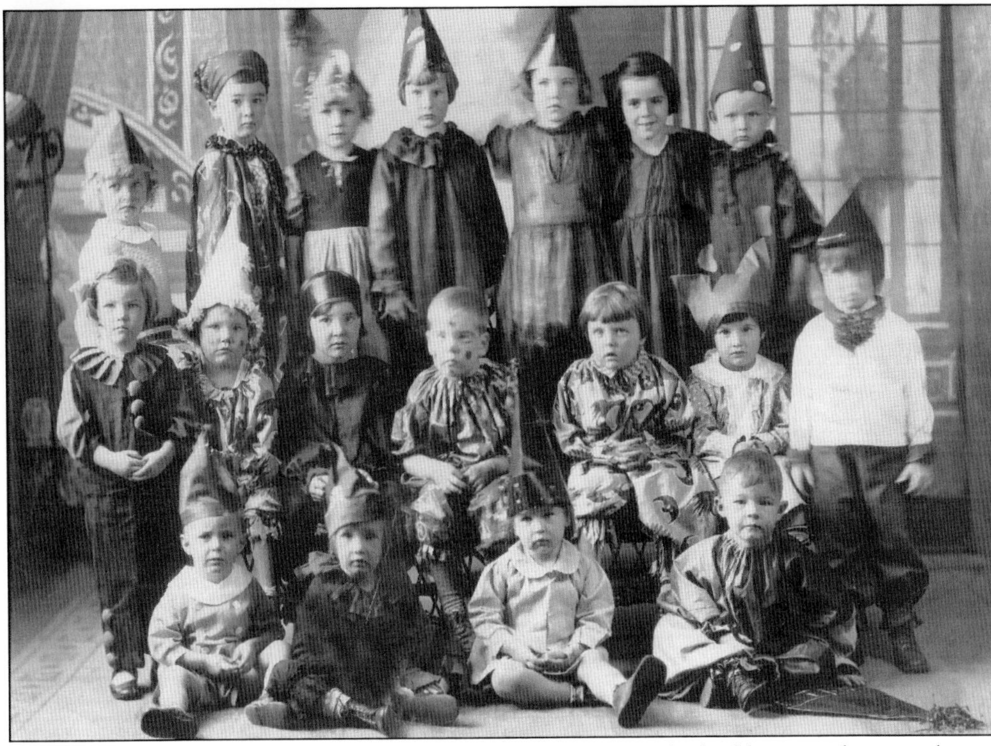

Harry Potter, the Early Years. Although this picture looks like a graduating class of Hogwart's School, it is actually an Albertville children's party from the 1920s

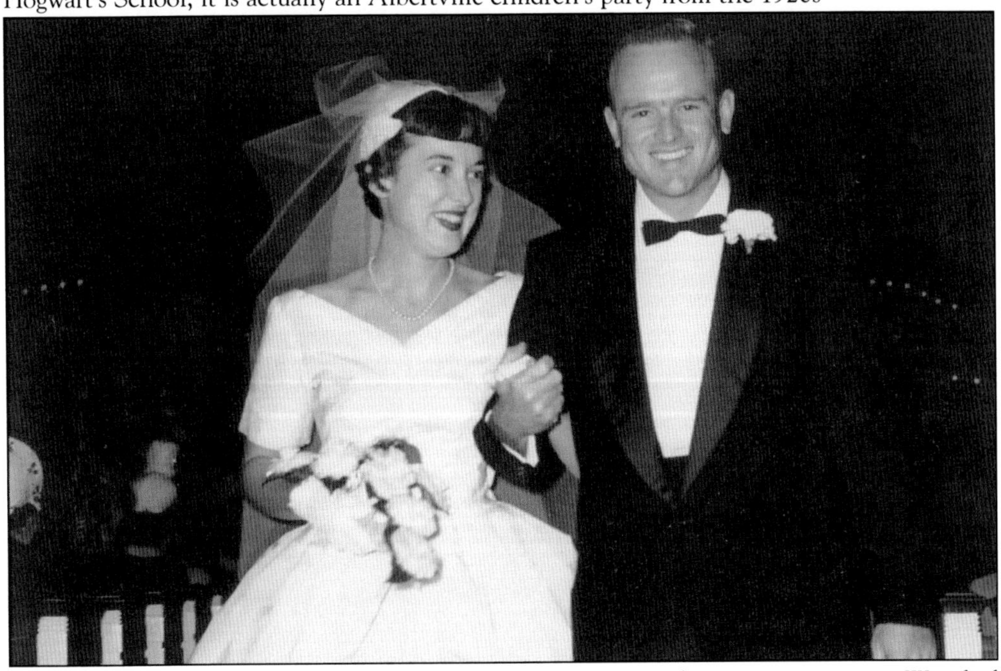

Wedding Day. On January 7, 1954, George D. Wells Jr. married Montgomery native Winifred Cardinal. The two met while both were students at the University of Alabama. They went on to have three children: Winky, Georganne, and Tom.

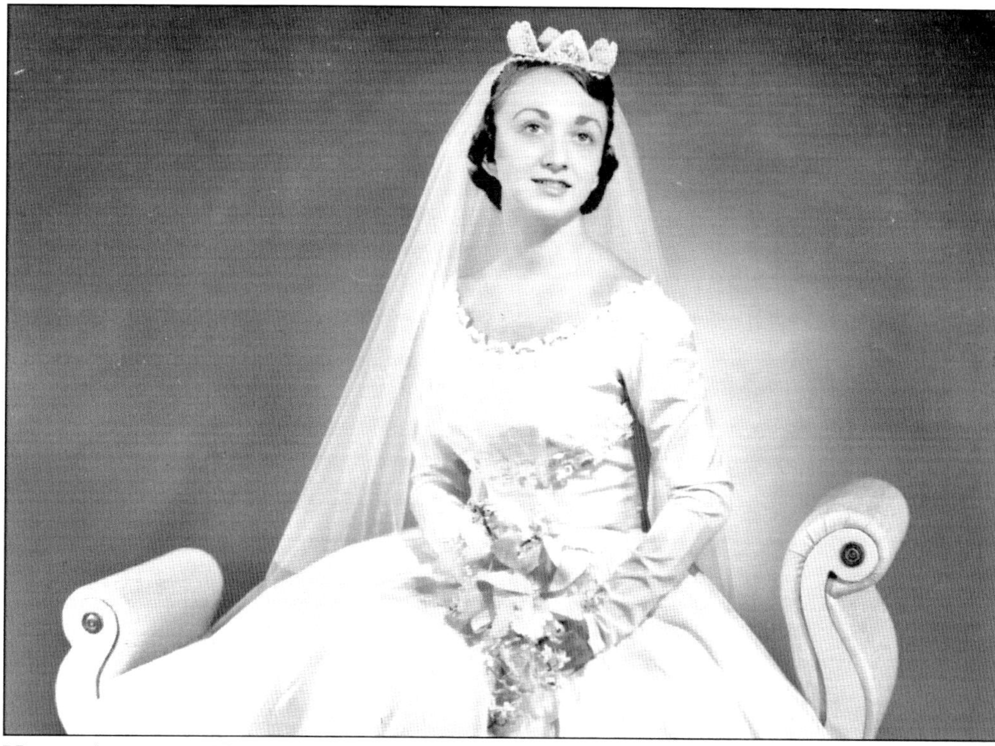

HELEN APPLETON HAYNIE. Pictured is Helen Appleton, the only daughter of Albertville dentist Shelton Appleton and his wife, Helen. She married Robert Haynie.

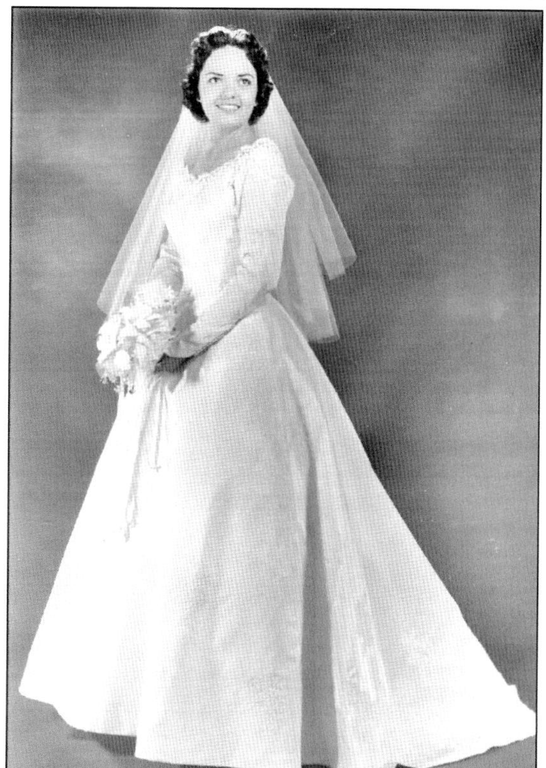

BETTY THOMAS JOLLEY. Pictured is a fourth-generation Albertville resident, Betty Thomas, the daughter of John Aubrey Thomas and his wife, Johnnie. Betty married Gene Jolley.

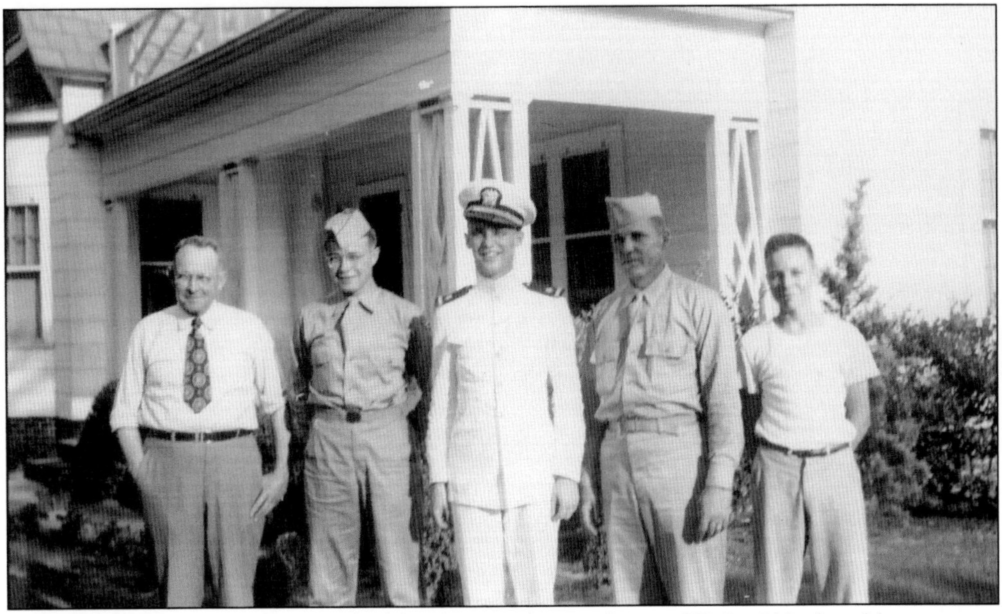

A FAMILY'S SERVICE. Photographs like the one shown above of B.A. Alford and his sons are part of homes across America.

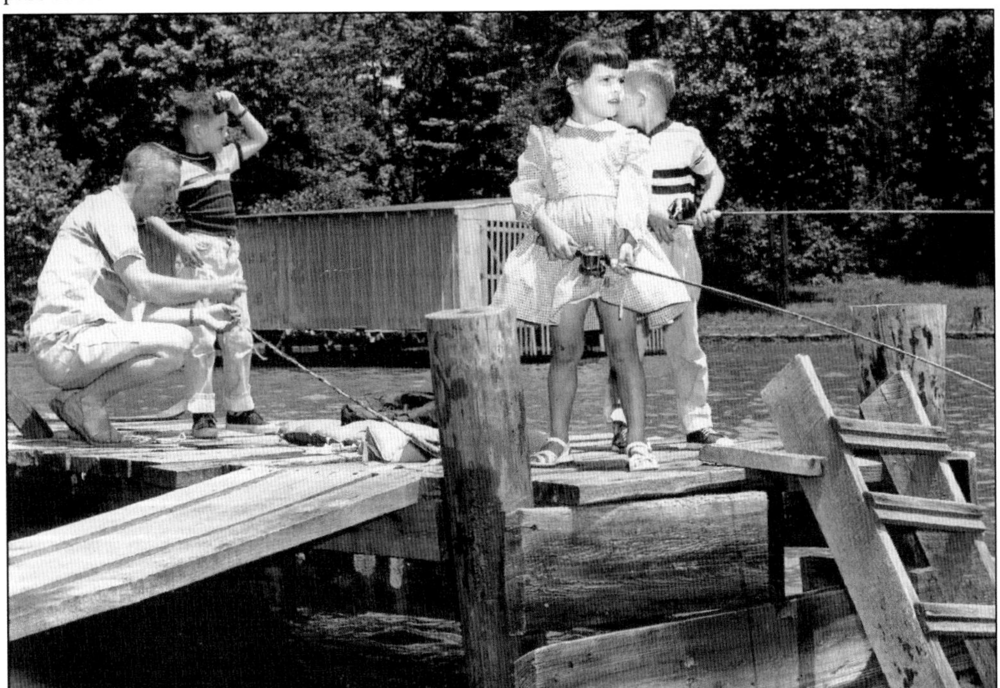

O.H. FINNEY JR. AND THE FOLSOM FAMILY. During the term of Alabama governor James E. "Big Jim" Folsom Sr., Albertville's Omer H. Finney Jr. served as his executive secretary and confidante. In this role, Finney became a member of the extended Folsom family; he was close to the governor, first lady, and their children. Pictured with Finney on a fishing outing are three of the governor's children; the one standing beside him is future Alabama governor James E. Folsom Jr.

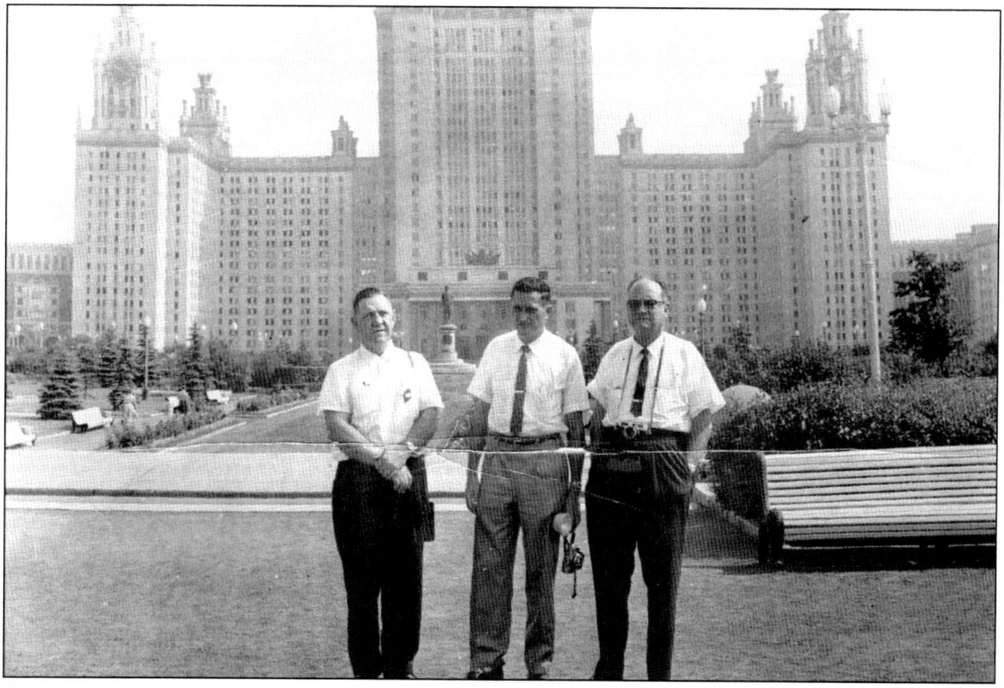

ALBERTVILLE IN MOSCOW. Albertville residents Olin C. Hearn, Jesse Culp, and G. Dewey Wells Sr. are shown in front of the Russian parliament building during a goodwill trip in July 1960.

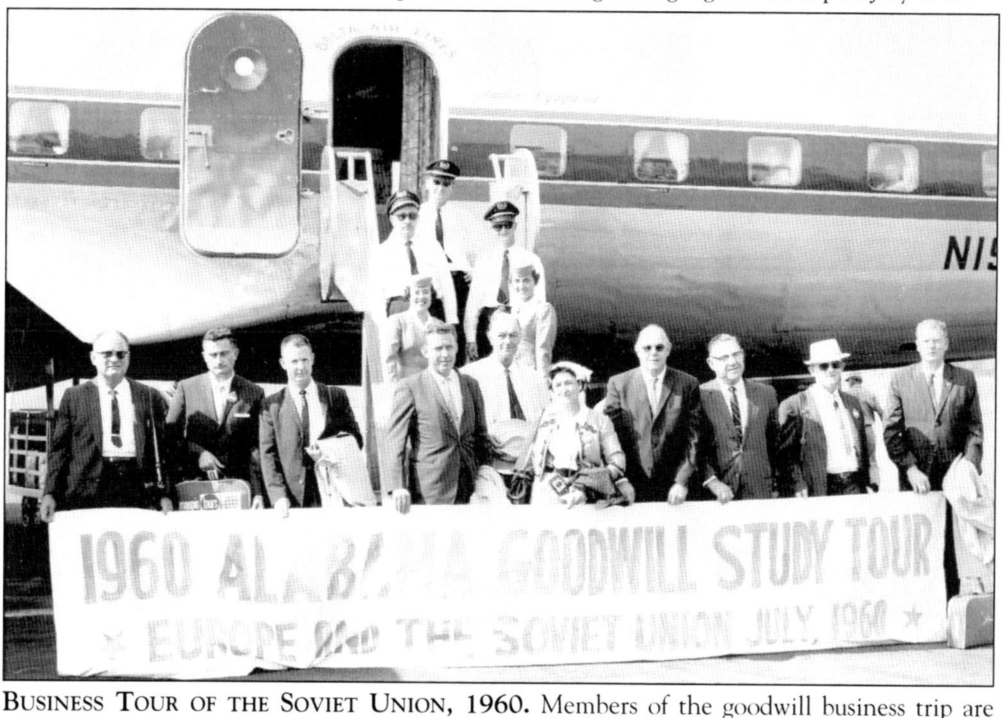

BUSINESS TOUR OF THE SOVIET UNION, 1960. Members of the goodwill business trip are pictured upon their arrival in Europe. According to his son, Dewey Wells was glad to return home. It seems that nothing made you appreciate home quite as much as touring the Eastern block during the height of the Cold War.

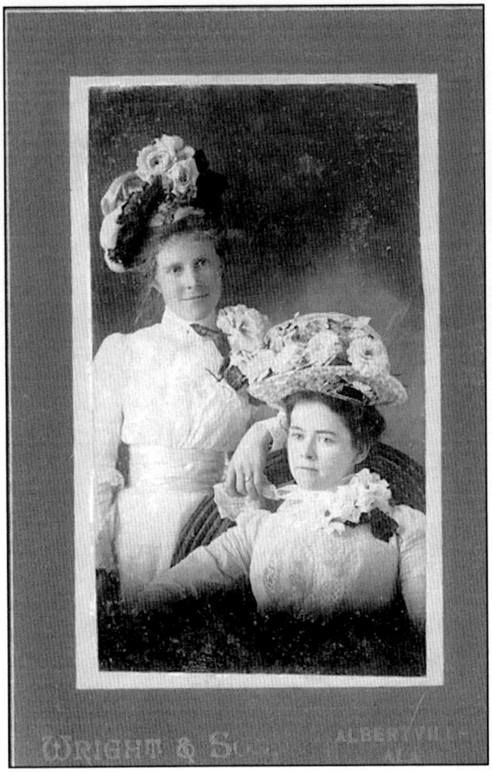

NOTHING LIKE THE RIGHT HAT. Standing at the left is the former Rebecca Hodges, who married James W. Walker a year after his arrival in Albertville. Seated is Walker's sister, Julia Walker Canterbury. During the late 19th and early 20th century, no mercantile or clothing store was complete without a millinery department just as a lady's outfit was not complete without a hat. One such store was Barron and Russell's, where Georgia Selman supervised the chapeaus.

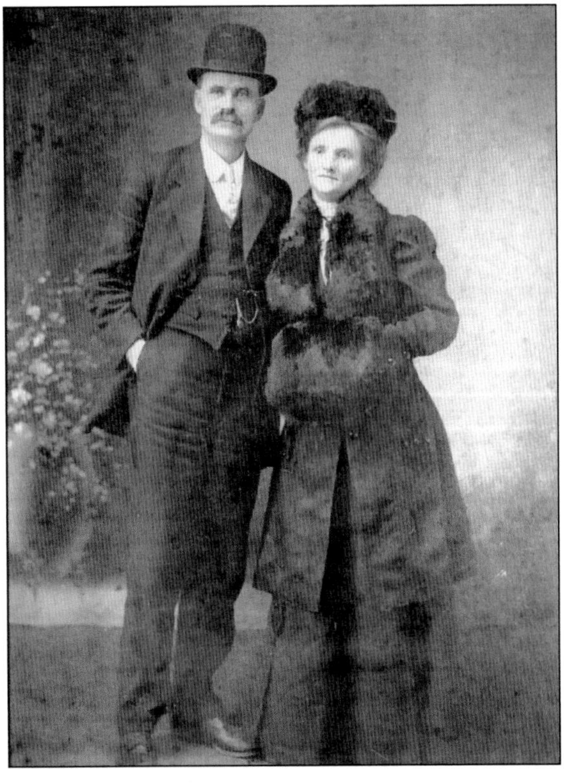

THAT GOES FOR MEN, TOO. Proving that men also know how to dress is Mayor E.O. McCord, pictured with his wife. They tragically lost their son in the cyclone of 1908.

Show Business. In the 1940s movie star and all-around showman Bob Hope came to the University of Alabama campus. Shown at the event directly behind Hope is Albertville's own George Wells Jr.

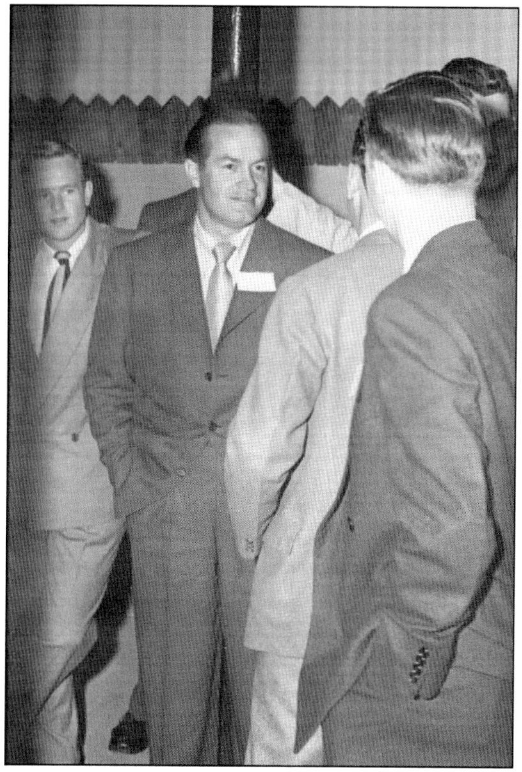

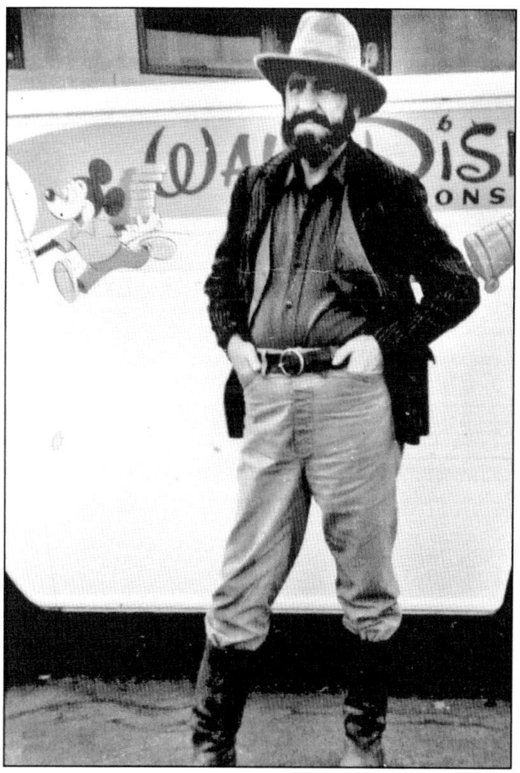

A Little North of Schwab's Drug Store. Roy Thomas, brother of John Aubrey Thomas and Josie Thomas, had a brush with celebrity while attending a Rose Bowl game; he kept being mistaken for actor Spencer Tracy. Though never rising to the fame of Tracy, he appeared in smaller parts and traveled to promotional events for movies around the country.

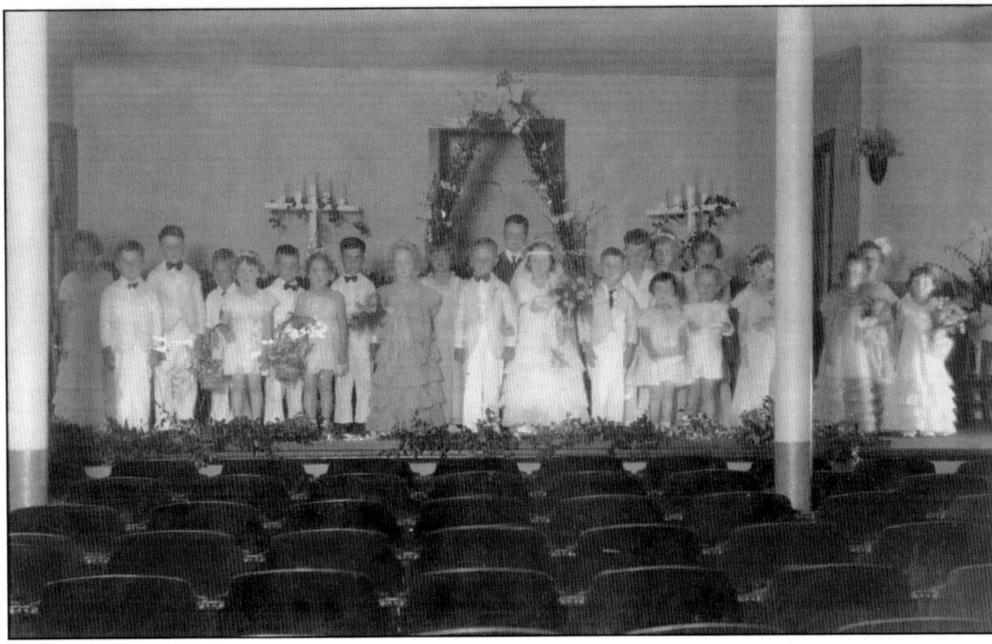

CHILDHOOD PAGEANT. Albertville children are pictured in a 1930s "wedding" pageant.

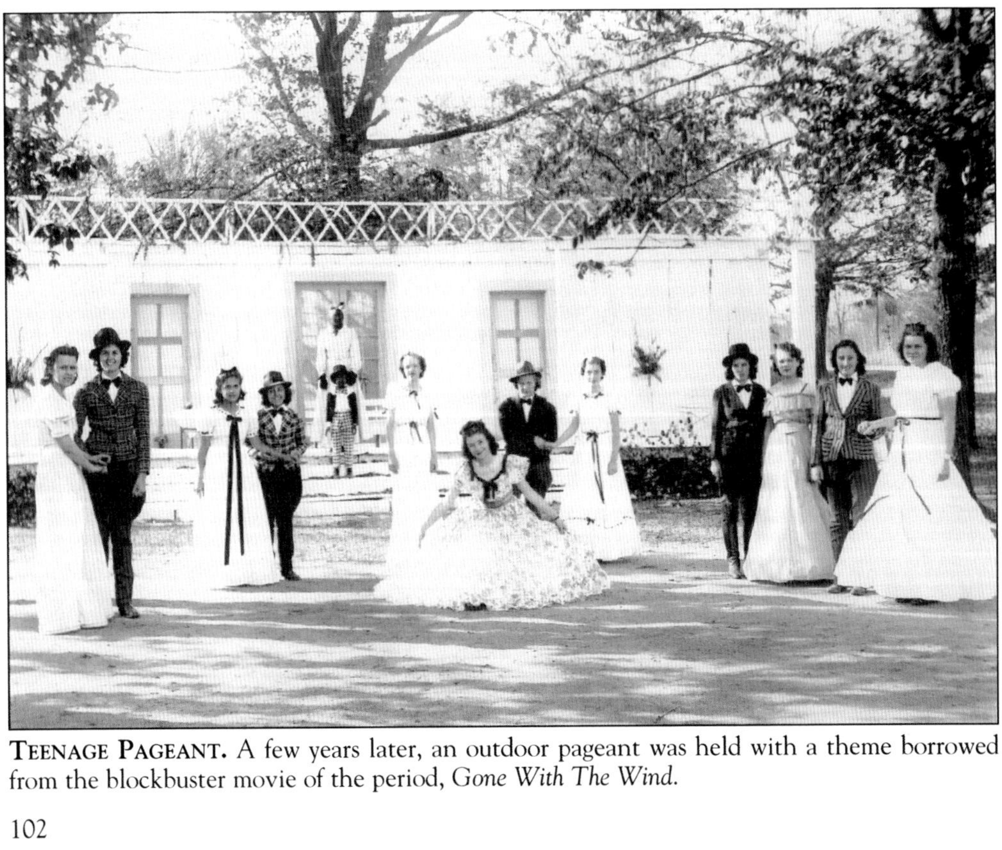

TEENAGE PAGEANT. A few years later, an outdoor pageant was held with a theme borrowed from the blockbuster movie of the period, *Gone With The Wind*.

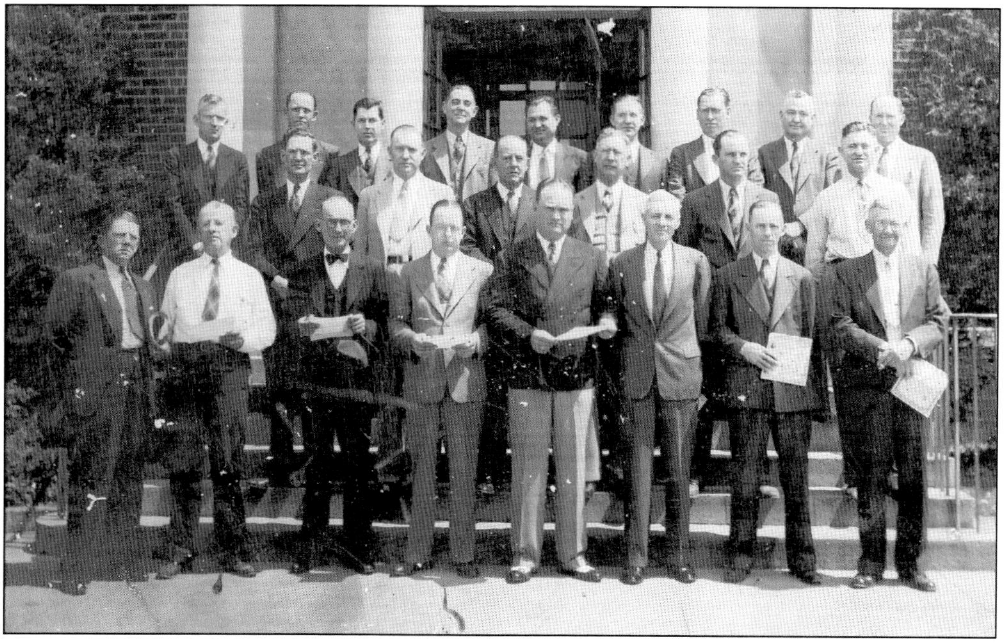

BOND RALLY. Members of the Albertville Civitan Club are pictured on the steps of the old post office. This photograph was taken on July 1, 1941, to mark that the Albertville Civitan Club was the first civic club in the country to have 100 percent of its members buy defense bonds.

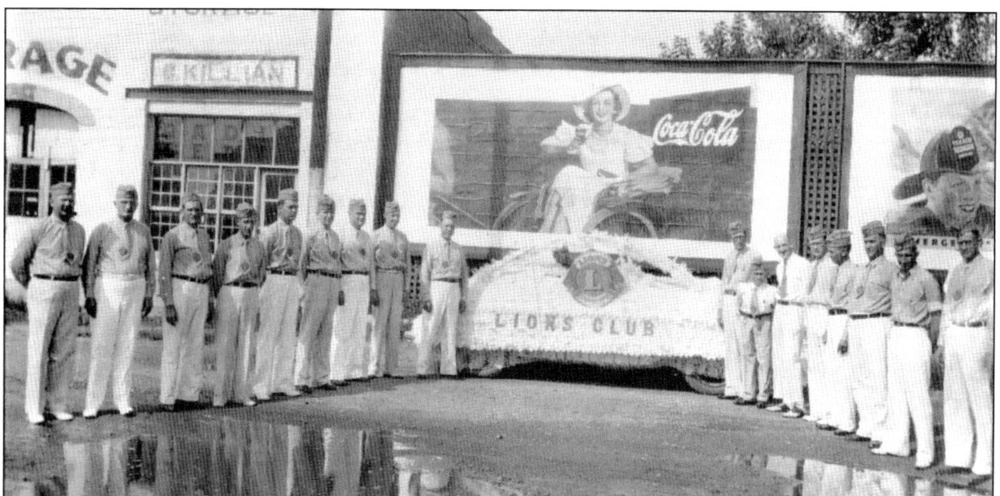

CIVIC CLUBS. From Albertville's earliest days, there have been civic clubs always stepping in when there was a need and championing the causes of those who could not. From the Lions Club with its sight conservation to the Civitans and Rotary Club with their multitude of causes, their support has often made the difference. A group from the 1930s is pictured above.

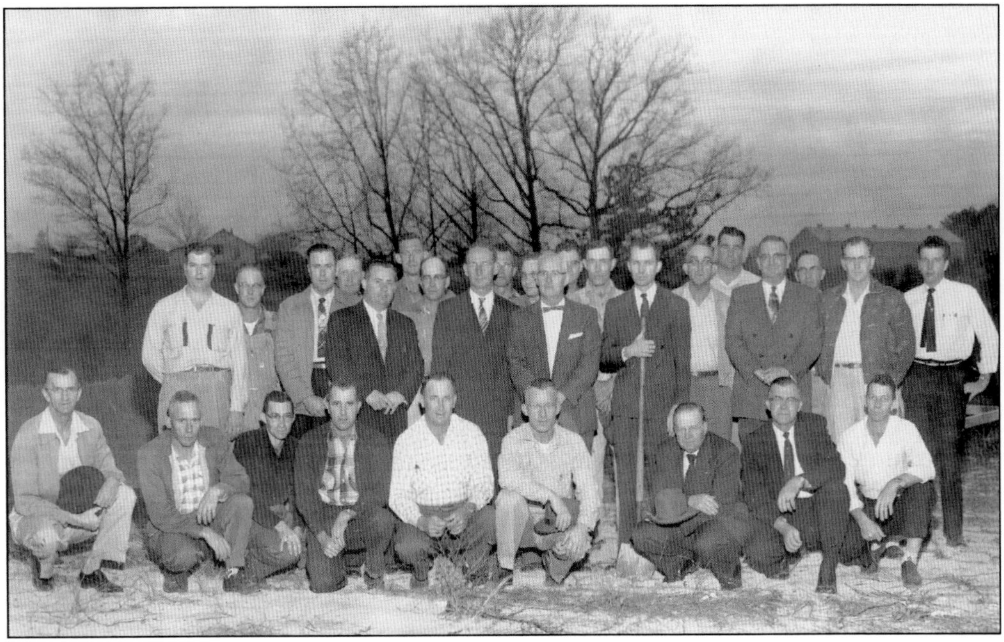

Groundbreaking for the New Masonic Building. In April 1956 members of the Albertville Masonic Lodge #430 broke ground for a new Masonic Hall. The two-story structure was built along Highway 431. The group rented the ground floor as business property. Shown among the lodge members is Lofton Upton, the lodge's Worshipful Master at that time.

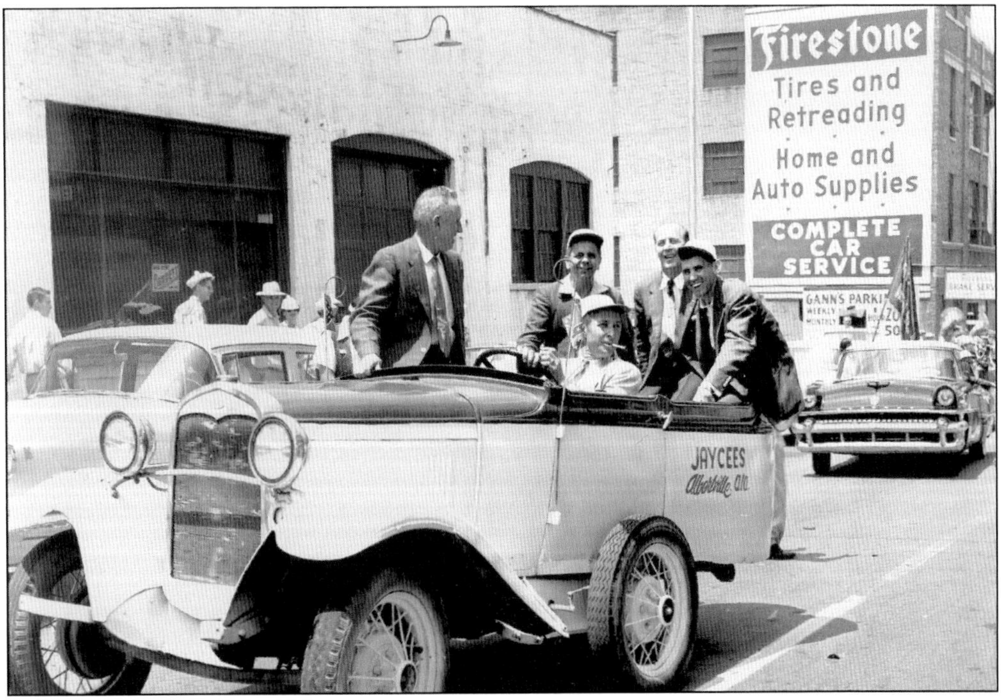

Jaycees in Atlanta. In 1940 Jaycees from Albertville attended the national convention in Atlanta. Shown in their parade car is the driver, Olan Spratling, surrounded, from left to right, by Buford L. Cryar, Robert O. Johnson, Dan Maddux, and John Mastin.

Ten
AROUND TOWN

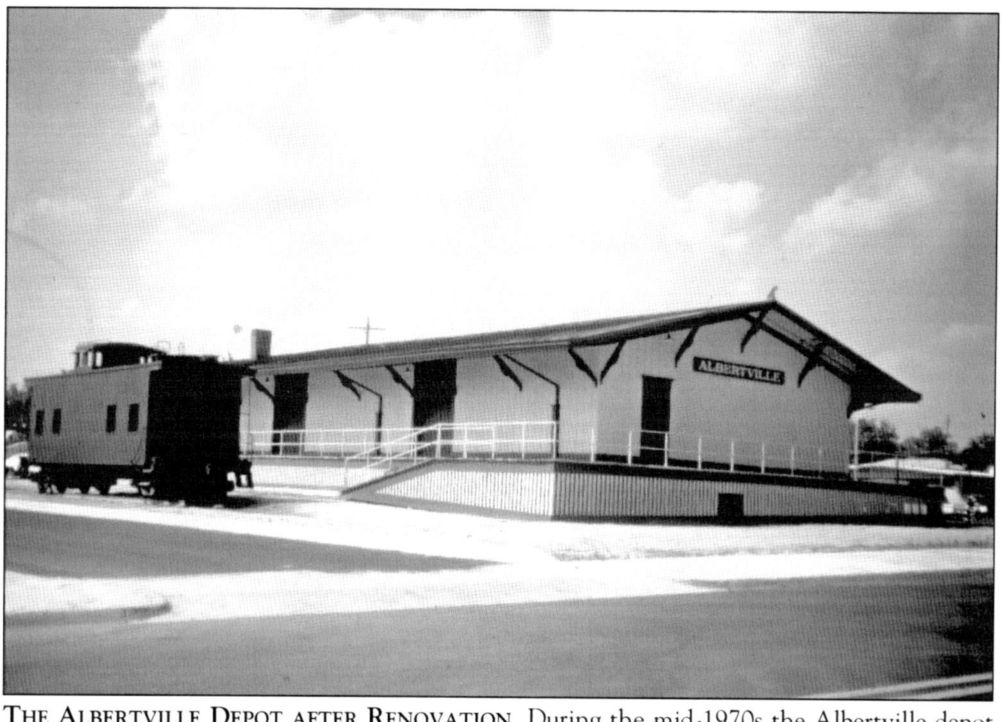

THE ALBERTVILLE DEPOT AFTER RENOVATION. During the mid-1970s the Albertville depot began to be restored to its former glory. In 1975 the structure was added to the National Register of Historic Places, a fitting tribute to a grand old building that withstood time, use, misuse, and the great cyclone of 1908.

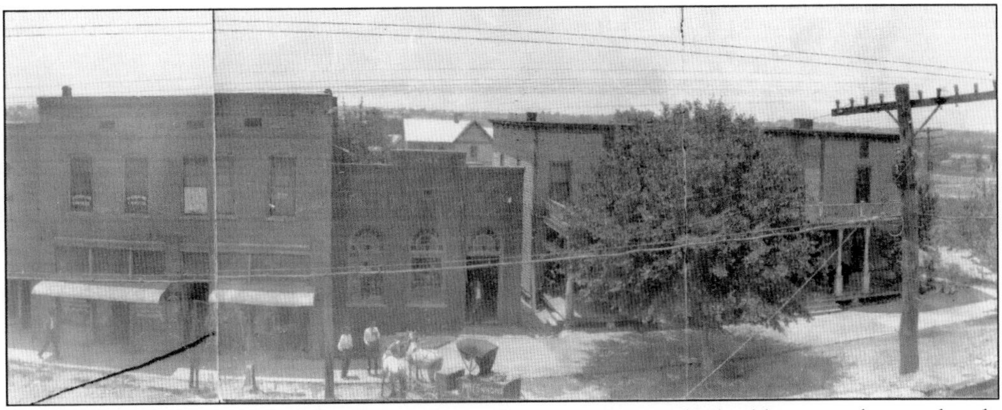

THE SOUTH SIDE OF MAIN STREET, C. 1910. Taken from atop the buildings on the north side of Main Street is this panoramic photograph showing the old Albertville Hotel, which burned in 1925, as well as the J.F. Hooper banking building.

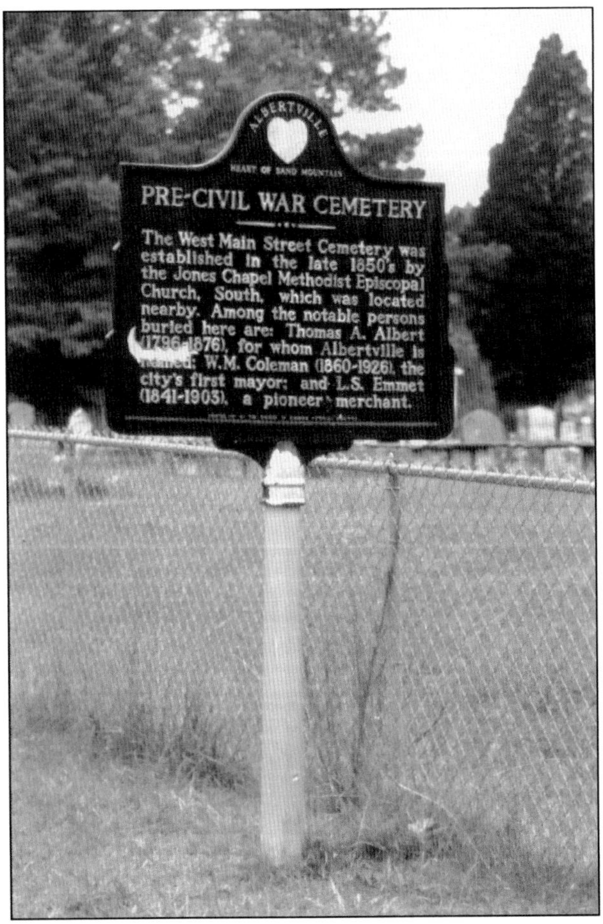

OLD ALBERTVILLE CEMETERY. The Old City Cemetery is located on West Main Street. As indicated by the historic marker, the remains of many of the town's forefathers, such as first mayor W.M. Coleman, founding merchant L.S. Emmett, and, most notably, the Thomas Albert family—the town's namesake—lie here.

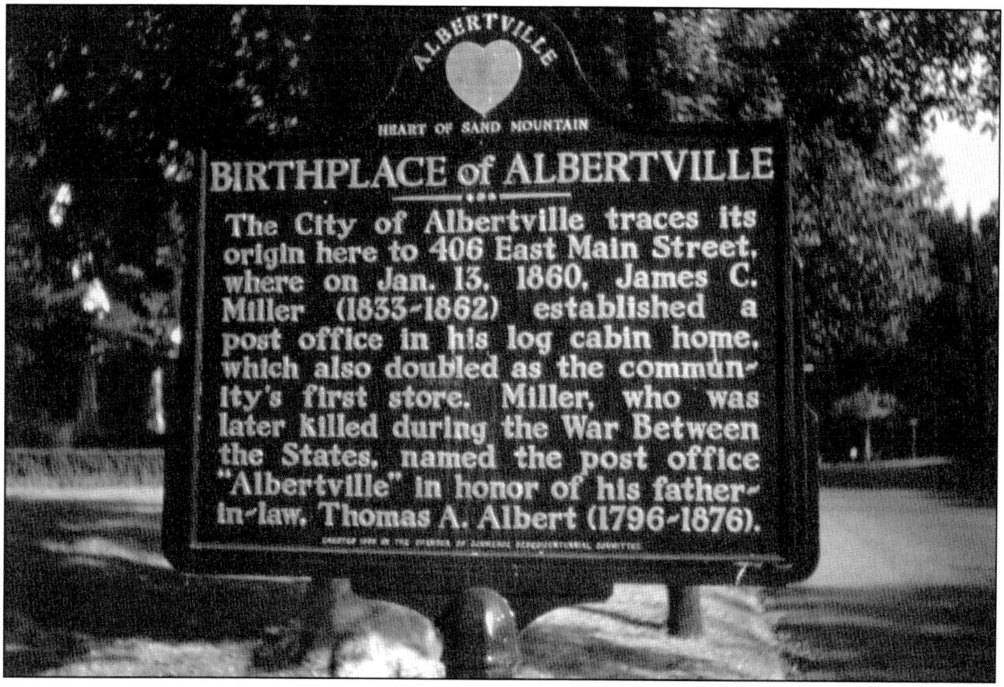

THE BIRTHPLACE OF ALBERTVILLE. A historical marker at 406 East Main Street proclaims that it was on this site that the city of Albertville was born. The first post office was established from the J.C. Miller log cabin and named for Miller's father-in-law, Thomas Albert.

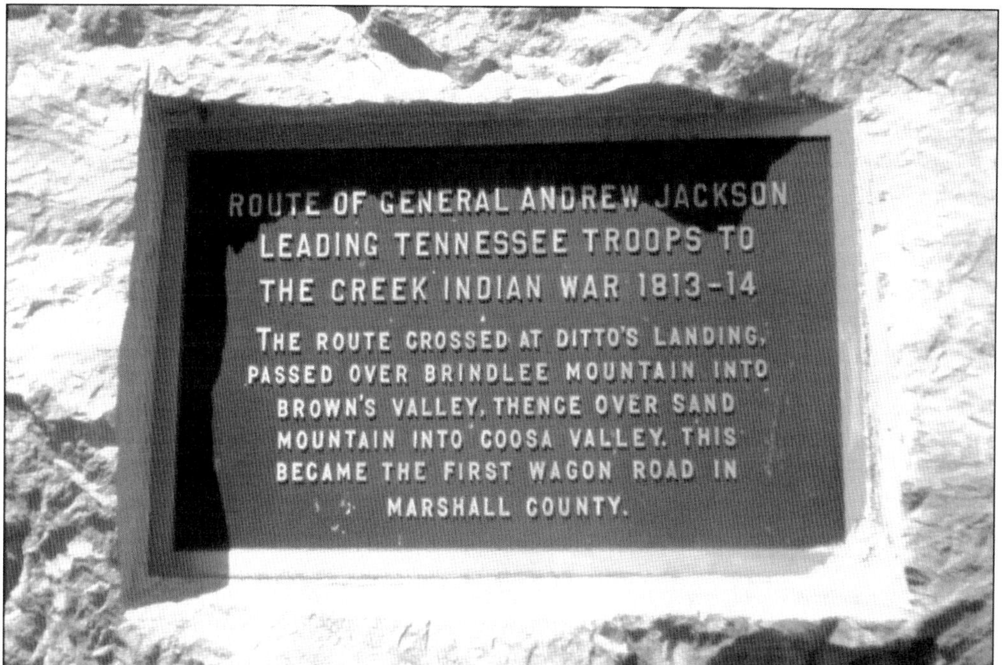

THE JACKSON TRAIL. The above marker sits at the intersection of Turnpike and Oneonta Cut-off Roads. It was across that spot that Gen. Andrew Jackson traveled on his way to battle the Creek Indians at Horseshoe Bend

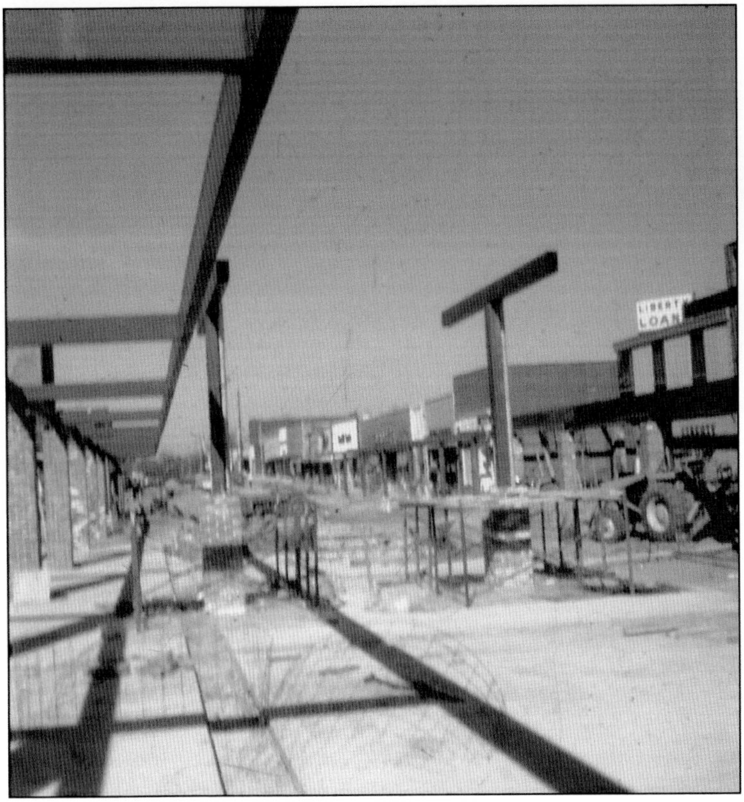

CONSTRUCTION OF ALBERTVILLE'S DOWNTOWN MALL. The steel skeleton of the Albertville Main Mall is pictured here.

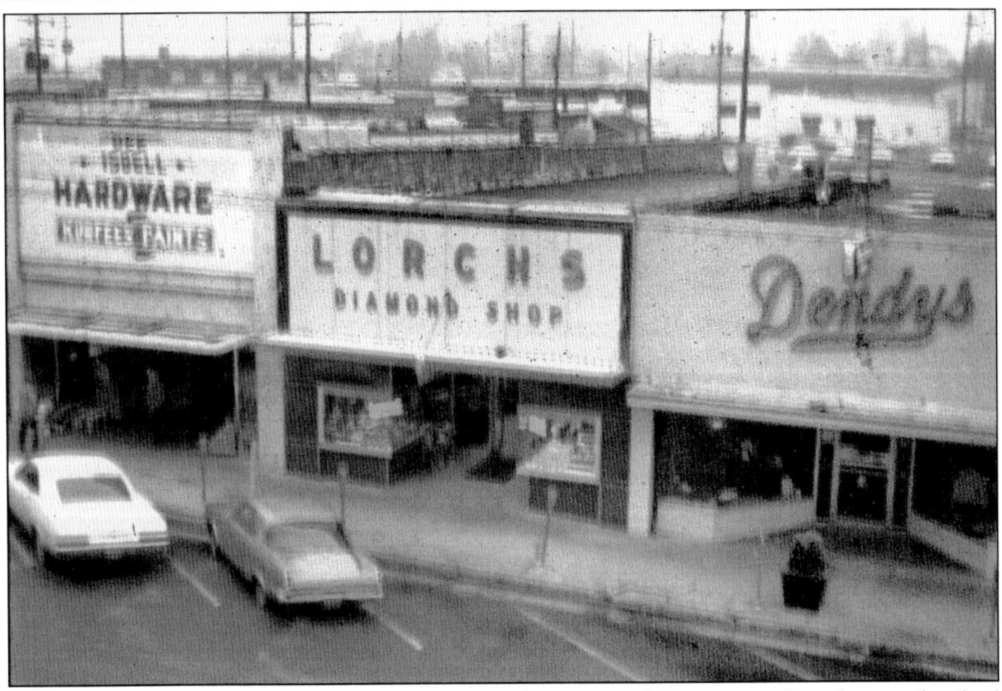

LORCHS DIAMOND SHOP. During the 1960s, Lorchs Diamond Shop opened on the site that had been occupied for 60 years by the Marshall Drug Company.

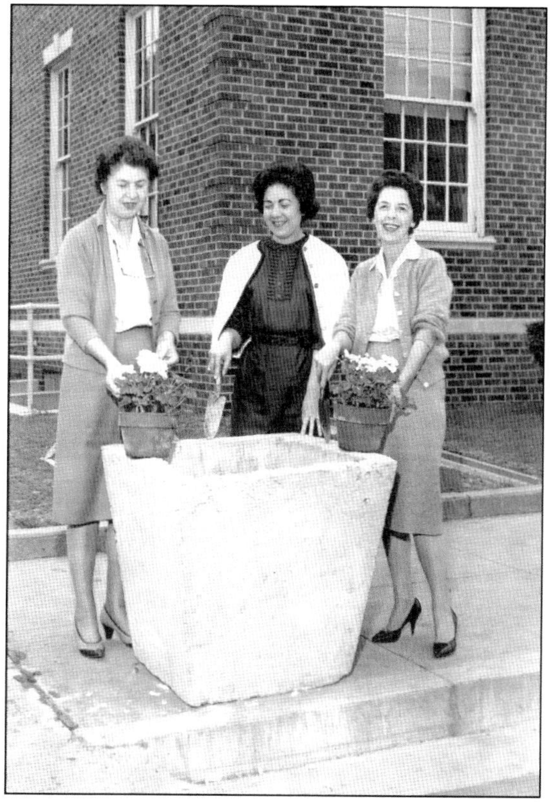

Beautifying Albertville. Mrs. C.J. Walker (left), Mrs. Bill Gullahorn (center), and Mrs. J.B. Roberts Jr. are pictured beautifying the flower boxes at the old post office.

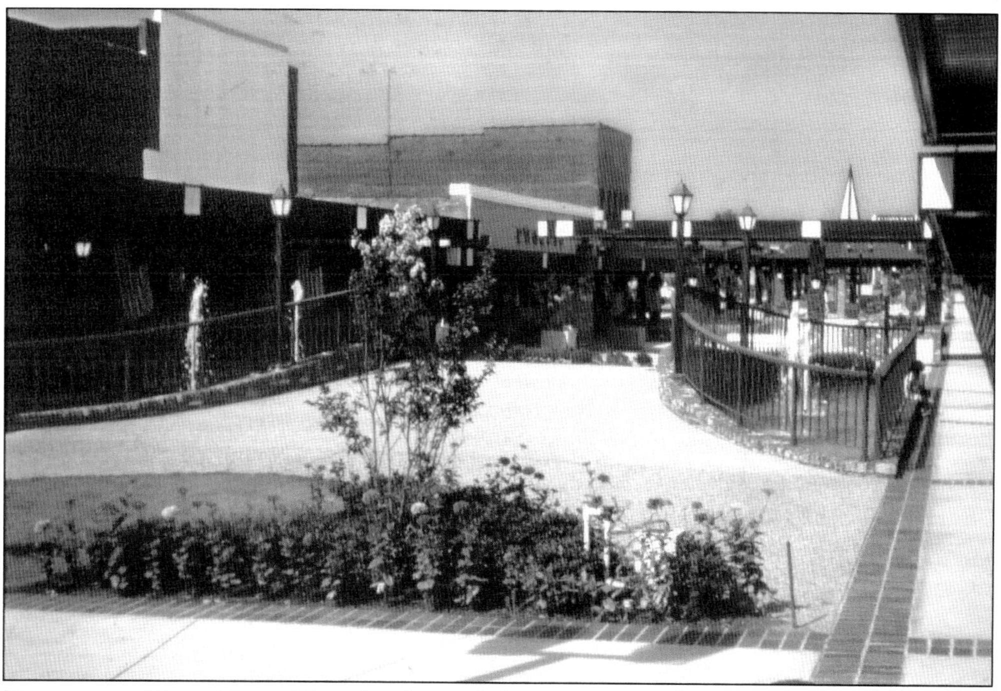

Downtown Main Mall. Though it has only been a matter of years, it seems a decade since downtown looked as it does in this photograph.

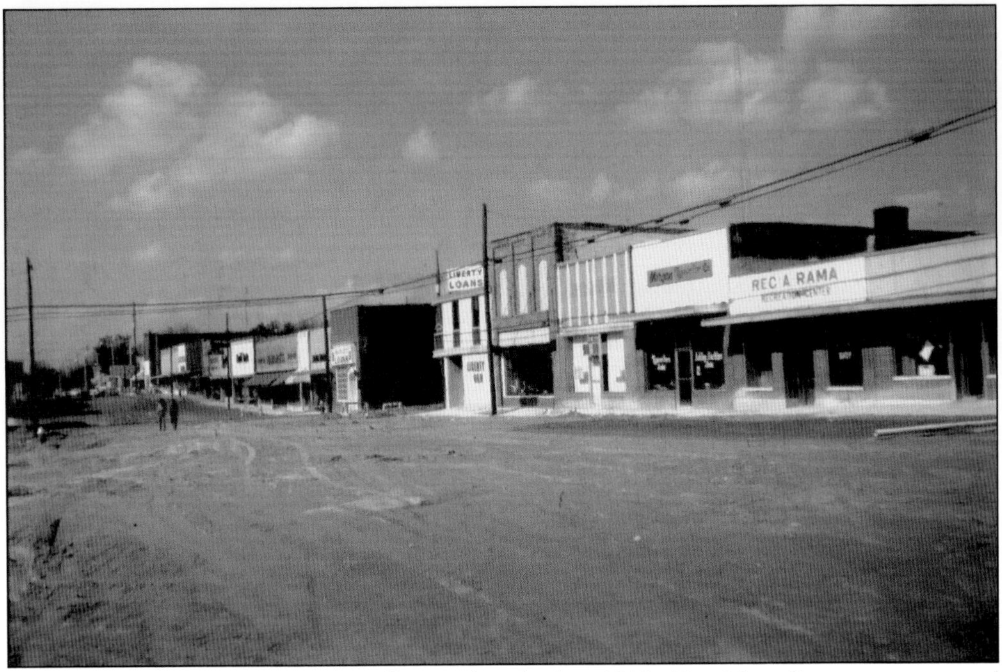

UN-PAVING MAIN STREET. Originally paved in the late 1920s, East Main Street was un-paved in preparation for the new downtown mall.

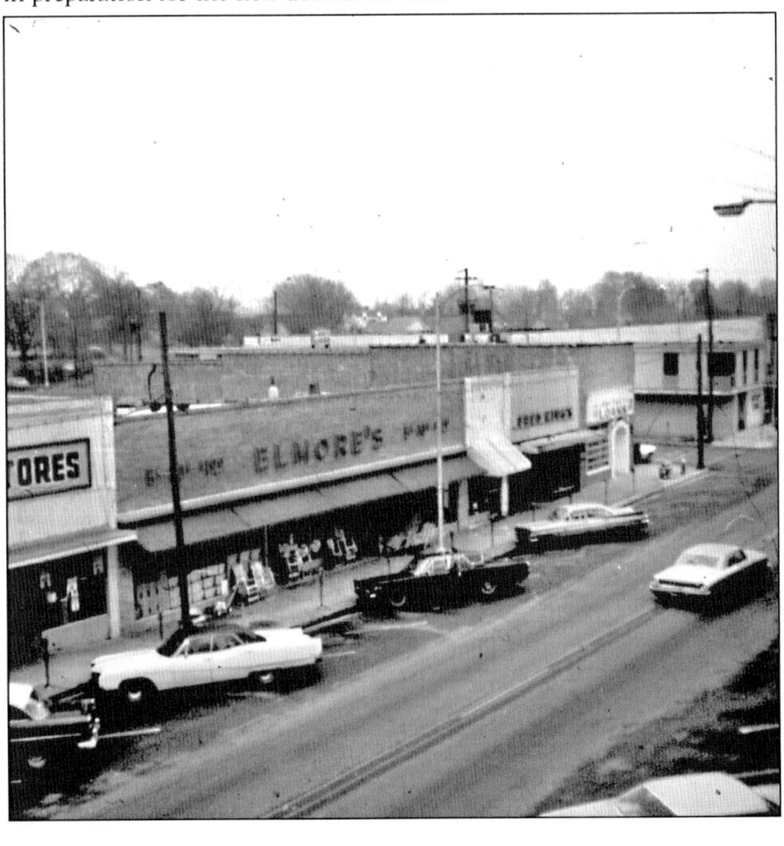

V.J. ELMORE'S 5 & 10. Growing up in Albertville, all children knew that there was the "new" dime store and the "old" dime store. The old dime store was on the south side of Main Street and was formally called Linn's; previously, it was known as Chester's. On the north side of Main Street stood the new dime store, V.J. Elmore's.

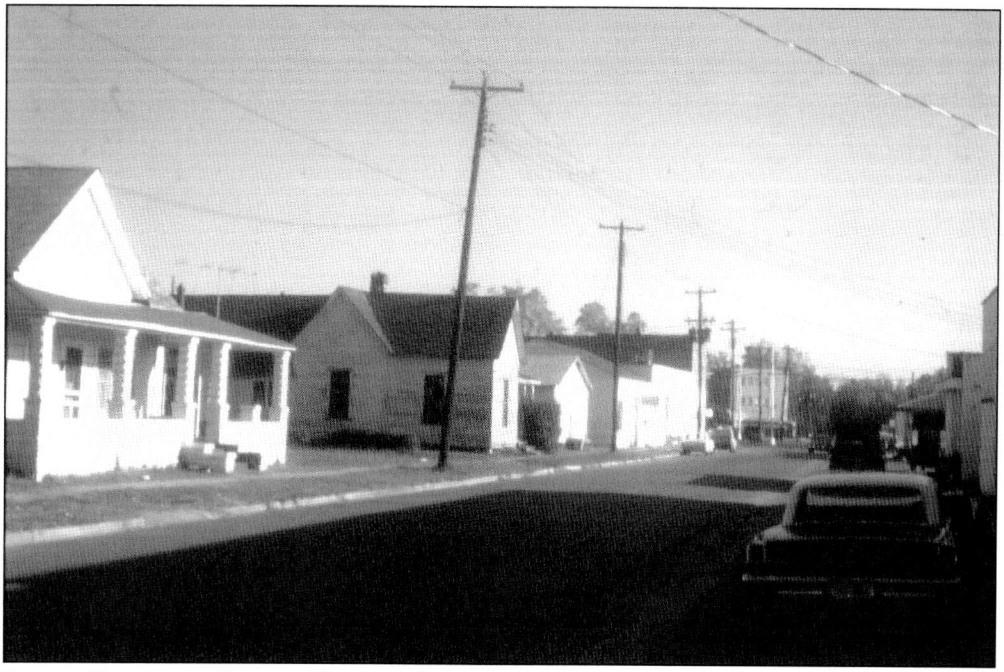

BEFORE EASTWOOD PLAZA. Shown is the row of houses that dotted the landscape along what is now Sand Mountain Drive. As a result of the urban renewal project, all the houses were razed and the Eastwood Plaza was constructed on the site.

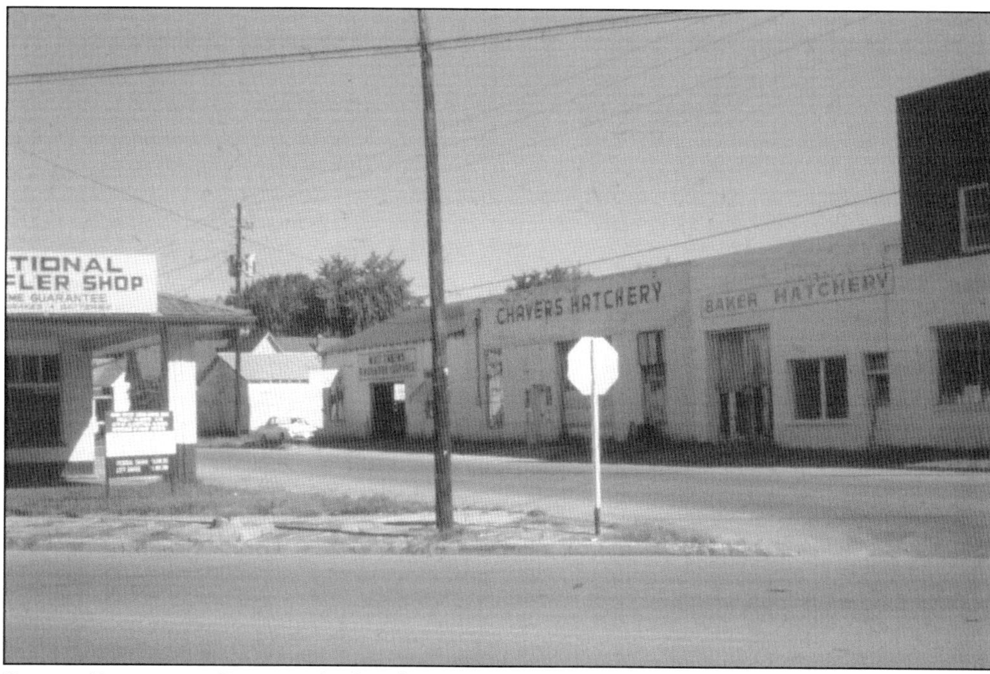

BEFORE EASTWOOD PLAZA. The hatchery businesses (pictured above) and, eventually, Bishop Pharmacy gave way to Eastwood Plaza.

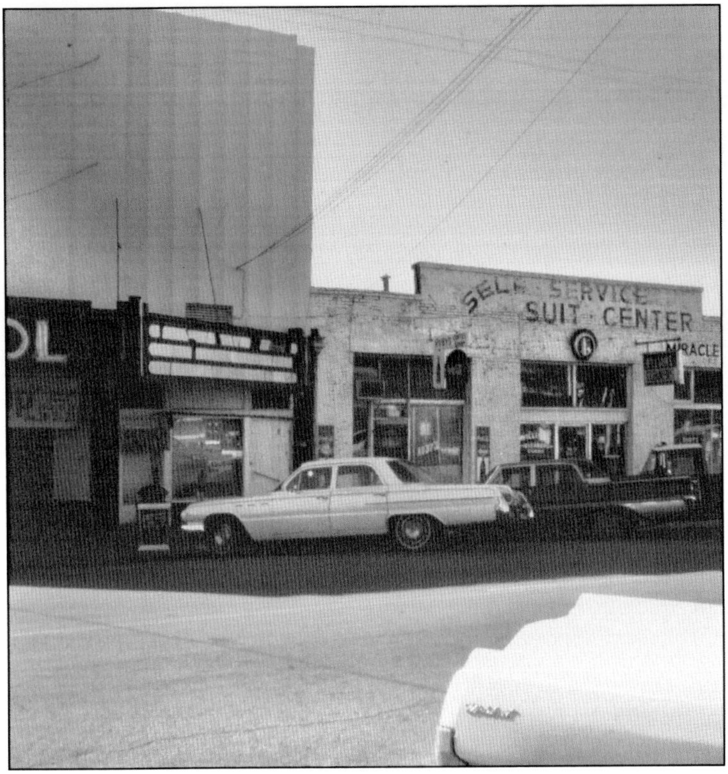

WILLIAMS CLEANERS. Williams Cleaners was located beside the old Carol Theatre. R.T. Williams was a minister of the Church of Christ and had served the North Broad Street Church of Christ for four years.

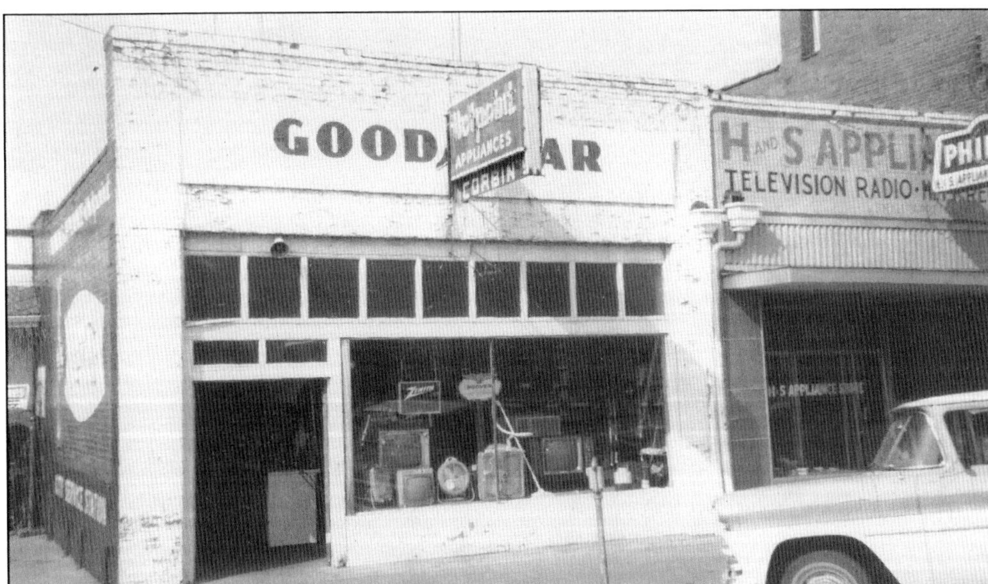

CORBIN'S APPLIANCE. In 1925 Hobart Corbin opened a garage known as Corbin and Smith, and in 1934 he purchased City Service Station at the corner of Main and Broad Streets. In 1944 Corbin began selling appliances for the entire home. Corbin's son, Ed, joined the firm upon his discharge from the service. The business was ultimately relocated to the old J. Pat Colvin site behind the Saunders Hotel. By this time, the third generation of the Corbin family was active in the business.

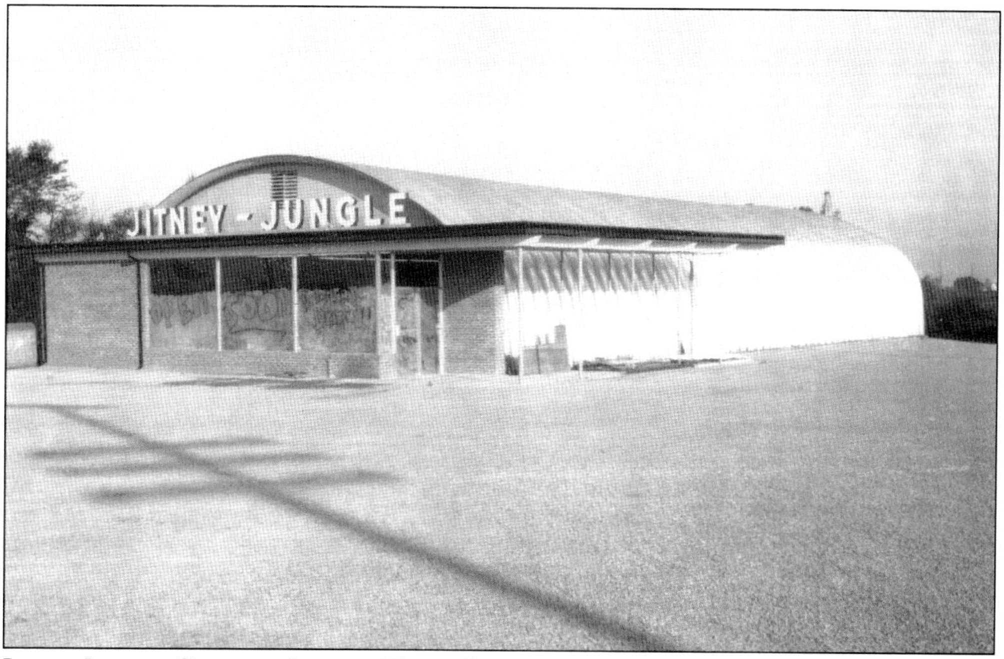

JITNEY JUNGLE GROCERY STORE. Albertville's original Quonset hut business first opened on Highway 431 as the Jitney Jungle grocery store. In more recent periods, the building has housed a car dealership and a pawnshop.

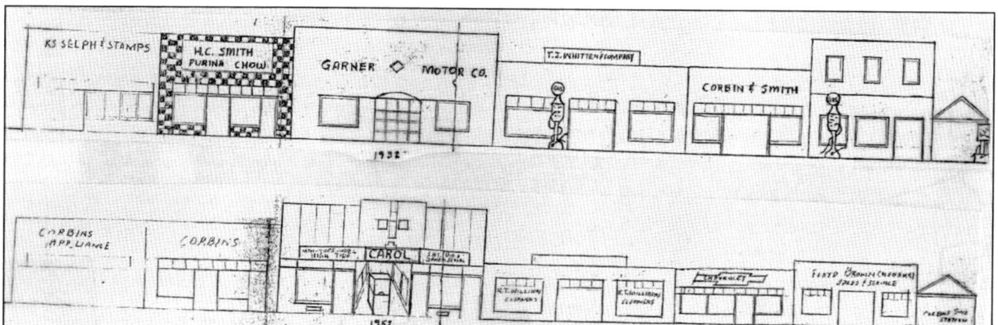

THE SOUTH SIDE OF WEST MAIN STREET. Shown above are sketches made by Albertville historian A.B. Hooper III contrasting the same stretch of downtown over two different time periods.

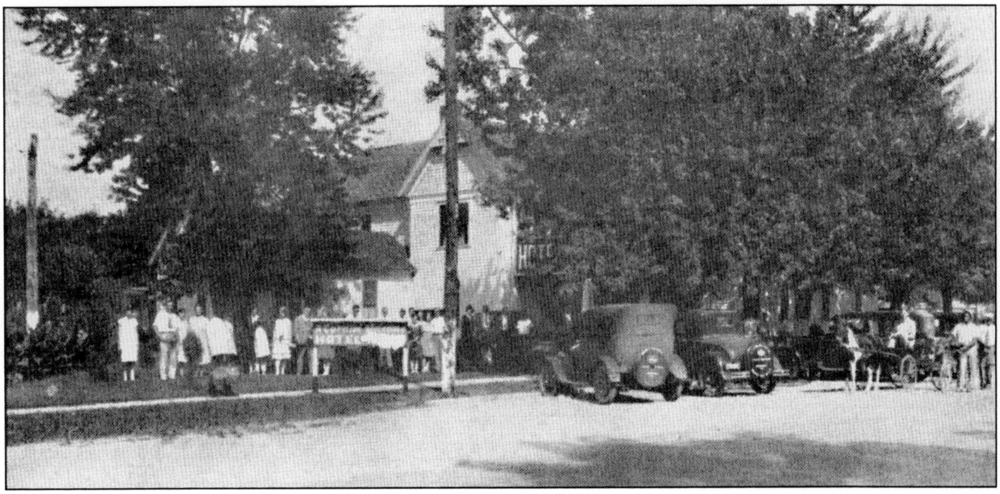

THE WITT HOTEL, C. 1930. The Saunders Hotel was always a centerpiece for town gatherings. The tradition was carried over from its predecessor, the Witt Hotel, shown above.

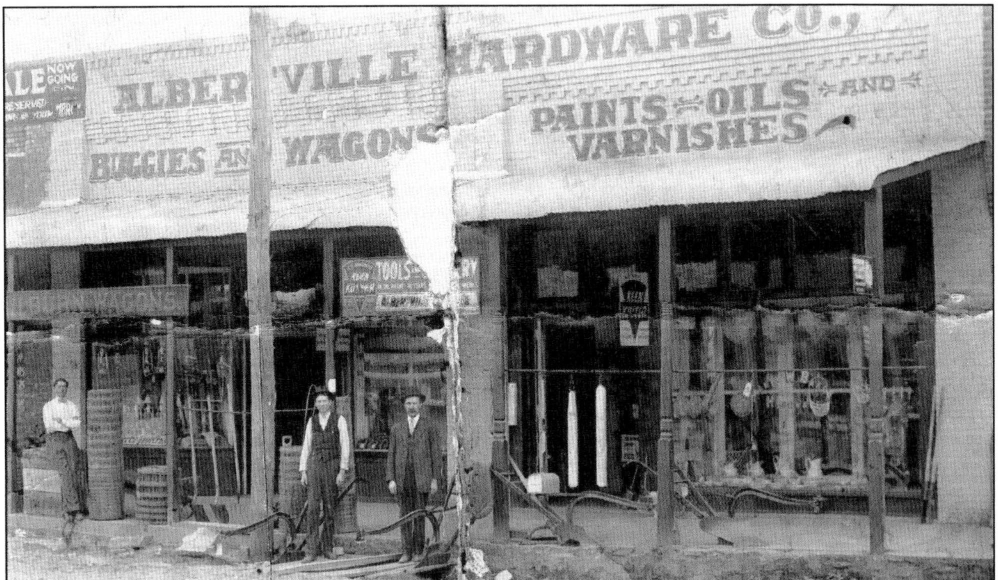

THE ALBERTVILLE HARDWARE COMPANY. The probable location of the Albertville Hardware Company shown here was East Main Street.

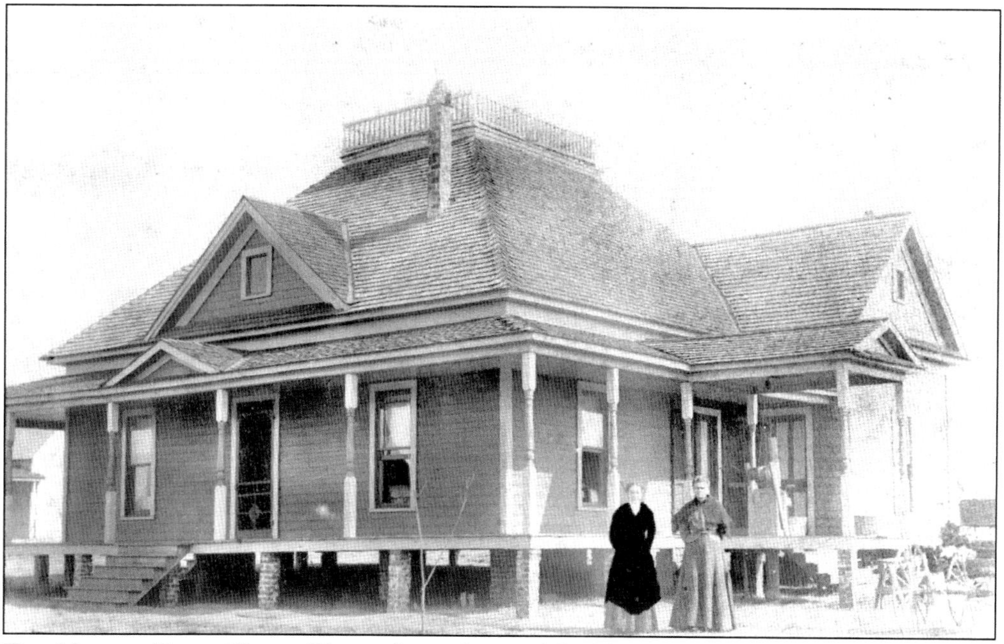

The Mercer Davis Home. This early residence of the Mercer Davis family was located at the intersection of Hambrick Street and Ober Avenue, now known as Sand Mountain Drive.

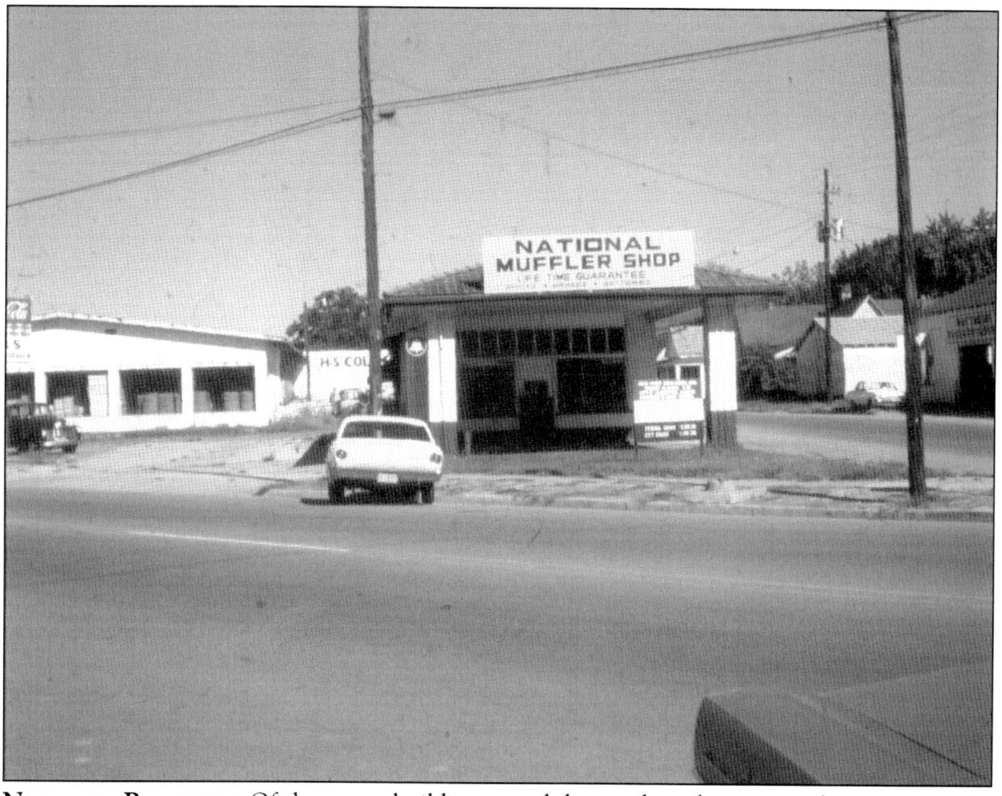

Near the Railroad. Of the many buildings razed during the urban renewal project was the one shown above on the north side of Main Street, just before the railroad track.

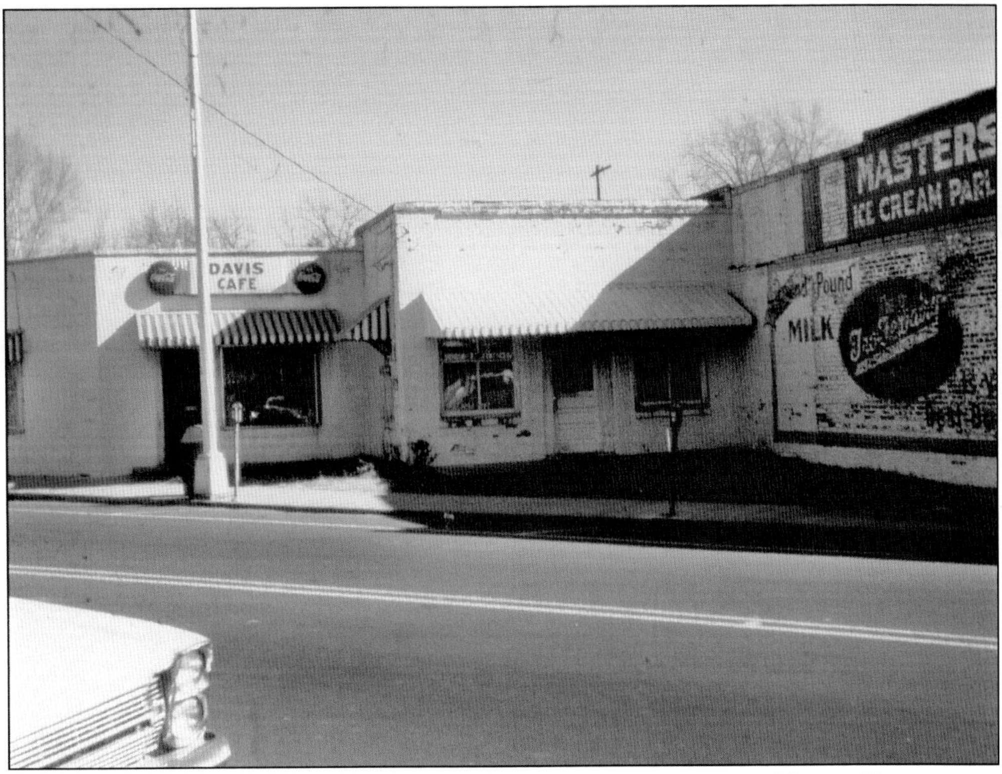

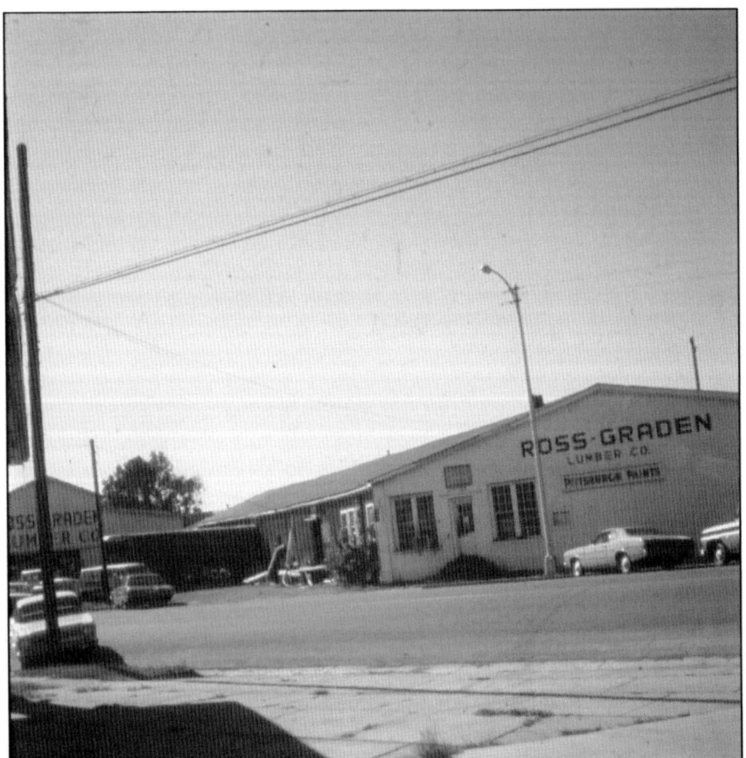

NORTH BROAD STREET. Pictured are the small storefronts located beside the old Checkerboard Store on North Broad Street.

ROSS-GRADEN LUMBER. The following buildings were demolished to make room for the urban renewal project. This one is in the vicinity of the Albertville Depot.

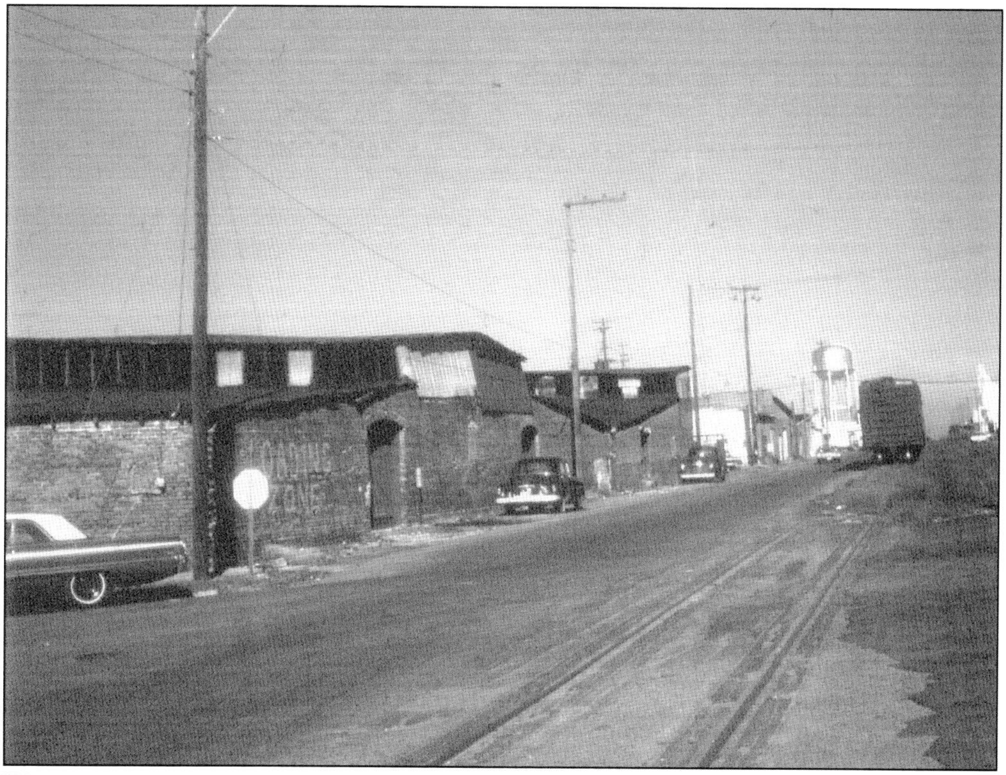

Warehouse Alley. Pictured above are the Roberts Warehouses located between Broad and Simpson Streets.

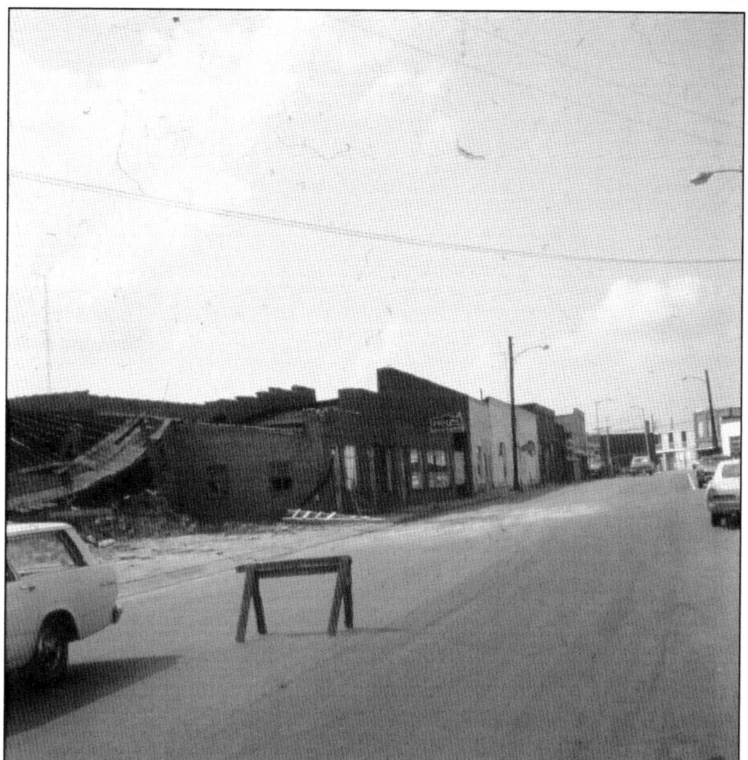

Raze and Fall. This photograph shows the demolition of buildings and warehouses down from the Darden Cotton Company, near the Reeves Rubber plant.

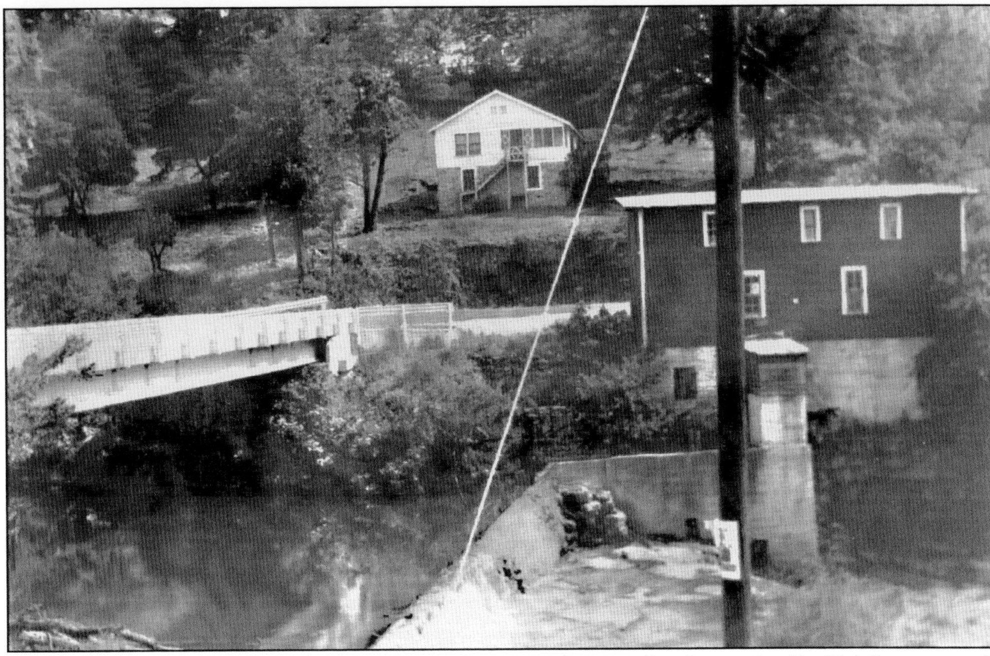

Red Mill. For years, a popular tourist attraction in the area has been the Red Mill, just north of Albertville. During the life of the mill, it was operated by a number of people, including I.E. Powell.

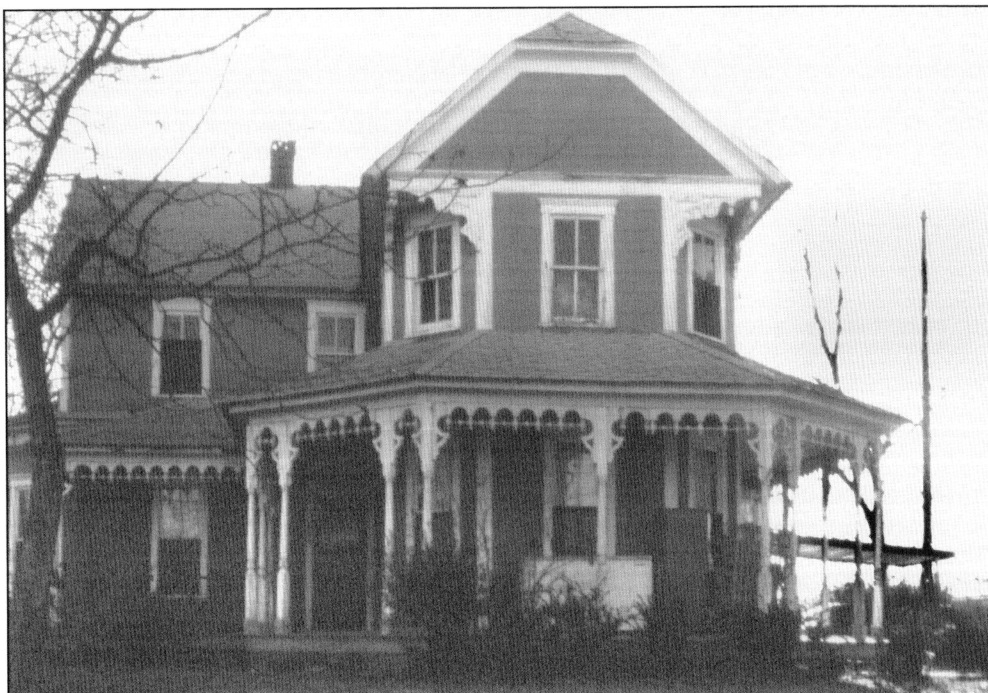

The Gingerbread House. Known for years as the Gingerbread House, this was the home of longtime Albertville police chief R.L. "Bob" Amos. When it was decided to develop an annual Christmas ornament for fund-raising purposes, this house was the inspiration for the first one.

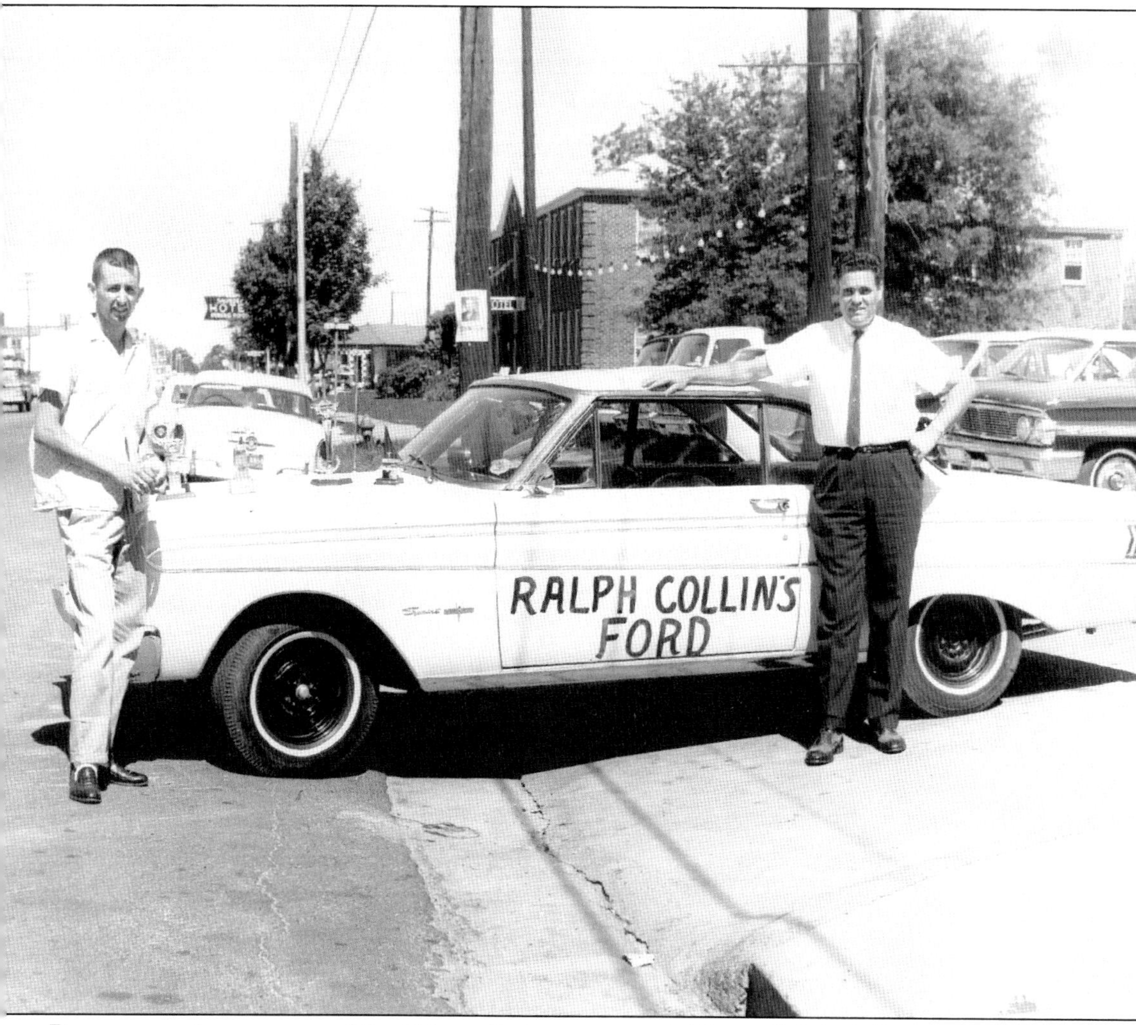

RACING TO ALBERTVILLE. The Falcon Sprint racecar of Albertville's Bob Dennis (left) is shown above in May 1964. The car was sponsored by Ralph Collins Ford and was on display at the dealership, located across from Albertville's First Baptist Church. Shown congratulating Dennis is owner Ralph Collins.

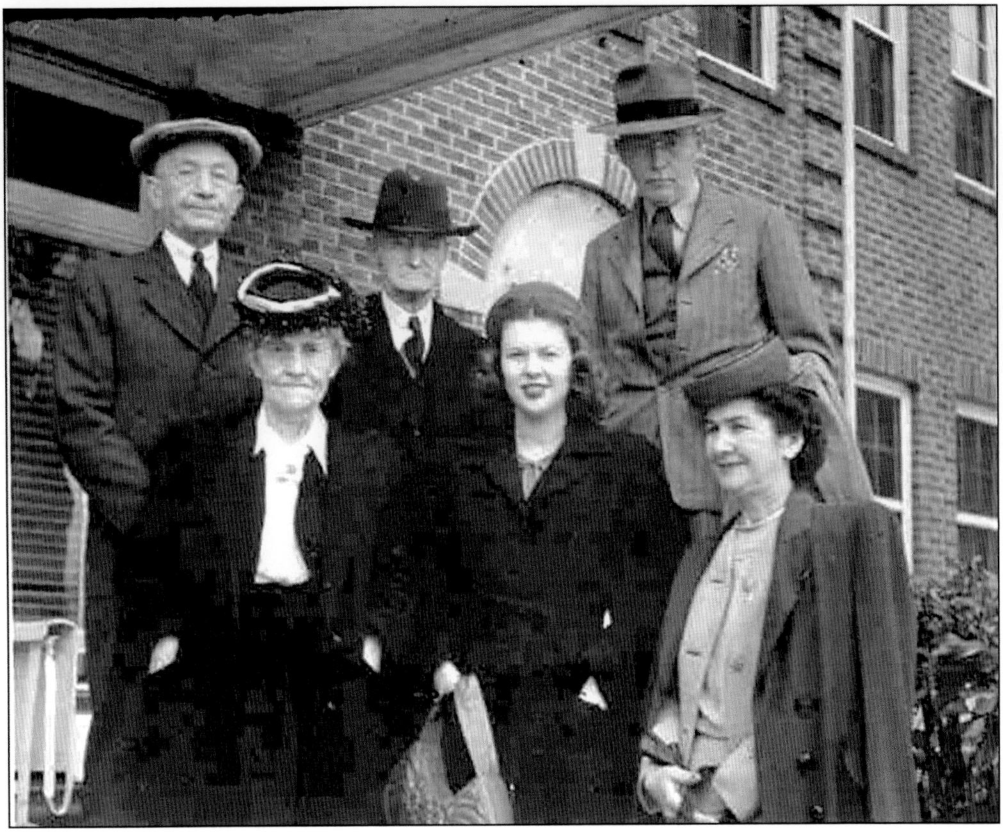

GATHERING AT THE SAUNDERS. Shown in front of the Saunders Hotel are members of the A.C. Walker family and a close family friend, E.W. Averyt.

Eleven
Personalities

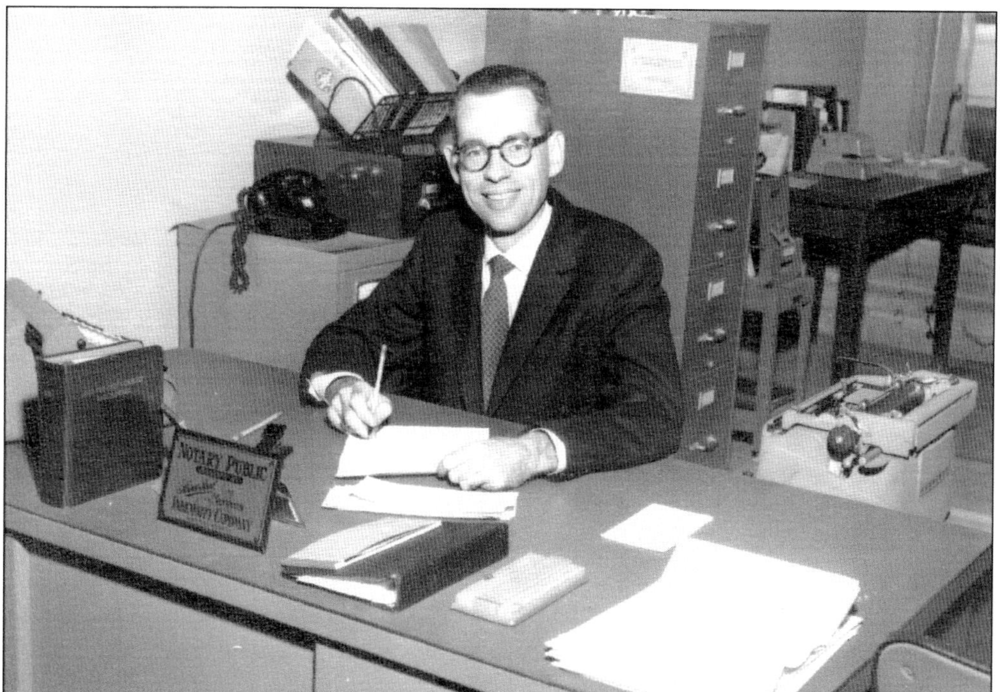

A.B. Hooper III. Pictured at his office in the Hooper building is A.B. Hooper III. His work as historian during Albertville's early years is immeasurable to later generations.

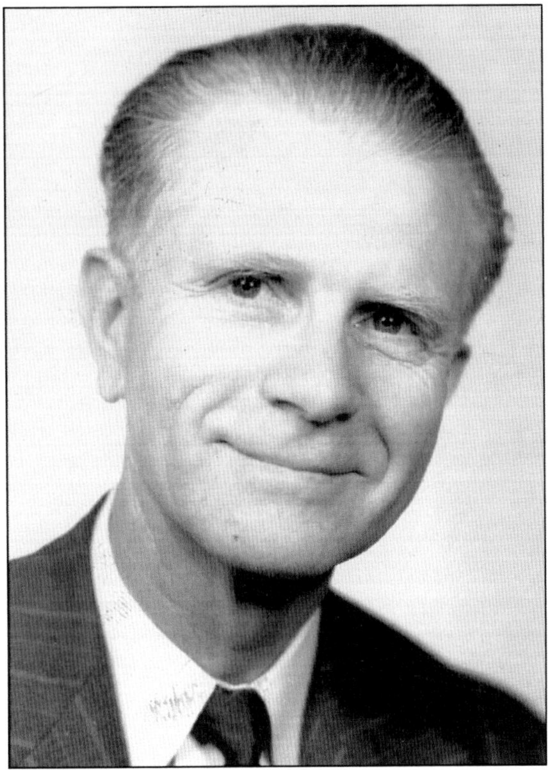

A.F. JONES SR. From his earliest days of youth, railroading was the centerpiece of A.F. Jones Sr.'s life. He and two of his brothers eventually followed in their father's footsteps—railroading. In the early days of railroad work, usually the first thing a fledgling worker was taught was how to use the telegraph. Jones always remembered that, when it came to the telegraph, sending was easier than receiving. When the opportunity came for him to move to Albertville and take over the depot, he jumped at the chance.

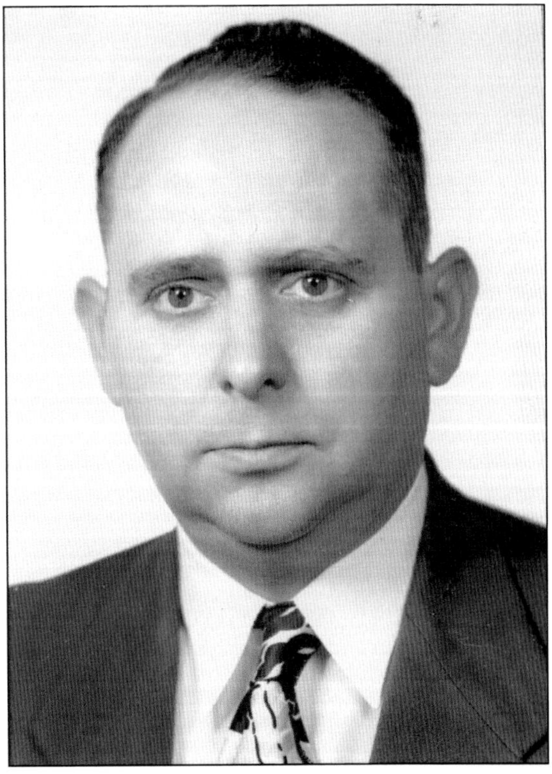

H. BROWN CRIBBS. In 1948 Sulligent, Alabama native H. Brown Cribbs moved to Albertville, where he established an Albertville institution, Cribbs Tire.

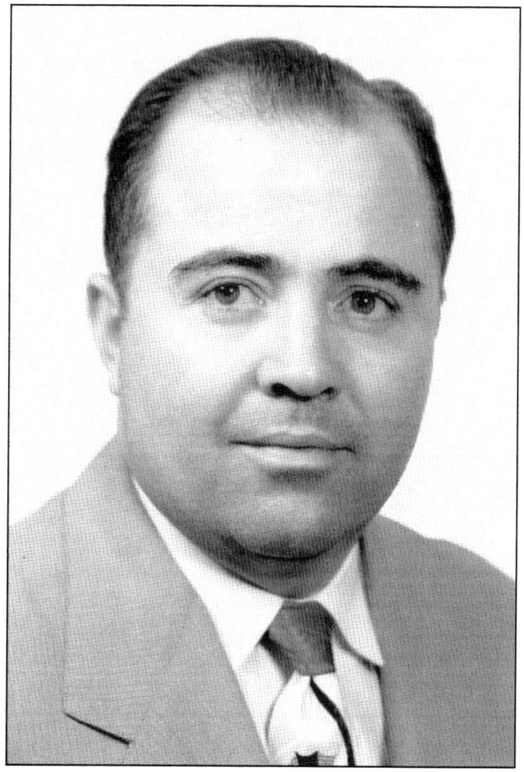

HAROLD GOLDEN. For years, the southeast corner of the intersection of East Main and Simpson Streets housed the Universal Photo store. Harold Golden operated the business for a number of years.

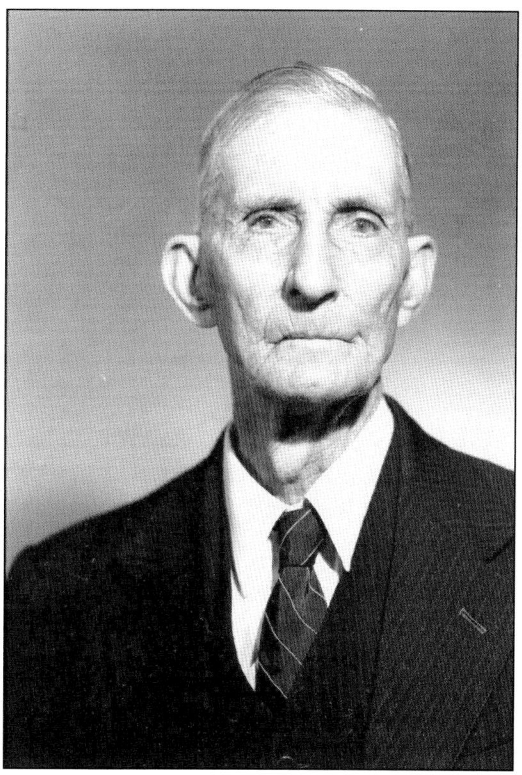

JOHN HENRY MOULTRIE. Pictured is the patriarch of Albertville's large Moultrie family. He and his wife, the former Nancy Camp, had a total of 12 children.

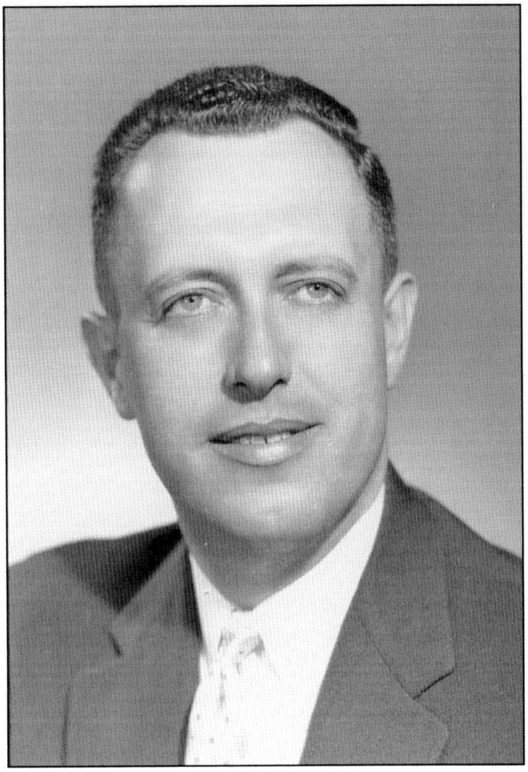

W.S. "BILL" RODEN. In 1928 W.S. Roden moved his family from Boaz to Albertville, where he established a wholesale business. Eventually, his sons followed in the business. The multi-ministry facility of today's First Baptist Church occupies the former spot of W.S. Roden Grocery. In addition to his business acumen, W.S. Roden designed and constructed a number of facilities around town.

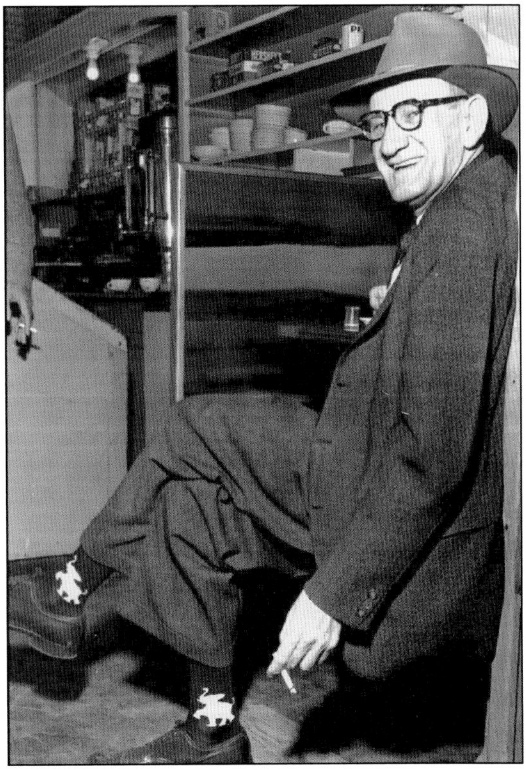

WALTER DECKER. Shown is Albertville resident and Republican party supporter Walter Decker. In this picture, he is shown sporting socks, but not just any socks—these are Republican socks. He recalled at the time of this photograph that prior to President Eisenhower's election, victories were rare for Republicans.

T.B. Mosley. Across Sand Mountain, singing schools were a popular pastime. Of all teachers, T.B. Mosley was considered to be the premier instructor. Mosley was also a prolific writer of gospel songs and a leader in the Church of Christ. Tragically, Mosley was killed in a traffic accident on October 2, 1927.

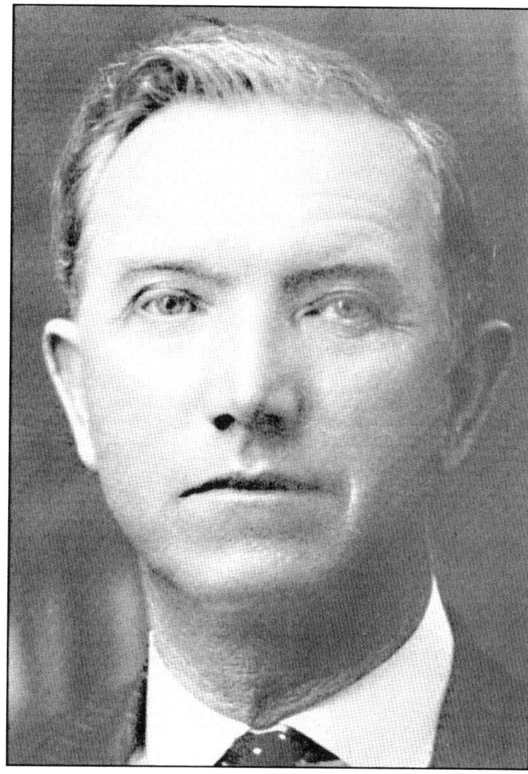

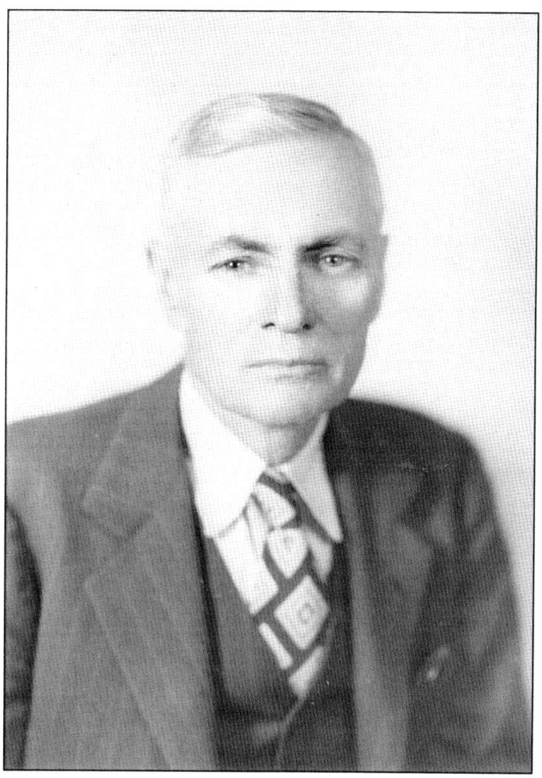

B.M. Rains. Shown is B.M. Rains, president of the Tennessee Valley Bank, the forerunner of Albertville's State National Bank.

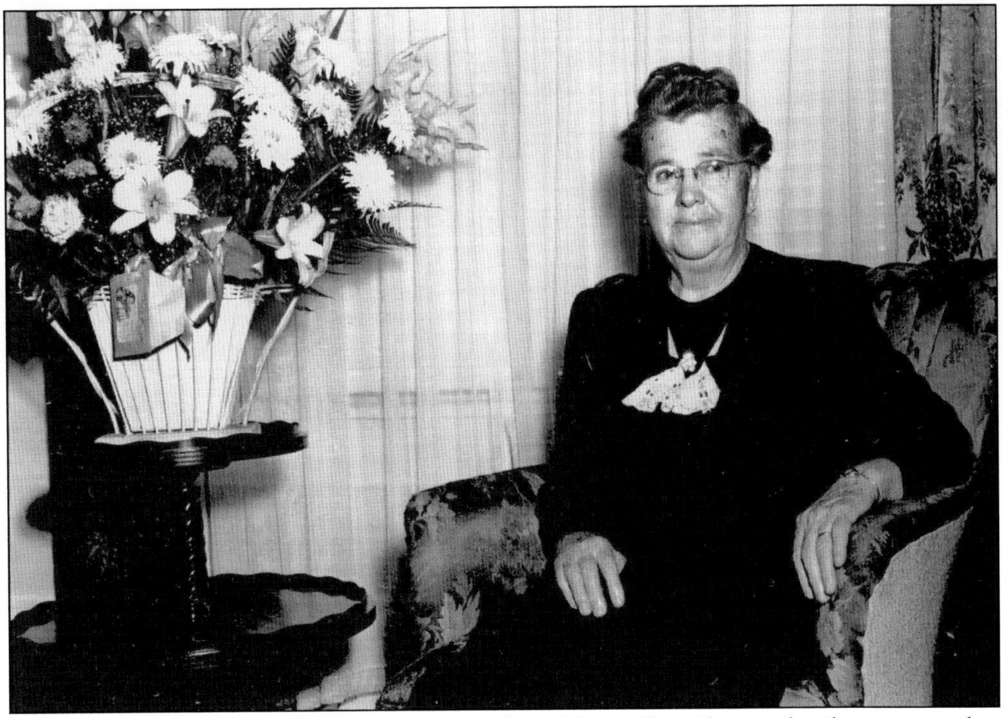

MRS. J.B. THOMAS. Ida Bell Thomas, matriarch of Albertville's Thomas family, is pictured in her later years.

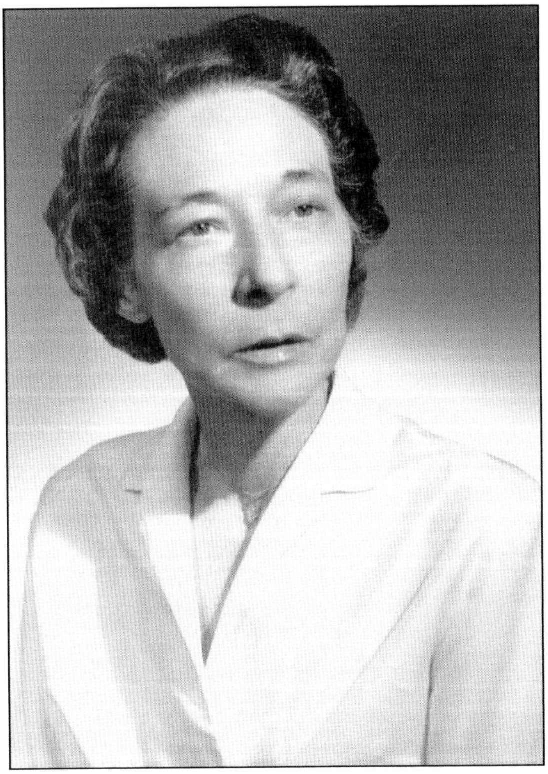

VIVIAN ALFORD WALKER. In 1920 Vivian Alford moved to Albertville with her brother and her father, B.A. Alford. On June 15, 1929, Vivian married James W. Walker Jr., grandson of Capt. Alexander C. Walker. The couple was married at the home of the bride's parents.

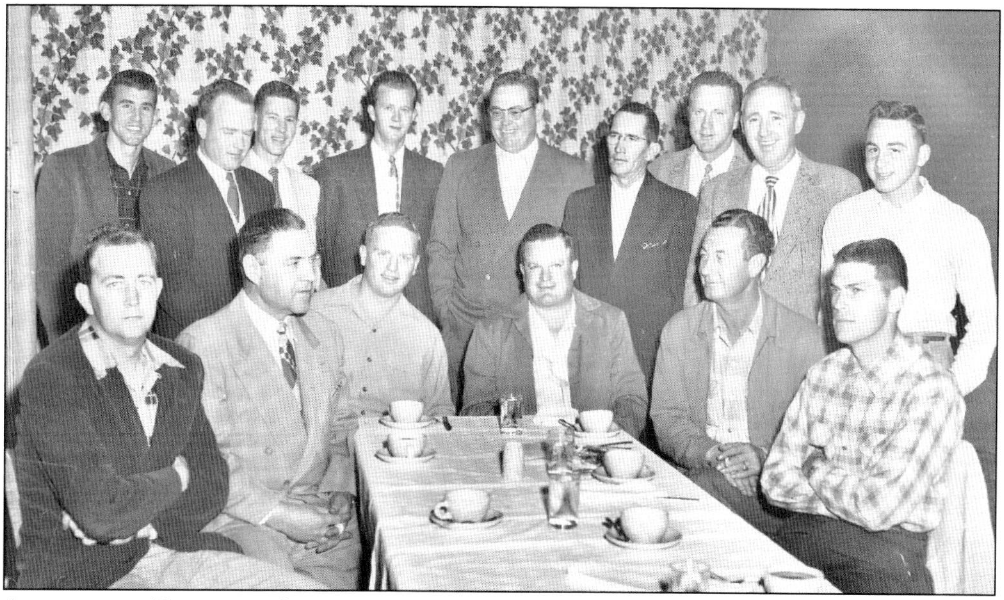

ALBERTVILLE BIRTHDAY GATHERING. On Saturday, February 6, 1954, a group of Albertville friends gathered at the Horsley Hotel to throw a surprise for their friend R.G. "Pug" Moore. The following guests are pictured from left to right: (front row) Richard Adams, Olin C. Hearn, Jack Wells, the honoree, L.P. Dickson, and Wayne Heard; (back row) John Mastin, George Wells, Dr. Harry Martin, Sonny Lackey, Bob Latta, W.P. "Peck" Williamson, Cullen Goss, Buford Cryar, and Dickie Latta.

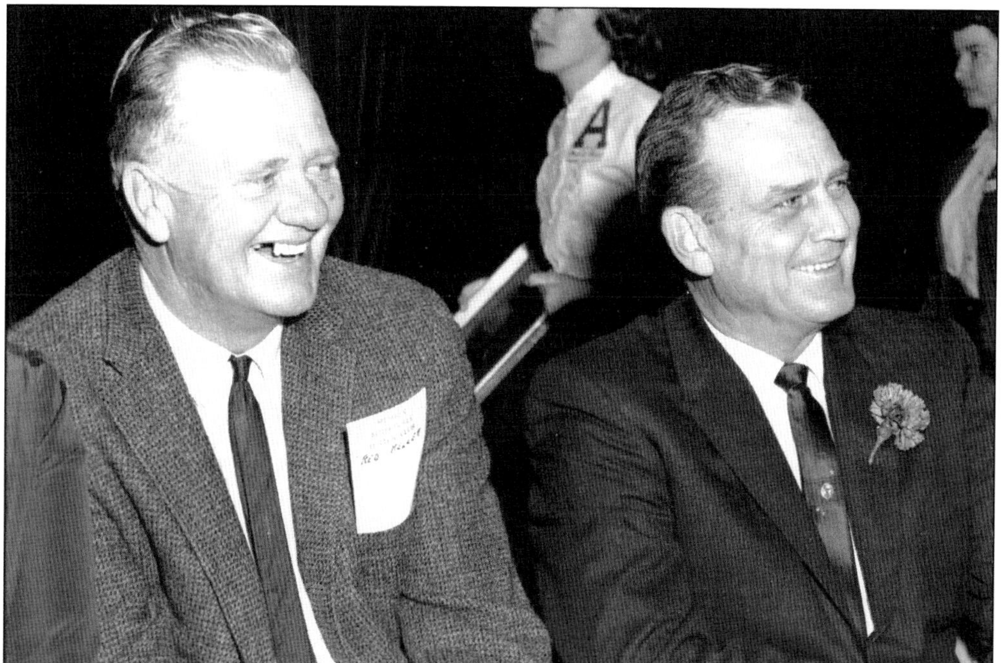

THOMAS B. "RED" KELLER AND PAUL "BEAR" BRYANT. Charlie Pell Day in 1963 brought together two larger-than-life characters, the University of Alabama's Paul "Bear" Bryant and Albertville's own Thomas B. "Red" Keller.

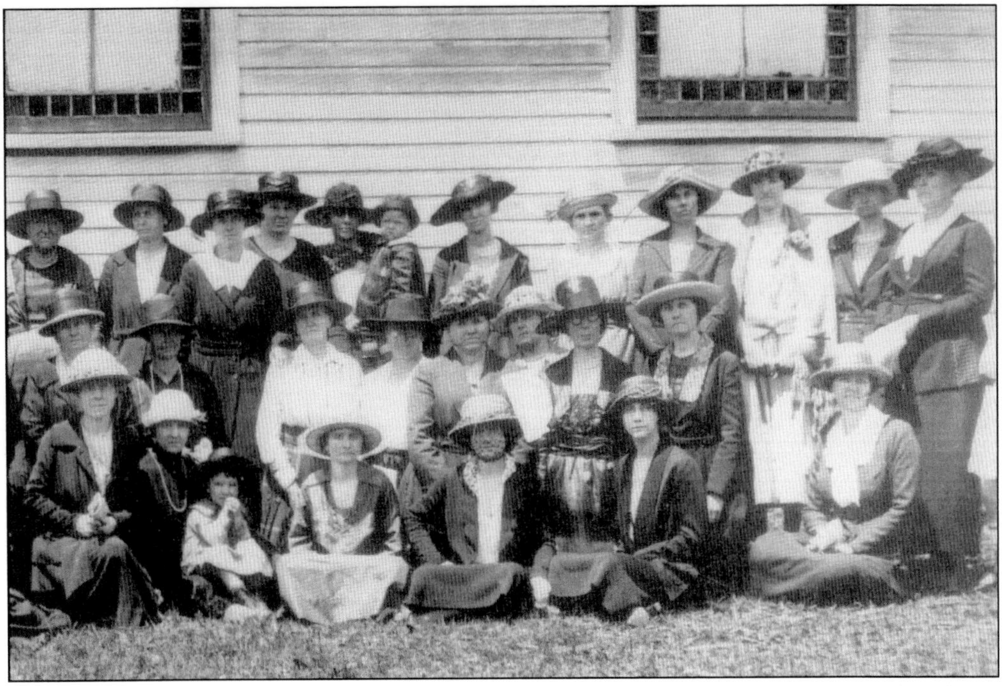

WOMEN OF THE BAPTIST CHURCH. The ladies of what is now the First Baptist Church are shown in a photograph taken *c.* 1915. These ladies would have probably enjoyed today's "Red Hat Clubs."

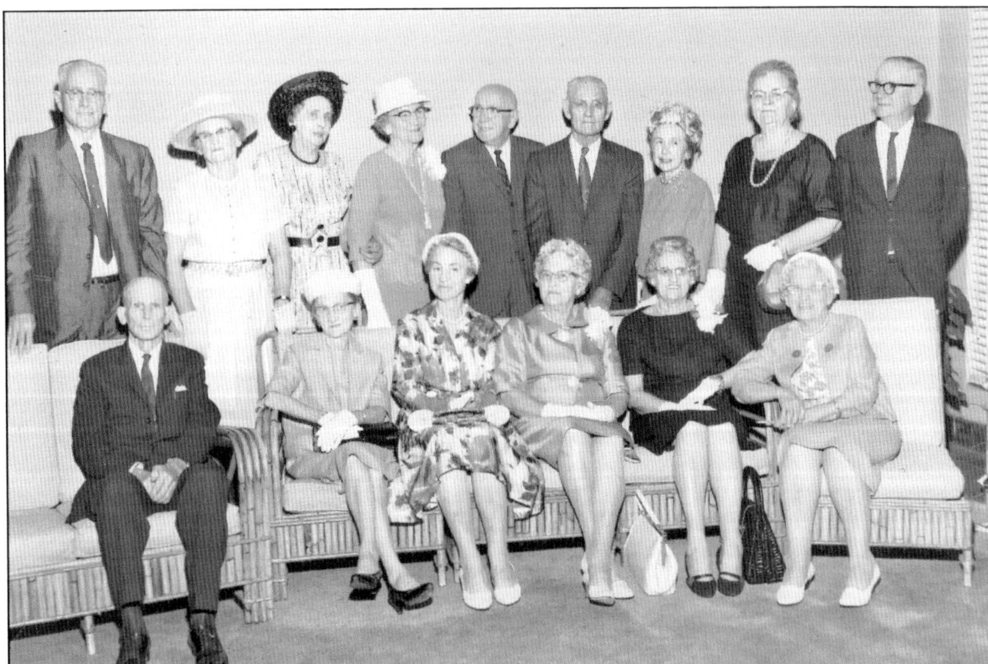

S.D.A.S. CLASS OF 1914. It seems fitting to close with this photograph of a class reunion of the Seventh District Agricultural School class of 1914. These folks can teach the lesson to make your steps count for the future but never forget the past.